ORGANIZATIONAL STRATEGY AND TECHNOLOGICAL ADAPTATION TO GLOBAL CHANGE

Organizational Strategy and Technological Adaptation to Global Change

Edited by
Frank McDonald
and
Richard Thorpe

MACMILLAN
Business

First published 1998 by
MACMILLAN PRESS LTD
Houndmills, Basingstoke, Hampshire RG21 6XS
and London
Companies and representatives throughout the world

ISBN 0–333–71396–6

A catalogue record for this book is available from the British Library.

This book is printed on paper suitable for recycling and made from fully managed and sustained forest sources.

10 9 8 7 6 5 4 3 2 1
07 06 05 04 03 02 01 00 99 98

Printed in Great Britain by
Antony Rowe Ltd
Chippenham, Wiltshire

To **Nuala Gallagher**
who did so much of the
early work for *Global Change*

and to **Herbert Thorpe**
for his work on the typescript

Contents

vii

Acknowledgements

This book is based on papers presented at the Global Change conference at Manchester Metropolitan University. The success of this first bi-annual conference was made possible only by the hard work of a large number of people who were involved in the establishment of this conference for various periods of time throughout its two years of planning.

The conference planning group consisted of Tom Lupton, Tony Lowe, Steve Little, Frank McDonald and Richard Thorpe and was ably supported administratively firstly by Chris Bagley and later by Eileen Seaston. The conference itself could not have taken place without the sponsorship of Brother International, Greenalls, British Airways and the Seton Healthcare Group, Greenall and the Manchester Training and Enterprise Council and, in particular, the personal support of Kay Tazaki and Paul Kitchen.

Between the conference and the completion of this book the bulk of the secretarial work has fallen to Louise Tanner and Richard Dewhirst who has completed the indexing and bibliography. We are most grateful for their continued patience and enthusiasm without which the project would not have been completed.

FRANK MCDONALD
RICHARD THORPE

Notes on the Contributors

Richard Brown joined the International Monetary Fund as an economist in its Young Professional Programme after graduating from the London School of Economics. Subsequently he worked in its European Department specializing in Mediterranean economics. He then joined the Bank of England, and his final job there was coordinating global economic analysis. In 1987 he left the Bank to become an economic consultant. He has given courses in international economics, banking and macroeconomics at several universities including Manchester, Malta and Wales, and contributes frequently to executive courses and the MBA programme at the MBS. He is also a Visiting Fellow at Durham University Business School. With DeAnne Julius he won the 1993 Amex Bank competition with an essay entitled 'Is manufacturing still special in the new world order?' Other activities include corporate consultancy and journalism. Current research interests include national competitive advantage and European monetary union.

Derek Channon is Professor of Management at Imperial College, London. Prior to this he was for many years Professor of Strategic Management and Marketing at the Manchester Business School. He was also a founder and subsequently Director at Manchester of the International Financial Services Centre. Before becoming an academic, he worked in a variety of marketing roles for the Royal Dutch Shell Group in the UK and abroad. He attended the Harvard Business School where his thesis on the Strategy and Structure of British Enterprise won the Irwin Prize. He was a founder of the Strategic Management Society and its President from 1985–88. He has consulted widely around the world for many major corporations including IBM, ICI, Shell, Exxon, Barclays, Citibank, Swiss Bank Corp., Phillips, Tarmac, Kodak, Prudential Insurance, Royal Insurance and many others. He has specialized in service industries and especially financial services and retailing. He is the author of many books, articles and cases in the field of strategic management. Amongst these books are *The Strategy and Structure of British Enterprise, Cases in Strategic Management, Multinational Strategic Planning* and *Global Banking Strategy*. He was also at one time Chief Executive of Evode Holdings and served for many years on the Board of a number of companies including the Royal Bank of Scotland.

Paromijit Hayers is a PhD student at the Liverpool Centre for HRD, Liverpool Business School, where she is researching the dynamics of international project teams. A former teacher, Ms Hayers has an MBA and has recently acted as a consultant on equal opportunities to the Littlewood's Organisation international division, where she helped write guidelines on recruitment and selection, and employment.

Lethos Hethy was for several years the Director of the Institute of Labour Research in Budapest, Hungary, and is currently the Political Secretary of State for Labour. He has thus been involved both as a researcher and a politician in the transition from communism to capitalism.

Eva Hrabitova is a lecturer at the University of Economics, Prague. Research interests are HRM, work organisation, working conditions, and cross-cultural management.

Richard Hudson-Davies is a lecturer in Marketing at the Business and Management Studies Department, Crewe and Alsager Faculty of Manchester Metropolitan University. His main research activity is centred on the impact of creative problem-solving techniques on individuals, groups and organizations. The particular orientation of this research is towards the impact on the effective marketing of products and services. The major research project currently relates to innovation and the marketing impact of loyalty credit cards within financial services.

Paul Iles is the Littlewood's Professor of HRD at Liverpool Business School, Liverpool John Moores University. He is a chartered psychologist and fellow of the IPD, and heads the Liverpool Centre for HRD. His research and consultancy interests are in managerial assessment and development, career and organization development, equal opportunities and diversity, and international HRM/HRD.

Roland Kaye holds the Royal Insurance Chair in Information Management and heads the Centre for Information and Innovation at the Open University Business School. He has led research into the impact of information technology on accountancy with publications in the areas of financial modelling, accounting information systems and computer based teaching. He has written a number of books and articles on financial planning and modelling and the strategic management of information technology, and has received a number of research grants.

György Kaucsek is an industrial psychologist, engineer, MTM expert, and Head of Department for Working Conditions in the Institute of Labour Research, Assistant Professor at the Academy of Craft and Design, invited lecturer at several Hungarian universities, manager of SZIGET Consulting Company, professional manager at the International Summer University for Ergonomics (Györ, Hungary), member of GfA (Gesellschaft für Aerbeitswissenschaft) and DPG (Deutsche Gesellschaft für Psychologies), and has 90 publications. The main topics in different national and international research programmes and consulting activities are as follows: job evaluation and wage systems, working conditions and work organization, work content, shift work, the impact of new technologies on the management of human resources, assessment of employees' values and attitudes, organizational development and communications training, ergonomics assessment and improvement of working conditions, mobbing (psychoterror) in the place of work, the organizational and management behaviour of multinational companies in Hungary, and the relationship between productivity and employment at different levels in Hungary.

Andrei Kuznetsov is Senior Lecturer on International Business at the Manchester Metropolitan University. He holds a PhD in Economics from the State Academy of Finance in Moscow and a PhD in Social and Political Sciences from the European University Institute in Florence. He has published extensively on the issues of post-communist economic transition in Russian and English including the book *Foreign Investment in Contempory Russia*, Macmillan, 1994.

Olga Kuznetsova is Post-Doctoral Fellow at the Centre for Policy Modelling of the Manchester Metropolitan University. Her current research includes work on changes in managerial behaviour in transition economies. She has published on this subject in such academic journals as *Europe–Asia Studies* and *Communist Economies and Economic Transformation*.

Stephen Little is Senior Lecturer responsible for postgraduate research within the Department of Business Information Technology (BIT) at the Manchester Metropolitan University following eleven years in Australia based at Griffith University, Brisbane and the University of

Wollongong NSW. He also held visiting fellowships to the Urban Research Programme at the Australian National University and the Fujitsu Centre for Managing Information Technology in Organisations at the Australian Graduate School of Management.

Tom Lupton has had extensive involvement in management education and development since 1959 when he became Head of Department at the then Birmingham CAT (now Aston University). His claim that he was the first British Industrial Anthropologist is well-founded, and his research and publications have covered such fields as industrial relations and personnel management, wage payment systems and change management. Most recently Tom has been working through EADA in Spain on a number of European initiatives to both assist in and to research the changes taking place in Central and Eastern Europe.

Robin Matthews is Professor of International Business Policy at Kingston University Business School. He has taught in many different countries in economics, strategy, organization theory and global business, and published over 25 papers and books that range over the disciplines. His current research interests include complexity and co-operative games. He works as a consultant with international companies and has carried out major work for the Confederation of British Industry. He is a director of EIS Consultants. He is also involved extensively with management training in the Russian Federation.

Frank McDonald is Head of the International Business Unit, Manchester Metropolitan University, and Jean Monnet award holder on the impact of EU integration on business activities. He has research interests in the area of the impact of economic integration on business strategies and operations and assessing the importance of the development of industrial clusters in the internationalization process.

Lawrence Reavill is a chartered chemical engineer with extensive experience of the management of research, development and technology in the chemical and metallurgical industries, particularly the management of technical innovation. He lectures in the management of technology in the Department of Management Systems and Information of the City University Business School. His research areas include management of change, innovation and technology, and holistic management – the application of a systematic approach to

management. His book, *Management for Engineers*, co-authored with
A.C. Payne and J.V. Chelsom, was published in 1996.

Gordon Redding is Affiliate Professor of Asia Business Schools at
Insead, and previously Professor of Management Studies at the University of Hong Kong, where he was also founding director of the
Business School. In Hong Kong from 1973 to 1997, he has researched
and published extensively on the subject of Asian business and comparative management. Present research projects include Asian systems
of capitalism, the operating issues for multinationals entering Asia,
and the management of expatriates.

Sir Bob Reid was Chairman and Chief Executive of Shell UK Limited
from April 1985 until September 1990, Chairman of the British Railways Board (on a full-time basis) from October 1990 until January
1995, and subsequently Non-Executive Chairman of Sears plc in June
1995. Sir Bob became Chairman of London Electricity in April 1994
and retired in February 1997, and is a member of the President's Com-
mittee of the Confederation of British Industry.

Bob Ritchie is Head of the Business and Management Studies Department, Crewe and Alsager Faculty of Manchester Metropolitan
University. His research interests and publications have been in risk
management, innovation and global strategic development. Current
research projects include international comparisons on Risk and
Crises Management and the development of management skills within
SMEs.

Reza Salami is Iranian, and completed a three-year PhD programme
at City University in 1996. His research examined the contribution of
international technology transfer to the industrialization of a number
of developing and newly-developed countries, and applied critical success factors derived from this study to the development of a technology
transfer strategy for Iran.

Lee Shuang is Senior Lecturer in the Strategy and Enterprise Division
at Staffordshire University Business School. His primary research interests are oriented around cultural issues within the fields of strategic
management, technology management and innovation. Current research projects are related to collaborative research with colleagues in
Mainland China and the Pacific-rim countries.

Thomas Steger is an assistant at the Department of Organization, Technical University Chemnitz-Zwickau (Germany), and its major areas of research interest include transformation processes in East Germany and Eastern Europe, organizational transformation and organizational culture.

Ian Taplin is Associate Professor, Department of Sociology, and Research Associate, Graduate School of Management, Wake Forest University, North Carolina. He has written extensively on restructuring in the US apparel industry as well as on the relationship between new technology and work organization.

Richard Thorpe is Professor in Management at Manchester Metropolitan University, Faculty of Management and Business. He has worked with colleagues in Central and Eastern Europe in projects relating to both research and development. He has published in the areas of motivation and reward, management learning and change, and research methods.

Will Williams is a Senior Lecturer in Strategic Management at the University of Glamorgan's Business School, where he is a lead lecturer on a number of undergraduate and postgraduate business strategy modules. He is currently researching the influence of national, regional and sectoral cultures upon organizational effectiveness, as well as the development of the Private Finance Initiative in the UK.

Jonathon Winterton is Professor in the Work Organization Research Unit of Bradford University. He has published extensively on restructuring in the clothing and coal mining industries.

Introduction

Frank McDonald and Richard Thorpe

BACKGROUND

This book is based on papers presented at a conference on the theme of Global Change held at Manchester Metropolitan University in 1996. The conference covered a wide range of topics in areas connected to changes in the international business environment. Sir Bob Reid, formerly chairman of Shell UK, gave a personal view on the major changes in the world business environment that were affecting the business community, and outlined some of the major challenges that were posed by global change. Experts in the areas of East Asia and Central and Eastern Europe provided overviews of the changes that were taking place in these regions. This book has been constructed from the three main themes of the conference which were focused on the implications of global change for: company strategy, technological change and organizational change.

Major issues that emerged from the conference were: (1) the implications for employment and working practices of the changes in the competitive environment brought about by internationalization, and (2) the need for companies to adopt strategies that take into account the wide variety of changes that are affecting the international business environment. Issues connected to cultural and institutional diversity across the major trading nations also emerged as a common feature in the papers and discussions at the Conference.

The presentation by Sir Bob Reid, the overviews on East Asia and Central and Eastern Europe, together with a selection papers that illustrate the main themes of the conference provide the content of this book.

CHANGE IN THE INTERNATIONAL BUSINESS ENVIRONMENT

The international business environment has experienced significant changes in the last two decades. The major changes, the main implications and the responses by companies that arise from these changes are outlined in Figure 1.

1

Figure 1 Major global changes

Changes

Liberalization Programmes
- WTO programmes to liberalize trade in goods and services
- Liberalization of capital markets

Regional Economic Integration Programmes
- Single European Market
- Economic and Monetary Union
- Regional integration agencies, e.g. NAFTA, APEC

Emergence of New Major Trading Nations
- Japan and the Asian Tigers
- China and India

Development of Market-based Economies
- Reforms in Central and Eastern Europe
- Imposition of market-based reforms in developing countries by the IMF/World Bank

Government Policies
- Privatization
- Reform of many product and labour market regulations
- Increased marketization of the means of delivering publicly provided goods and services

Technological Factors
- Growth of international standards
- Fast technology transfer
- Development of new technologies, e.g. IT, biotechnology

Political and Social Developments
- End of Communism in Europe
- Rise of Islamic power
- Opposition to the adjustment costs arising from the internationalization process
- Growing pressures to improve the environment

Implications

Increase in competitive environment requiring improvements in price and non-price competitiveness

New market opportunities and threats – expansion into new markets, contraction of mature markets, and loss of market share to companies from the new major trading nations

Adjustment to new market environments arising from privatization and deregulation

Need to adjust to fast technological change and to large-scale international technology transfer

Emergence of political and social movements with diverse views on how companies should relate to the societies in which they operate

Requirement for enhanced social, ethical and environmental awareness

Responses

Growth of direct foreign investment and other types of international business activities

Development of customer-driven supply chains

Introduction of flexible working to improve competitiveness

Increasing use of international strategic alliances to enhance competitiveness

Focus on leaner and fitter organizational structures, e.g. development of core competencies, re-engineering and lean supply chains

Development of R&D potential as a key method of creating and maintaining competitiveness

Use of technology transfer to boost competitiveness

Improvement of external relations by changing policies and by use of public relations exercises

These changes have not had equal effect in all parts of the world, or indeed across different sectors within single countries. Nevertheless, a number of tendencies can be identified that have wide-ranging effects across most companies in particular parts of the world.

In Western Europe the development of the Single European Market and the progress towards Economic and Monetary Union is leading to a growing rationalization of the European operations of companies. Furthermore, companies in many sectors in Western Europe and in North America face strong competition from Asian companies. These Asian companies have developed organizational structures and new production processes that appear to give them competitive advantage over their American and European counterparts. Trade liberalization programmes, enhanced capital mobility and easier technological transfer have encouraged companies to relocate activities to countries that provide a better base from which to develop a competitive advantage. Consequently, American and West European companies have been seeking to adopt new organizational structures, develop new production systems and engage in the relocation of activities to enable them to compete against leaner and more competitive Asian companies.

The evolution of regional economic integration, privatization and deregulation programmes in sectors such as telecommunications and the need to develop customer-orientated and directed supply chains have encouraged a significant amount of direct foreign investment into Western Europe and North America. As a consequence, global changes have not led to a one-way traffic of investment out of Western Europe and North America, and as privatization and deregulation programmes have been most actively pursued in America and in parts of Western Europe companies based in these regions have been able to acquire expertise in operating in this new competitive environment.

In another part of the world the reforms in Central and Eastern Europe have led to considerable restructuring of their institutional and organizational structures. Companies located in this region are adapting to global changes and adjusting to the rigors of operating in market-based economic systems. Multinational companies who relocate to Central and Eastern Europe are seeking to transfer western technology and management systems into a system that lacks many of the basic institutional requirements required by market-based systems. Given these problems it is possible that the direct transfer of western techniques is not an effective solution to the problems that face this region. In addition, the adjustment processes connected to the transformation of Central and Eastern European economic systems are leading to significant economic and social problems. Technological changes have also added to the pressures on companies to alter their activities. New technologies, especially the development of information technology-based systems, have led to new products, improved production systems and to obsolescence of many existing products and production systems. The growth of direct foreign investment, international joint-ventures, strategic alliances and other types of international business activities has also added to the pace and volume of international technology transfer.

Differences in culture and institutional frameworks across the nations and regions of the world may well provide a means whereby competitive advantage can be developed in the face of global changes. The success of East Asian countries may be, at least in part, due to the characteristics of their cultures and institutional frameworks. These unique cultural characteristics may mean that attempts to directly transfer technology and management systems to countries and regions that have different cultures may prove to be difficult or even counterproductive. Effective solutions for Central and Eastern Europe, for example, may well be different from those which would be successful in East Asia or the USA. Nevertheless, because of the pressures from common global forces there is a tendency, by countries that are heavily involved in international business transactions, to move in the same direction, albeit with implementation processes for new organizational and technological systems that take into account differences in institutional frameworks and cultural characteristics.

Global changes are leading to rapid and extensive changes in company strategies and operations. These changes often lead to high economic and social adjustment costs, arising especially from concentrations of unemployment in particular geographical areas or sectors of the economy. Concern about the implications for the physical environment as a result of past activities has led to pressure to force companies to curb or alter their operations that harm the environment. The growth of international business activities has been identified as a major contributory factor in environmental damage because of the increase in industrial production combined with the resultant demands for non-renewable resources and the growth in activities that pollute the environment. These changes have led to the growth of political and environmental groups who urge companies to alter their activities to reduce the stress on environmental, social and political systems that are caused by adjusting to increased international competition. In addition, pressures are increasingly being exerted on companies to face up to the social, ethical and environmental consequences of their activities. Clearly companies are faced with a variety of pressures as a result of the many global changes that they have, and are continuing, to experience. In response to these pressures they seek to improve their competitiveness but these attempts often lead to high adjustment costs as companies alter their organizational structures and introduce new technology. As globalization spreads, companies are increasingly operating in a number of countries and have to function in a variety of institutional and cultural settings. This diversity requires companies to adjust their operations to obtain the best possible outcomes in the many different environments in which they do business. These pressures, which can often result in conflicting incentives, are outlined in Figure 2.

There is a recognition that global changes are creating complex and perhaps conflicting pressures on companies. The chapters in this book examine these issues. Different views are expressed – some advocate the need for the adoption of a fairly uniform approach, often based on the adoption of Asian practices, others favour an approach that is tailored to the cultures and conditions that prevail in different countries or regions. The chapters examine these questions in a variety of areas – strategy, technological change and organizational learning. Therefore, the book provides a balance of views and opinions on the questions that arise from a consideration of the implications of global change on company strategy and operations.

SUMMARY OF THE CHAPTERS

The book has four main parts. The first contains the papers by Sir Bob Reid and the overviews of important issues facing East Asian countries and the countries of Central and Eastern Europe. The four chapters in Part 2 explore strategic issues arising from global changes. The third part examines issues connected with technological change, and Part 4 explores some of the lessons for organizational change.

Overview of the Key Issues in Global Change

In Chapter 1 Sir Bob Reid highlights many of the key issues that are raised by global changes. The background of the author, a major

6

Figure 2 Pressures arising from global changes

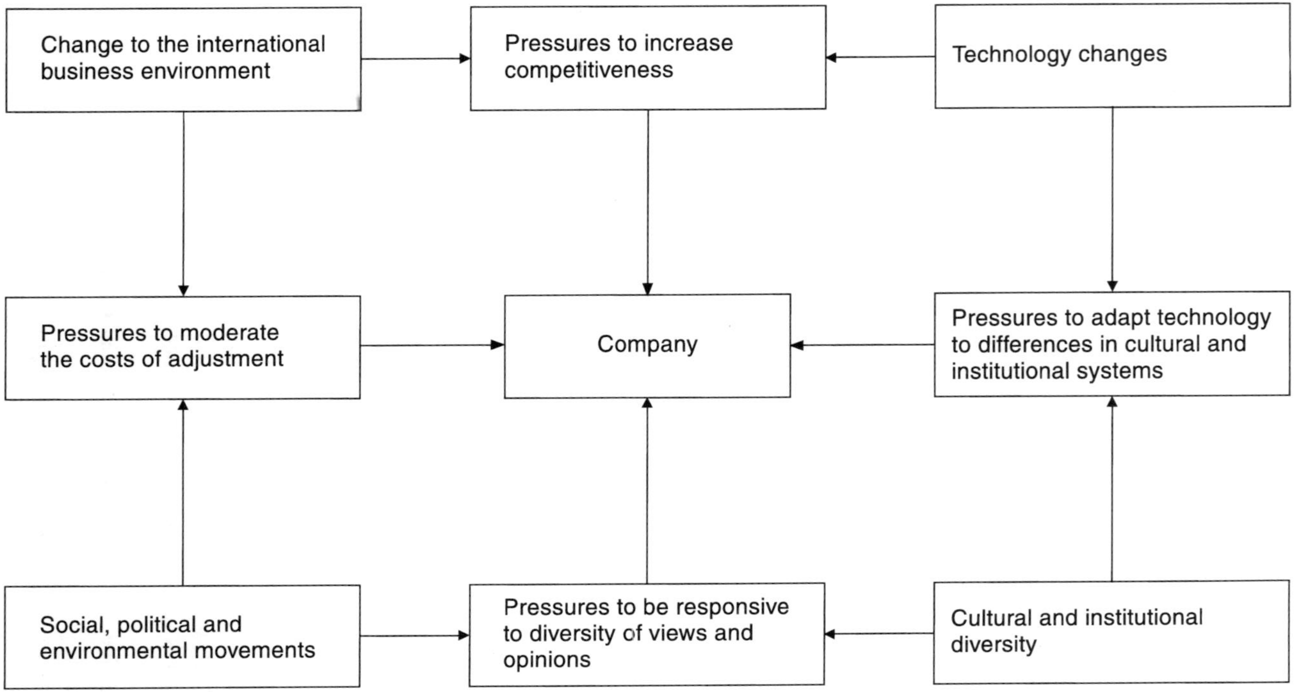

Technology changes

Pressures to adapt technology to differences in cultural and institutional systems

Cultural and institutional diversity

Change to the international business environment

Pressures to increase competitiveness

Company

Pressures to be responsive to diversity of views and opinions

Pressures to moderate the costs of adjustment

Social, political and environmental movements

executive figure with experience of managing many large successful international companies, provides the reader with an insight into the thinking of a leading industrialist on the main issues that companies face in adjusting to a range of global changes. Two major issues are considered to be paramount; problems of poverty, in the midst of plenty, and the pressures on the environment caused by the greater freedom, mobility and wealth that have, at least partially, arisen from the expansion and development of business activities. The chapter considers the impact of major political changes, the end of imperialism and the death of communism. These developments have left capitalism as the only viable form of economic interrelationship between individuals, groups and nations. However, differences in cultures and political and social frameworks have led to a variety of capitalist models. Companies, he argues, have to learn how to operate in this uncertain and diverse world. Moreover, they have to contribute to finding solutions to the problems of poverty and environmental degradation that have arisen in the modern world. The author argues that managers must develop a stronger ethical dimension to their work. This chapter indicates that companies must not only grow and develop to take advantage of the new opportunities that arise from global changes, but they must also make significant contributions to finding solutions to the economic and social problems that arise from the globalization process. In effect, this chapter suggests that companies can not leave economic and social problems to governments; companies themselves must become part of the solution rather that the creators of these problems.

Redding (Chapter 2) provides a thoughtful analysis of five forms of capitalism, individualistic (Anglo-Saxon capitalism), communitarian (West European capitalism), the *keiretsu* of Japan, the *chaebol* of Korea and the Chinese family business model. The chapter concentrates on the Chinese family business model of capitalism. This type of capitalism is based on a complex interaction between institutional structures, cultural factors and ideology. Redding argues that this form of capitalism is very different from western types of capitalism and from the Japanese and Korean variants as a consequence of the prevailing Chinese historical, cultural, legal and economic conditions. This model is emerging in China and other Asian countries where Chinese businesses constitute a significant proportion of economic activity. The argument he develops is that as these countries have some of the highest growth rates in the world they are certain to become major players in the world trading system. Therefore, a new vibrant and very different form of capitalism is likely to become an important driving force of global change. The chapter suggests that existing companies in the West, Japan and Korea will have to adjust to this phenomenon in order to compete and survive.

Chapter 3 by Hethy focuses on the problems of transforming Central and East European countries into modern market-based systems. The chapter highlights the problems that have arisen from concentrations of high unemployment in geographical areas as a result of the closure of uneconomic plants. He argues that long-term unemployment is increasing due to obsolete production technologies being replaced by modern systems that require different skills. Hethy argues that achieving macroeconomic stability can be painful, but that it is achievable if appropriate policies are adopted. However, creating the institutional frameworks that can ease the economic and social costs of the transformation programmes is proving to be the most difficult task. These issues are also explored by Kuznetsov and Kuznetsova (Chapter 11), Steger (Chapter 13) and Lupton *et al.* (Chapter 14).

Strategic Implications of Global Changes

Channon (Chapter 4) contrasts the strategic management practices that are predominately used in Anglo-Saxon countries with those of Asian companies (mainly in the Japanese version of capitalism). The author clearly favours the adoption of a more Asian (Japanese) approach to strategic management. One aspect of this is a move away from financially-determined and short-term strategies towards more long-term and production-driven strategies. Channon also explores the importance of an interventionist approach by governments as an aid to the development of company competitiveness. This issue is also considered, in the case of Singapore, by Ritche *et al.* (Chapter 10). The chapter by Channon outlines a case for western strategic thinking to be more influenced by the approach taken by the Japanese.

By using a game-theoretic framework Matthews (Chapter 5) illustrates the complexities that should be taken into account when assessing strategies that seek to boost the competitiveness of companies. Attempts to create and sustain competitiveness by the use of organizational change strategies such as re-engineering and lean production techniques may, he argues, be self-defeating if the implementation of these strategies leads to redistribution of the payoffs between the participants to the games. If strategies do not take into account the wider social and cultural implications of the pursuit of competitiveness, they are unlikely to achieve their purpose of boosting the net payoffs to companies. This chapter encourages the use of more rigorous tools of analysis to examine the strategic implications of global changes. His conclusion is that importance must be given to the tools of analysis that are best able to incorporate the complex interrelations that exist between the players of games that seek to attain international competitiveness.

Chapter 6, by Brown, outlines a simple method of assessing the ability of western countries to adjust to the pressure of increasing international competition. The author argues that existing forecasting models, such as those provided by econometric methods, are unable to provide useful information on the ability of countries to adjust to the pressures that arise from global change because these models can not incorporate, within their frameworks, the capacity of a country to achieve structural change. Brown calculates an index of the capability of major western countries to adjust to global changes and uses this to assess their prospects of successful adaptation. The ranking system, developed in the chapter, is also used to assess the ability of European countries to adjust to the changes that are likely to arise from the creation of European monetary union.

Taplin and Winterton (Chapter 7) provide an examination of the restructuring of the clothing industry in six high-wage countries in response to the growth of competition from lower-waged economies. They develop a model of the forces that both drive and constrain the adjustment processes in these six countries. From their analysis they observe a common pattern of adjustment which centres on the use of such strategies as outsourcing, niche marketing with higher value-added products, and the use of more advanced production technology. They also detect significant differences across these six countries which they attribute to the prevailing cultural and institutional conditions. They conclude that, overall, the clothing industry in these high-waged economies are not creating a new production paradigm as many have suggested, but, rather that new variants of *Taylorist* production systems are being created.

Technological Implications of Global Changes

The need for workable systems to ensure compatibility of standards to allow for effective technology transfer within business systems is explored in Chapter 8, by Little and Kaye. They consider that the growing internationalization of business activities is encouraging the development of business systems that encompass a variety of organizational and cultural systems. As a consequence companies must find ways to agree on and implement technological standards systems that will allow business networks to be effective in a wide variety of cultures and organizational structures. The authors examine this issue by use of several case studies.

An examination of the necessary policies that are required by developing countries to successfully utilize imported technology is provided by Salami and Reavill (Chapter 9). They do this by developing a model that takes into account the experience of East Asian economies. The ability to develop supporting infrastructures such as domestic R&D facilities and skilled labour emerge as the major requirements for the successful use of imported technology. Highlighted as important is an open policy towards the importation of foreign technology by use of direct foreign investments and other types of international business activities if successful international technology transfer is to take place.

Ritche *et al.* (Chapter 10) explore the importance of a number of cultural values in the process of aiding technological change. They use the case of Singapore to illustrate the importance that government policies play in creating a culture that is conducive to fast technological change. The authors argue that lessons may also be learned by western governments from the experience of Singapore. Cultural factors are considered to be of particular significance in the process of technology change. Moreover, they argue that governments can play an important role in encouraging the development of appropriate cultural conditions.

Implications for Organizational Change

Kuznetsov and Kuznetsova in Chapter 11 consider the problems connected to the privatization programmes in Russia. Their chapter highlights the difficulties of achieving the desired aims of increased efficiency when large-scale privatization programmes are used. The main problem identified is that Russia lacks the appropriate institutional frameworks to allow western-style organizational structures to generate efficient outcomes. They advocate that a policy of adapting western organizational structures to Russian conditions should be considered together with some reforms to a number of institutional frameworks in the Russian state.

The benefits that can arise from the use of culturally diverse project teams are considered by Iles and Hayes in Chapter 12. The authors argue that competitive advantage may emerge from the learning effects of using culturally mixed project teams because the learning process forces people to adjust to new and different ways of thinking and conceptualizing. A model of cultural diversity is constructed and this is illustrated through an assessment of two case studies where international project teams have been used.

The contribution by Steger (Chapter 13) considers the impact of organizational change in the context of the changes faced by East German managers as a result of the reunification of Germany. The case study approach adopted uses a qualitative approach based on a sociological model of how people react when faced with radical change.

The study by Lupton *et al.* (Chapter 14) offers a series of interviews with managers and workers as the basis of an assessment of the impact of foreign investment on labour markets and the management of companies in the Czech Republic and Hungary. The results illustrate a number of key issues that are raised by the radical changes that organizations have undergone. In particular, the need for governments to provide stable and effective institutional frameworks to allow both companies and workers to better adjust to changes. The study goes on to indicate that the problems caused by the economic and social adjustment costs that follow from radical change in the business environment must be tackled if these countries are to successfully integrate further into the world economic system.

As we have stated at the beginning of this introduction, the chapters in this book do not provide a common method for analysing the phenomenon of global changes. Neither do they indicate any agreed set of policy prescriptions for business organizations. Instead, the book highlights a variety of analytical tools, used in quite different ways, that lead to a diversity of scenarios and outcomes. These tools range from formal game-theoretic systems to inductive models based on observations from case-studies. Likewise the policy prescriptions that are suggested come in a variety of forms. Some, such as Brown and Channon's call for policies that are based on a fairly simple synthesis of existing data. Others, for example, Matthews or Little and Kay, argue for more rigorous analytical systems that would allow for the construction of policy prescriptions that would more accurately reflect the complexities of global changes.

The editors regard this diversity of approach as helpful as it offers the reader different perspectives that permit for a fuller understanding of the multitude of complex factors that arise from global changes. We believe that by providing a variety of policy prescriptions the chapters contribute to the debate on how business organizations may best respond to the challenges raised by global changes.

Although a variety of different approaches and views are reflected in the chapters, a number of common factors are repeatedly identified as being of significance. The most common reference was to the importance of differences in cultural characteristics and institutional frameworks as important factors contributing to the complexity of global change. In addition the political, social and environmental costs of the adjustment to increasing international competition was also identified as a major factor that affected both the direction of global changes and the responses of business organizations to these changes.

The editors hope that this book will stimulate business managers, academics and students to develop, extend and clarify the many complex factors that arise from the global changes that are having an impact on business organizations.

Part 1

An Overview of Key Issues in Global Change

1 An Industrialist's View of Global Change

Sir Bob Reid

This chapter begins by defining its context: firstly, there is the political context of the day and how the resolution of one problem can produce through its outcomes more uncertainty and issues rather than less. My conclusion suggests that there will be many question marks as we depart this century. Secondly, there is the economy, and in this section I wish to deal with the primary issue of energy and link this to the environment, mobility and poverty. Poverty I see linked in its turn to widespread societal disaffection within industrialized societies. Unfortunately, the chapter will not address the case of the many millions of people, mostly children, who die from malnutrition and starvation without access to professional health services or even to clean drinking water. The plight of these human beings is unlikely to be touched or influenced by global change unless that change is much more fundamental than anything so far conceived.

In 1789 the French witnessed the storming of the Bastille which marked the beginning of the French Revolution; exactly 200 years later in 1989 we witnessed an event perhaps at least as important, in the ending of the Cold War. It was in 1989 that the ideological confrontation between capitalism and communism came to an end in favour of capitalism. This confrontation had been a long and arduous struggle which had not ended in war in Europe, but instead saw defeat coming out of the total collapse of a system that could not be sustained economically nor be supported any longer by its individual citizens. When the challenge came as to which direction to take, Gorbachev chose to let go of the reins and the whole system collapsed.

From a purely political point of view the victory was for the democratic system over totalitarianism, and totalitarianism in the shape of German national socialism had already been spectacularly defeated in 1945. Democracy, at least for the time being, had won the day and the forces that had brought matters to a head in 1989 had been consolidated by concern for the welfare and material well-being of individual citizens. Through television and media this had become increasingly apparent to the Eastern Bloc countries. The Berlin Wall between East

Germany and West Germany may have prevented mass emigration but it did little to stop the citizens in East Germany seeing how well their brothers and sisters in West Germany were doing and how prosperity had grown in comparison with their own relatively poor circumstances. So, in the end, it could not deliver what the citizens wanted, and the opportunity fell to the politicians to pick up the challenge and help to begin to undermine the system which was not delivering and no longer had the controls and the will to ensure survival. Hence the emergence of Gorbachev and all the relaxations in control which could then take place after he began to make changes. But how often is it the case that it is sometimes easier to explain what you don't want rather than what you do want?

With the collapse of communism that question is very much in the fore. If capitalism is what the citizens want, what changes and modifications would the citizens like to see in its present form? As the battle against communism intensified in the immediate postwar years it would be wrong to assume that the political systems of the West were themselves not undergoing a process of change. The forces of imperialism which had been rampant in the nineteenth century were no longer as important in the middle of the twentieth century. Rather the reverse, the advantages of an empire were increasingly outweighed by the responsibilities Empire brought. Keeping different countries and their expatriates under control and in some form of acceptable prosperity had become too heavy a responsibility even for the wealthiest countries. So it is probably true to say that the successes of independent movements owed as much to the shedding of responsibility by the imperial powers as they did to the leaders of the newly-independent countries. It was perhaps only in the case where energy was involved, particularly oil and gas, that any form of imperial relationship or behaviour was still relevant. As a consequence, by 1948 Britain's withdrawal from India was followed during the 1950s and 1960s by all the old colonial countries of Africa becoming independent, and the withdrawal of Portugal from its colonial responsibilities in Angola and Mozambique. The British withdrawal was in many ways quite well-managed despite the occasional outbursts of frustration about the speed and the timing of the change.

By the mid-1960s imperialism was dead and buried, and with the death of imperialism came the application of international responsibility; minding your own business was as good an excuse as any to stop any foreign involvement which might be expensive and politically unpopular, particularly when the body bags began to arrive home. Even so, the determination to stop the threat of communism saw America involved in Vietnam and from time to time making sorties into South America. These conflicts I would contend were as unpopular in America as they were unsuccessful. However, the fact remains that the world does not always behave in a perfect way and with the television cameras the problems of individual countries are ever present and available to be seen by the electorates of America and Europe. This has on a number of occasions meant that non-involvement is just not possible.

The problems of Central Africa and the difficulties in Bosnia all produce public support for action. It is impossible for politicians today to stay uninvolved whether it be troops in Bosnia or talks to ensure a continuing peace between Arabs and Israelis. Many of these actions can now be conducted through the medium of the United Nations which from being only a debating house 10 years ago has become the instrument which legitimates direct military action. The care with which the Americans obtained approval for their move on Iraq in 1992 is a very clear example of this process in action. Twenty years ago this would have been inconceivable.

So to summarize on the political front, looking back over the post-war years, change has become global, dramatic and in a way disturbing, if not downright dangerous. I believe the year 1989 was a seminal point in the history of the twentieth century; whilst it solved the Cold War it left many questions unanswered, and above all it put a huge question mark over Russia and its satellites and perhaps, even more worryingly, over China. How China will develop in the next 20 years and how its political and economic revolution will impact on politics and prosperity of the whole world will be crucial. Drawing scenarios against this background is certainly a much more difficult task than it was in the more certain days of the 1980s.

Turning now to the second theme of this chapter, the economy. Here there are fundamental forces at play which I believe need to be identified and understood. Firstly, there is the role of the state in a free market economy. This is not as simple an issue as it is often purported to be by some political parties or pundits. In Britain, the answer has been different from France and different again from Germany. Privatization is symptomatic of the question posed at the beginning of the chapter: 'what do we want?' We know what we don't want, the positive answer is slightly more difficult to find; suffice it to say that the role of the state is gradually being redefined and with it the role of the private sector. The transfer of responsibility is not a simple matter – reward is one thing, risk is another. It is not unusual for governments to happily transfer the neglect of decades one year and charge the successor corporations for inadequate assets and incompetence the next. Never have the words been more relevant when you want to consider privatization. Secondly, there is the issue of energy which was one of the top problems of the 1970s and 1980s and which has now virtually disappeared. In those days of the oil shortage much was written and much spoken about renewable reserves and the need for smaller cars, insulated homes and energy conservation in every possible form. These concerns have been suppressed as cheap energy has reappeared, but the problems have not gone away. Now that we have had military action in the Middle East it is unlikely that the oil flow will be disturbed by negative political action. The Iraq war set a precedent and let the world know that the West was not prepared to suffer a destruction of the energy flow that fuels industries and heats and lights individuals' homes. The cost of obtaining the answer may in the future cause embarrassment, but in many ways a precedent has been set. The question of price however is another matter. It is clear that with the present fuels and the present reserves shortage will not be an issue for some time in the future, but it will be an issue that will have to be faced sometime in the future. What is more certain is that pressure on energy is more likely to come from the problems the environment faces and the need to reduce hydrocarbon emissions. This is a political problem which will not go away and which is already climbing up the agenda as more of our children suffer from asthma and public health concerns grow apace.

If I dwell on this problem of energy and transport for a moment two points can be made. Firstly, freedom of speech was a freedom hard won in the nineteenth century and one which we are increasingly abusing in the twentieth. Personal mobility is the freedom of the twentieth century which we are now increasingly abusing, and in doing so seriously damaging the environment. However, the politician who interferes with personal mobility with a view of containing it is on a total loser. What the politician must address is how this desire to be mobile may be satisfied in a way which is less damaging in its impact on the environment. This problem has had much political comment but so far very little positive action. It will remain a persistent concern and will affect the framing of economic policies well into the next decade – with the environment and its protection a priority of the next century. A second related issue is that the technology already exists that makes personal communication so much easier; modern designs and new materials can produce much lighter, more fuel-efficient, smaller motor cars, trains can go faster and hold more people. Even the molecular structure of gasoline can be created from a variety of sources. Each of these factors properly managed could lead us to the conclusion that we may not have an energy problem. The ingenuity of human beings to solve their problems is infinite and like our fore-fathers we have more than enough creativity to find a path to the future. For example, it has been shown that a brown-water kelp farmed on a racecourse in the United States could easily satisfy all the natural gas requirements of that country. Now brown-water kelp is a simple plant easily reproducible and no doubt in the face of a continuing energy crisis it could be made to do what the public requires. Equally, gasoline from sugar could result in Australia becoming the refinery for Japan. So with our technological prowess, matched with our under-standing of botany and our knowledge of agriculture, the fundamental problem of an energy crisis need not arise.

Turning now to the issue of the economy in terms of wealth and the distribution of wealth. It is undoubtedly the case that over the last 30 years the gap between the rich and poor has grown in virtually every country in Europe except Germany and Scandinavia. There are a var-iety of reasons for this, beginning with the way the move from industrial societies to information societies has put a premium on the knowledge worker. As knowledge workers are involved in every aspect of business from financial services to retailing and from production to telecom-munications, their expertise and even confidence commands a premium which the majority achieve. The gap becomes even wider when an examination is made of the new information workers' relations with one another. Put simply, if an assessment is made of the wealth of two knowledge workers living together without children, and this is con-trasted with the single mother living on her own in a council flat bringing up say two children, it can be seen how the gap grows. The DINKY's (Dual Income No Kids Yet) income rises as the single mother's sinks. However, if you consider that members of the next generation are living with her and not with the knowledge workers, then a different complexion is brought to the problem. This simple fact multiplied many times over becomes an issue for society for the next century.

The United States is already beginning to find that there is a shortage of people required to run and operate businesses with all the complexities this entails. The degradation of the manpower resource is causing concern that there will not be the people with either the mo-tivation, the education, the ability or the qualifications to make up for the shortfall in this important economic activity. By contrast, in Germany the gap has stayed much smaller because of the power of the unions, and while this has kept the skill aspect of the problem under control it has raised the more fundamental problem of the competitiveness of the German economy in the short and longer term – this itself may have equally serious implications. Poverty, however, is only one side of the equation. An even darker side is the disaffection members of society may feel and the development of an underclass which can, by crime and drugs, destroy the basic fabric of society. The most fundamental debate requires to be held on education and the broader issue of just how we prepare our citizens for participation in the world of tomorrow.

Over this century we have advanced in areas far beyond the imagination of those conceived in 1900. Our transport and communication systems are at a level of sophistication which even 50 years ago would have been incomprehensible. Our ability to satisfy basic human needs is no longer in doubt. Our ability to understand technological processes and biological developments has advanced and will continue to advance with the strides in computing technology. We have progressed in medicine and this is reflected in the longevity of our citizens which in turn presents its own problems and its own opportunities. Our economic processes have become much more successful, not only in monetary terms but in the quality and reliability of outputs.

Where we have advanced little, or perhaps we have regressed, is in our understanding of ourselves. If Dunblane had happened in the middle of a ghetto in New York or in the degradation of an inner city in any country in Europe, the solutions would have been much more easily defined. Obviously there would have been drugs involved, there would have been hate built up over a period of time against society and against the collection of innocent individuals who perhaps appeared to the perpetrator to be much happier and more content about their own personal circumstances than himself. The fact is that it happened in Dunblane and so it poses a question which we all ponder.

What is it that makes individuals conduct themselves in a sensible and reasonable way towards their fellow human beings and what is it that does not? This is a problem which has not been subject to change, which is still there and which we must all address. Recently I have been working, and continue to work, on a project which is dealing with what young people – the next generation – want in the next century. The art work and the poetry they have produced depicts deep concerns of many of the issues touched on in this chapter. They turn away from the rational and the scientific analysis and instead their thinking is intuitive. They feel that the world is wrong and they want to play a part in putting it right. In a way it is as if they want the responsibility of imperialism without the material advantage. The force of their view is strong and the fundamental question I raise is: are we entering one of the great transition phases of our civilization as the adequacy of scientific analysis is challenged as the primary process by which we should solve our societal problems, as the decline of patriarchy radically revolutionizes our value system, as materialism fails to satisfy our real need to contribute to the community and the common will? Certainly the environment of the twenty-first century has less certainty and a less clearly defined impetus than its predecessor. In this situation – one of turbulence and change – we all have a chance to guide and shape a revolution which is worthy of a new millennium. The Chinese see the word 'change' as synonymous with crisis, and that in turn means danger and opportunity. We have a chance to play our part in ensuring it is opportunity.

2 The Changing Business Scene in Pacific Asia

Gordon Redding

There are three issues of particular relevance to the western world as it comes to terms with understanding Pacific Asia:

1. There are currently five successful forms of capitalism able to compete effectively in world markets. In simple terms these are:

    a) the western individualist form represented in the large divisionalized firm;
    b) the western communitarian form found commonly on the European mainland;
    c) the large Japanese network of firms now usually called *keiretsu*;
    d) the Korean *chaebol*;
    e) the Chinese family business.

    It is necessary for managers who work in one form to understand that the other forms are viable alternative structures answering organizational challenges by the use of methods grounded in historical traditions of their own societies.

2. The emergence of new large business groups built by the ethnic Chinese of the Asian region is a new feature now having an impact on world markets. For western firms going to do business in Asia these are potentially very significant as partners, competitors, suppliers or customers. Their significance in western business environments is so far limited, except in the context of parts supply or made to order (MTO) manufacturing where their impact is not obvious, but is substantial.

3. Changes in China, despite the difficulties of predicting future trends, are potentially very important for the future balance of world business. The most important change is the tendency for the influence of capitalism to increase markedly. This is visible in the growth of a healthy private sector, now moving towards 25 per cent of the economy, but more significantly in the behaviour of the collectivist, or town and village enterprise sector, which increasingly adopts the behaviour patterns found in capitalist societies.

This latter sector is expected to grow to 50 per cent of the economy by the year 2000, and is ahead of expectations now in doing so.

Western managers coming to terms with the Asian system of capitalism may find it useful to take note of the huge variety of business environments in the region, and of levels of economic development and sophistication. At the same time, certain common themes remain to pose constant challenges, and to prevent the effectiveness of simply transferring techniques and assumptions from back home. Some of the more frequently found issues are:

1. The need to co-opt political support locally because of the greater involvement of government in the economy.
2. The need to understand that in societies where trust is not handled by using institutions like law and contract, and widely accepted principles of rationality, the establishing of reliable business deals and relationships rests heavily on the moralities of interpersonal obligation.
3. Particularly for the ethnic Chinese, the drive to own their own businesses is very strong, and employing entrepreneurs is not easy in western systems.
4. The labour markets of the region vary greatly, and in many there is a serious shortage of executive, professional and technical talent.
5. The availability of reliable information on restrictive government behaviour is often unpredictable and markets can appear very unstructured. The level of uncertainty is threatening to most firms entering for the first time.
6. The type of authority seen as legitimate in most Asian cultures is paternalistic. More participative styles are often not understood.
7. Many large western firms do a poor job of preparing executives for the region, and also retain a high level of ignorance about methods of doing business there. Ethnocentrism in head office remains a common complaint among executives working in Pacific Asia. Also, assignments of three years do not make it easy to develop the network of personal ties seen as necessary in such environments.

FIVE FORMS OF CAPITALISM

This chapter aims to give some perspectives on South-East Asia as seen from that part of the world, Pacific-Asia; the aim is to highlight three

particular aspects which are useful in understanding the changes taking place. One is that there is not one form of capitalism required to
compete in world markets today, but in fact five. A second is to discuss
one form which very few people know about mainly because there is
very little literature, that is the ethnic Chinese model of Pacific-Asia,
and a development of this is to speculate what is happening in China.

It is recognised that the five forms of capitalism which are internationally competitive rest upon work in fact which is ongoing. As a
result there are several versions of what these actually are, but generally they are agreed as follows: the first and most obvious form is the
western individualist form of capitalism which most clearly manifests
in the classic multi-divisionalized bureaucratic firm, this is the form
that is in the majority of text books. The second form of capitalism
which is apparently still very competitive is sometimes referred to as
the communitarian form of capitalism, this is more typical of western
Europe outside the United Kingdom, for example in Germany and
France and some other countries. It is communitarian in the sense that
the number of stakeholders involved in the strategy-making of those
firms is much wider than in the Anglo/American model, and there is a
much more open debate between interested parties and stakeholders in
the enterprise which include even the banks, government and the
public, as well as labour, management and customers. Many would
argue that this is a much more difficult form of capitalism to manage
than many, and one which is much more frustrating for managers than
many other forms. Viewed from some perspectives the model can even
appear extreme. Whilst on a visit to Peking the Head of Daimler-Benz
in China received this comment from the Chinese President. He had
been bemoaning the problems of making money in western Europe,
saying how labour was difficult in Germany with all the attendant
problems of margins and cost structures, and at one point in the
meeting the Chinese President stopped him and said 'In China we
couldn't possibly afford the Marxist–Leninist extravagances of the
German labour-relations system'. The way the world looks depends
upon the shape of the window.

In putting forward the view that there are in fact five forms of capitalism, – individualistic (Anglo-Saxon), communitarian (West European), *keiretsu* (Japan), *chaebol* (Korea) and Chinese family business
model – the argument is for the development of a conceptual framework within which to understand their emergence. Often what develops in these capitalist systems is partly a result of culture, history and
accident and partly a result of the standard processes of economic

history, all being worked out in different contexts. It is the contexts which make the difference, and what is meant by 'forms' of capitalism is the merging of these variables as they run together and interplaying with each other. In the Far East, for instance in Japan, the most representative firm is the large conglomerate, *keiretsu* in Korea the *chaebol*. The *keiretsu* is publicly owned and professionally managed, and the *chaebol* is privately owned and family managed. Together with the Chinese small family businesses, these are three quite different types of organization.

The relationship between firms in an economy which make up a form of capitalism also vary in some societies. In some there is permission to form cartels, often unspoken but still there. In others much more elaborate networks between organizations exist. This will be discussed in more detail later. In other societies, particularly the western individualistic ones, there is a belief in perfect competition and hence the need to break up cartels, and the need to try to create a level playing field for a 'fair game'. This is not universal, it is a peculiarly western form of understanding about how economic behaviour should be structured. And, finally, there is the way the firm holds together, the glue, the psychological cement which holds it together.

All these forms emerge out of the particular history of modernization which a society goes through, and this has taken place over the last 100–150 years in some cases, although much more rapidly in countries such as Korea where it has really only taken place from the 1950s onwards; in Japan it has taken place from about 1860, in the UK from about 1780, and in the USA from about 1820. Different forms of organizations take different periods of time to modernize. But in modernization what occurs is that the way in which firms have access to capital shapes things differently; so one society will invent a joint-stock company regulated through stockmarkets, and there will be a free press and an accounting system that is open to audit and an intense form of rationality which drives firms to satisfy quarterly returns. Another kind of society in working out how to get access to capital will come to the conclusion it is best done through the government. Yet another will achieve this through the banks, which happens in Japan. The ethnic Chinese do it through social networks. So the means whereby capital is accessed and directed to those areas of business where there is the maximum potential for profitability is different as each society has quite different understandings about its institutional structure, and the accidents of different political philosophies, their experiences, their borrowing and ideals create different structures.

The same is also true of the access to skill. This is particularly visible in management where the western world has relatively recently invented the discipline of management which has become codified and professionalised. It would be a big mistake to believe this is universal. The Japanese to a greater extent do not do this, neither do the Germans. This factor is also part of the formulae that creates different kinds of organizations. They are of course embedded in the societal matrix which is called culture, which goes much deeper and endures for a much longer period in evolutionary history, and which of course varies in the clarity with which it gets expressed. It has always struck me that the three main components of culture which make a difference to what emerges later in our institutions, our companies and our practice are trust, identity and authority (see Figure 2.1).

Figure 2.1   The main components of culture

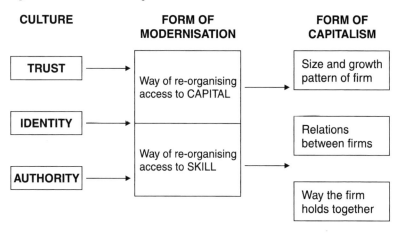

A society which institutionalizes trust is very different from a society which is based on personal trust. Both have a moral base, but the moral bases and the behaviour patterns are different, and as a consequence the trust structures and therefore the transaction structures are also different, so that the economies are different. So, in most of Pacific-Asia business people operate by interpersonal obligation as a basis of trust. There is little resort to law or institutional trust as in the West. The same is true of identity, the collectivist as opposed to the individualist, and so too with authority, the hierarchical versus the autonomous, so that the kind of authority that is considered legitimate varies with the culture.

Using a model like this makes some explanation for some of the crucial differences between western forms of business and Pacific-Asian forms of business. There are of course many others which could be said to be hybrids or which are not yet fully developed to a level of international efficiency. What appears to me to be happening is a game being played in which there is a first division, and a series of second and third divisions. The first division contains the western individualist and the western communitarian, Chinese, Japanese and Korean, the five forms of capitalism.

The purpose of this chapter is to open up one of these boxes that people in the West know little about; this is the Chinese form of capitalism. The Chinese operate over a range of different kinds of organizations, and their most successful form is the family business, particularly outside China among the ethnic Chinese of Pacific-Asia. These people are emigrants, and they left China over the last hundred years or so moving south in sub-groups – 'tribes'. The dispersion of these tribal groups can be seen in Figure 2.2.

Moving down the South China coast there is in the area just opposite Taiwan, the Fouchow, then the HocChia, Henghua, Hockien, Teochew, Hakka, Cantonese and lastly the Hainanese. These groups all speak different languages from each other, dialect groups which are mutually unintelligible more or less, but which hang together and can be made to be understood in places like Indonesia, Malaysia, Thailand and the Philippines – as in the case of poor emigrants and coolie labourers a hundred years ago. There such groups they make money and build large companies out of small companies. The result has been amazing. In Indonesia, for example, a recent study by the Australian government (Table 2.1) showed that in 1988 the Sino-Indonesian (the ethical Chinese in Indonesia) held 74 per cent of total assets in the top 300 conglomerates in Indonesia. By only 1993 this percentage had grown to 80 per cent, yet they represent only 4 per cent of the population. In the Philippines they hold 68 per cent of the sales volume of all commerce with only 1 per cent of the population. In Thailand, the picture is the same with 70 per cent of sales controlled by the ethnic Chinese who represent only 8 per cent of the population. The biggest companies in Thailand are shown in Table 2.2, where those marked[*] are owned by overseas Chinese; the only one that isn't happens to be owned by the king.

If one considers the gross level, the macro-economic level, there is a sense in which these ethnic Chinese are in total charge in places like Taiwan, Hong Kong and Singapore. The volume of money that has

28

Figure 2.2 Main towns and ports of Chinese emigration to Singapore

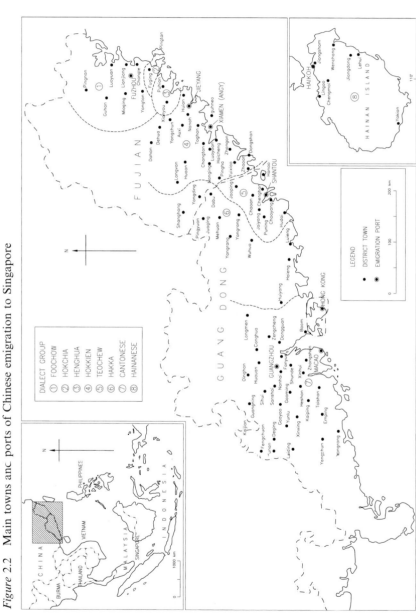

Source: Adapted from figures 1.1 and 2.2 in Cheng, Lim Keak, *Social Change and the Chinese in Singapore* (Singapore: University Press, 1985).

Table 2.1   Ethnicity of Indonesia's top 300 conglomerates (as at 1993, by gross assets)

Ethnicity	1988		1993	
	Number	Total Assets (%)	Number	Total Assets (%)
Sindo-Indonesian	191	74.6	204	80.1
Pribumi Joint	98	23.4	81	16.4
Pribumi/Sino-Indonesian	11	2.0	15	3.6

Source: Pusat Data Business Indonesia, *Conglomeration Indonesia*, 2nd edn, Jakarta, 1994.

Table 2.2   The ten largest business groups in Thailand

Group name	Family owner	Main business line	1988 sales in millions of US $
1. Siam Cement	The Crown Property Bureau	Cement, pulp, steel, autoparts, petrochemicals	1,613
2.*Bangkok bank	Sophonpanich	Financial conglomerate (finance, insurance, textile, sugar, real estate	1,571
3.*Charoen Pokphand (CP)	Chiarawanon	Feedstuff, broilers, prawns, meat processing, petrochemicals	1,222
4.*Thai Famer's Bank	Lamsam	Financial conglomerate (finance, insurance, food, real estate)	921
5.*Siam Motors	Phornprapha	Automobile assembly, autoparts, manufacture, flourite	711
6.*Saha	Cholkwattana	Daily goods, apparel, food, shoes, electronics	630
7.*Metro	Laohathai	Fertiliser, flour milling, tapioca, steel, silos	597
8.*Bangkok Metropolitan	Teechaphaibuun	Financial conglomerate (finance, real estate, liquor, beer)	531
9.*Saha-Union	Darakanon	Textiles, apparel-related goods, shoes, electronics	516
10.*Sukri	Bodiratnangkura	Textiles, apparel, polyster production	504

* Owned by overseas Chinese.

been accumulated over the last 30 years is astonishing. The foreign reserves of these three countries – US $ 223 billion – puts them in the top five economies worldwide. What is even more significant is that they are all very small countries. If the income per capita figures are examined (from world economic forum data) they indicate that in terms of per capita purchasing power parity Hong Kong is now the third largest in the world.

If the focus is put on investments in China (see Table 2.3) we find that enormous sums of money are flowing from all over the world, but by far the biggest investors are the overseas Chinese. These are largely individuals and, except for one, nearly all are Chinese and take the form of family businesses. They come from Hong Kong, Indonesia, Malaysia or wherever they are settled. These businesses are pouring money into China at a far higher rate than anybody else. In terms of organizational structure and culture they can be characterized as a form of guerrilla army troop designed and trained for guerrilla warfare, and they could be our competitors in an unwinnable game if we're not careful. Their characteristics (see Table 2.4) are small size, simple structure, centralized decision-making, and the way they are controlled by a dominant owner. The style of management is paternalistic and distinctly so, even nepotistic again distinctly, and coupled with an intense concentration on efficiency and an obsession with money and cash flow. These business-owners believe in making money sweat as well as people and they do this for 24 hours a day, 365 days a year; and if the data on the use of working capital is examined you can find textbook examples of how not to waste a penny.

Table 2.3   Ten largest investors in China (by total project costs)

Rank	Investor	Total project costs (HK$bn)
1	Hopewell	100.1
2	Cheung Kong	90.5
3	New World Dev (1)	56.2
4	Kumagai Gumi	49.9
5	Hutchison Whampoa	38.7
6	China Light & Power	33.0
7	Wharf	16.8
8	Henderson	13.2
9	Paliburg	9.7
10	Lippo	9.2

(1) For nearly 50% of investments. Total Project Cost was unavailable.

Table 2.4   Chinese family business

---

1. Typically small scale and simply structured.
2. Centralized decision-making by dominant owner.
3. Paternalistic company culture.
4. Nepotistic.
5. Intense concentration on efficiency. Lean and mean.
6. Tendency to focus on specialized field based on owner's expertise.
7. Long term strategic alliances and flexible networks.
8. Weak in complex integrations/international brand marketing requiring decentralization to professionals.
9. Highly adaptive, opportunity seeking.
10. Large-scale versions now appearing
    – diversified
    – professional

In terms of markets and products there is a tendency to focus on a specialized field, one that is aligned with the owner's own expertise. Typically, the owner immerses himself in an industry concentrating on that which is known thus keeping the knowledge at the centre of the business and protecting it. This enables a clearer view of the long-term strategic alliances, and flexible networks that might be developed (see Table 2.5). What they don't have are complex integration systems or strong international brand marketing competences which require decentralization to professionals; but what they do have are ways of getting into other markets by MTO, there are highly adapted and opportunity seeking, and there are large-scale versions now appearing which are diversified and beginning to become more professional.

To illustrate this point, Figure 2.3 shows the kind of picture one might get of the region if we were to ask a merchant banker the

Table 2.5   Common denominators in successful Asian business recipes

---

1. Long term relationships behind business deals.
2. Long term financial perspective (especially Japan).
3. Often bank-driven rather than capital-market driven.
4. Paternalistic corporate cultures.
5. Tight performance control.
6. Long term co-opting of political support.
7. Relationship-dominated sourcing and marketing.
8. Internal labour markets (especially managerial).
9. Use of network alliances.
10. Home government co-operation (Korea, Japan)

Figure 2.3   The 70 major Chinese family business groups in Pacific Asia

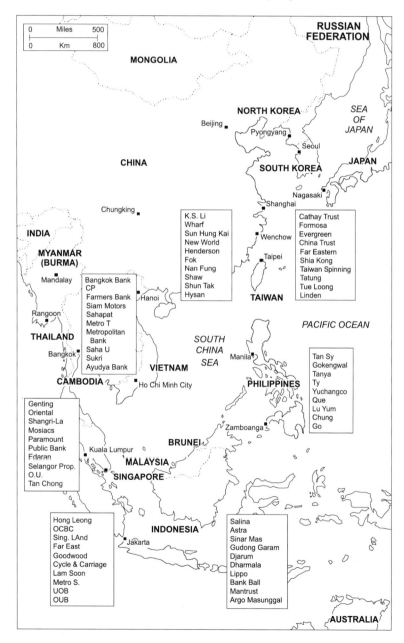

question, 'who runs the region?', 'who should such and such a firm deal with?', 'who should they set up joint ventures with?' and 'just who are the big players in the game?' The big players are shown in the seven inset boxes. For the sake of simplicity China is not included but all these companies extend into China, and in this sense the map is a very deceptive one. Figure 2.4 shows the actual trading relationships which have been established and the deals that have taken place over the last four years which amount to over $10 billion. The impression we wish to illustrate is one of networking, something which the ethnic Chinese are very effective at. Figure 2.4 illustrates the big players in each country who are in this case ethnically Chinese in Hong Kong, Thailand, Malaysia, Singapore, Indonesia, Philippines and Taiwan; a huge 'opportunity seeking' machine in which collaboration over very rare information is strategic.

This sharing of information which is unobtainable by other people because it depends on government contracts, bribery, inside information, long-term obligation and family connections becomes a strategic component of the firm's behaviour. Once such information about an opportunity is obtained before somebody else spots it, capital is provided to take advantage of the opportunity, and it needs to be borne in mind that these markets are very volatile and very uncertain. Their networks are needed to siphon in the capital, thus sharing the risk, but sometime in the future obligations may be called upon to share new opportunities in the other person's space.

Deals are therefore done one after the other, the game being not so much how much return on capital can be made (the minimum requirement in the region is about 25 per cent and the yield is required for four years), but rather what is the capital gain? And here companies are looking for 300–400 per cent. That is how US$ 223 billion is created from nothing in 30 years. It is a formidable machine and that machine is what is now beginning to operate in China; it has already taken over the region. At the moment the discussion is not about Japan, although Japan is also a major investor in perhaps rather different fields – mainly in heavy industry, large-scale manufacturing and sophisticated high-tech products. What this overseas-Chinese machine is focusing on are the rest – namely retailing, wholesaling, distribution, small-scale manufacture, OEM, service industries and so on – all the large sectors of most economies, and these are very large and employ large numbers of people.

Before concluding it is worth reflecting on one or two additional aspects to this huge economic machine sitting on the edge of China

Figure 2.4   Overseas-Chinese business webs

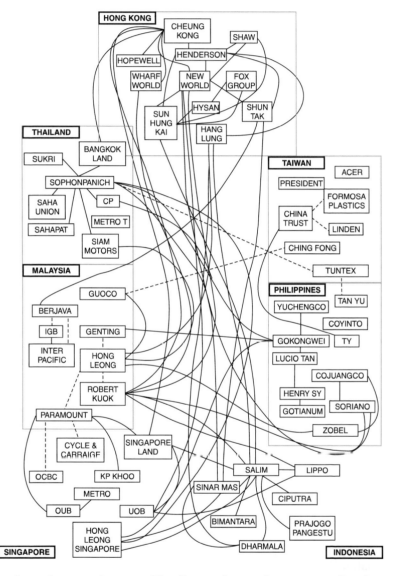

and moving to take over. The first and most important point that needs to be made is that China is undergoing a complete restructuring of its economy. Taking the sectors of the economy which appear most crucial, in 1980 24 per cent of the Chinese economy was what was called the collective sector – this consisted of township enterprises and neighbourhood organizations. The remaining 76 per cent comprised the state-owned enterprise sector. Two parts, both heavily tied up with the machinery of the state, and all with a communist party member in the boardroom, sometimes several. By the year 2000 (and the indications are that China is ahead of schedule), the aim is to have 27 per cent of firms as state-owned enterprises, 48 per cent in the collective sector, and 25 per cent will be private; quite simply the state-owned sector will have collapsed.

What is interesting is that most recent studies done on the collective sector indicate that a clearly entrepreneurial mindset is developing. Organizations are being built opportunistically by local government officials in conjunction with either foreign Chinese capital or technology, or they have developed through their own entrepreneurial skill and they are being run just like businesses, serious businesses, which are in competitive markets and use modern technology. If this is the case, and the private sector is the really booming sector in standard classical capitalist mode, then 75 per cent of the Chinese economy will be behaving in a capitalist manner only four years from now. That is a truly astounding revolution.

One explanation for this is that the state-owned enterprise sector is so hopeless. Examining productivity data it can be seen that Chinese productivity when adjusted in terms of capital productivity has a score of 120 against a US-adjusted score of 260 (see Table 2.6), in other words it is less than half as productive as a typical US factory in capital terms. Focusing on labour productivity gives a more devastating picture. Here the ratio is 10 per cent of the American figure (Table 2.6), the implications of which are quite frightening.

Finally, what is the role of Hong Kong? Hong Kong is in one sense another revolutionary cell. At present it behaves as an example of a capitalist system functioning with Chinese people. Thus far it has borrowed heavily on western infrastructure and western business practices. As a hybrid form of capitalism it is already also acting in a way that will change peoples' perceptions in China. Returning to the original models of culture (see Table 2.6), Hong Kong is in a situation where there is trust but it is interpersonal and limited – society is essentially full of mistrust like all Asian societies perhaps with the exception of Japan. But here it is filtered through a rationality heavily influenced by western ideas such as the laws, which make for a different ideology from the purely Chinese one. In terms of identity, family and the collectivist concentric degrees of belonging which are

Table 2.6   Capital and labour productivity comparison

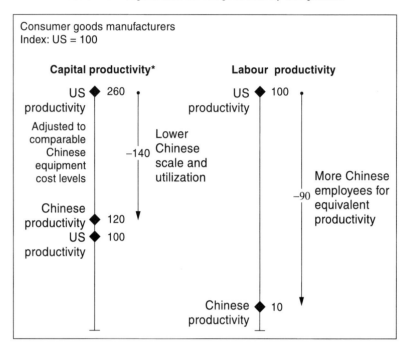

* Measured by tons per US$ invested.
Sources: *State Statistical Yearbook*; McKinsey analysis.

aspects of chinese culture, these are also filtered so that in Hong Kong even under a Chinese managerial ideology it becomes possible to do such things as employ professionals and build up a corporate culture independently from just the family. Their authority, which is essentially paternalist based on filial parity and a particular moral exchange, mainly personal and tied to ownership, is also filtered enabling Hong Kong to develop a hybrid ideology which is a kind of westernised version of the pure Chinese original, borrowing from both and perhaps in more than one sense getting the best of both worlds.

If the process of modernization of Hong Kong society is examined, this best of both worlds phenomenon can be observed – there is economic exchange based on institutional trust and backed by law. For example, there is a fully functioning modern stock market, but this is supplemented by the retention of personal trust. There is a decentralization of business decisions into larger corporations just like the big

Chinese conglomerates. There is now the entrepreneur as hero, which is a change in Chinese values where the traditional Chinese entrepreneur held the lowest status in society. There is no doubt that in Hong Kong they have been raised without question to the highest level. There is the rational use of capital which is served by an active free press, and a very high level of professionalism in the financial sector – this makes it a hybrid. In terms of skills the legitimate authority is paternalism which holds together the organization, but at the same time there is the emergence of an increasing degree of professionalism. There are paradoxes in this of course, but these never appear to bother the Chinese who simply absorb them.

Responsible, self-educated and promoted by individual obligations to their family, higher levels of skill acquisition are being created and these become consolidated through formal qualifications. There is also use of talent being promoted by new forms of organization and new forms of ideas. The consequences of all this are new economic actors, small stable networked family businesses, networked in ways that would not have been otherwise possible, large companies containing both paternalism and modern management at the same time. Business groups and conglomerates emulating those of the region in Figure 2.4 and a greater reliance on joint ventures. Hong Kong offers a fertile ground for this kind of hybridization. What appears to be happening for Hong Kong is that despite all the threats levelled at the colony, and despite all the ensuing political uncertainty and not knowing what the actions of the next rulers will be, the general context suggests that as China itself is becoming increasingly dependent on economic growth and therefore on these kinds of inputs, little will happen to disturb its evolution.

Dependence is therefore very simple, because if China stops growing at 8 per cent per annum they will experience unemployment on an unimaginable scale – the civil unrest that could be produced by 200 million people simply could not be contemplated. Therefore, there is little choice other than to continue to develop. They may do it carefully, but they will keep on going. As Deng Xiao Peng himself said, 'we don't know how to get across the river except to take it one step at a time, feeling the stones as we go across one at a time'. We don't know now whether they will ever make it, but the implication of this overview is that they probably will and in doing so produce a new form of hybrid capitalism which will occupy one-quarter of the world's people. So, a final warning – we had better watch out, they know how to do it.

3 The Changing Business Scheme in Central and Eastern Europe

Lethos Hethy

This chapter begins with an almost impossible – certainly challenging – task to attempt to explain what is happening in Eastern Europe. When we talk about globalization in the world economy, in many ways from the perspective of Eastern Europe and also from the perspective of each individual country, our primary responsibility is the struggle to survive and to attempt to keep pace with the rest of the world. Emphasis needs to be made that the intention is not to discuss Central and Eastern Europe as a kind of 'Eastern Bloc', because the differences between the individual countries are tremendous. For example, Hungary and the Czech Republic are faced with problems of a quite different nature than, say, Albania, Romania or Russia. What they all have in common, though, is the fact that they are engaged in two different processes, one is macro-economic stabilization, the second is restructuring in a broader context – what has been referred to as transformation.

To understand the whole problem requires an example: a Hungarian economic historian made some calculations about GDP growth in the world in two periods, the first between 1950–1973 and the second between 1973–1993. In the first period GDP per capital in the world doubled. During this period the Eastern European countries were in fact among some of the fast-growing economies. In the second period GDP growth was much lower, the average was about 28 per cent although this masked quite different rates of growth between the continents. Whilst Western Europe had a growth of 50 per cent, Latin America practically stagnated, and Africa declined slightly, dropping by a similar rate of decline (0.4 per cent) to that experienced in Central Eastern Europe (0.8 per cent). In fact in the past three decades there has been a steadily growing gap between Western Europe and Eastern Europe. Where the richest countries have GDP per capita of above $20 000 (United States $20 000; Switzerland $30 000) Eastern Europe hovers around an average of only $2500.

The new regimes that took power in 1989/90 were faced with the difficult problem of macro-economic stabilization, as these countries had serious economic imbalances – government budget balances and the balance of payments. At the same time they were compelled to do something about economic development and economic growth.

In many ways the economic strategy adopted was fairly uniform all over the region. The literature distinguishes between two kinds of strategies – shock therapy as was tried in Poland, with more gradual reforms taking place in other countries. In practice these strategies were very similar. They all included the liberalization of prices of imports, tight monetary and fiscal policies, highly-restrictive income policies in order to control wages and even measures to suppress, if not to reduce, real wages. In addition there were measures to cut social expenditure to cover budgetary deficits; usually the national currency was depreciated in order to improve the balance of trade, and of course privatization was regarded as a prerequisite of 'market'-oriented reforms.

With all these measures to what extent have they contributed to macro-economic stabilization? In this respect I think our answer can be positive. The second question is to what extent have they been successful in promoting restructuring in the wider sense, in terms of the ownership of production and the management strategies followed? Although the answer to the first question must be a qualified yes, the answer to the second is less certain. In many ways the stabilization of the macro-economy was a short-term one whilst restructuring is more long-term that on closer examination there are certain contradictions between the two. Those aspects of restructuring that have been achieved are those relating to a shift in favour of primary services, transport, commerce and the services sector, including financial services and banking.

What has been important has been, for example, the development of telecommunications. To take one country: Hungary had a telephone system which suffered from a lack of capital investment. It now has a very modern and highly-developed system important for business activity and economic growth. This is almost entirely due to American and German investment, and the same is true of telecommunications in Poland. In a similar way there has been dynamic development in the automotive industry. In Hungary there are several multinational companies – General Motors, Ford, Volkswagen and Audi. Over the same period, though, there has been a gradual decline in the traditional heavy industries of iron and steel, engineering and mining. But even accepting the expected job losses, the balance of this restructuring appears to be positive. There are two examples of this in practice from Hungary and Poland. In Hungary there has always been a highly-developed, high-quality industry for the production of optical and medical instruments – now it has practically disappeared. In Poland there was a successful relatively high-quality textile industry; this has also disappeared. It can be debated as to whether the economic policies that would allow these skills to disappear in this way were in general beneficial, or in fact, as some people consider, too liberal.

In terms of restructuring a major problem has been, and still is, the lack of capital. In Hungary it is extremely limited and the only capital available is foreign. In terms of foreign capital there are three possible sources. The first is credit, but the problem here is that the majority of Eastern European countries cannot rely on international loans because they are not creditworthy, save for Hungary and Poland and to some extent the Czech Republic. The second source of capital is international assistance. Here promises have not been fulfilled. In the early 1990s, 24 countries committed themselves to providing $26 billion of support for the region. By 1994, only $11 billion had been transferred and there is much debate as to why this should be so. One argument is that Eastern European countries cannot work out and produce well-founded projects; on the other hand it is also thought that the main target for western assistance has been the financing of western-based institutions through western know-how, and there is little gain in such schemes for the Eastern European countries. Whatever the reason, the result has been a fairly low transfer to the region. A third source of capital is foreign direct investment. Unfortunately this has also been rather limited compared with the needs of the region – with perhaps Eastern Germany being the exception for obvious reasons.

The comparison is stark: until 1994 foreign investment in Eastern Germany per capita amounted to $5900. In the rest of the region it amounted to only $30 – only one-two-hundredth of East Germany's figure. Of all the Central and Eastern European countries, Hungary benefited most by foreign direct investment up until 1994 with about 60 per cent, but foreign investment per capita even in Hungary amounted to only $600, which is still ten times less than Eastern Germany. Today it is about $1000 per head as a result of selling the electricity and gas industries. Restructuring has therefore been patchy, whilst macro-economic stabilization seems to have proceeded relatively successfully.

The next question is just what are the major economic indicators and what lies behind them? One is certainly GDP growth. GDP growth is important not just for the population but also for foreign investors because in a sense it is related to the size of the local market. In the early 1990s there was a very sharp GDP drop all over the region. On average it amounted to 25–30 per cent which in size can be compared to the great depression of 1929/33. In Hungary it reached 20–25 per cent, but in some countries of the former Soviet Union the decline was 40 per cent. Since then as a result of the economic policies applied the GDP position has improved. In 1992 economic growth began to restart in Poland; it restarted in the Czech Republic and Hungary in 1994. By 1995 several other countries experienced economic growth including Albania, Slovenia and Estonia, and in several of them GDP grew to about 6 per cent which is a high figure for the region and bodes well for the future.

However, there are always concerns that when economic growth begins there is a danger that the economic balance is upset as changes lag behind in the economic infrastructure. For example, when Hungary attempted to begin the process of economic growth in 1986, it was a catastrophe. Some would argue that Hungary's international indebtedness can be attributed directly to this experiment. A similar experience occurred in 1994, following which there had to be very strict adherence to economic conditions. There are also indications that in the Czech Republic economic growth has tended to add to imbalances in trade. What is being attempted is a moderate but sustainable growth, so in Hungary it is envisaged to average 2 per cent growth for the forthcoming years.

As for unemployment, there are very mixed experiences. In 1990 there was no unemployment so the rapid growth was a big shock for all of the economies and their peoples. In 1990 in Hungary unemployment was below 1 per cent, it is now 11.6 per cent and this masks quite a wide differential between regions – higher in the East and lower in the West. However in some countries like Poland and Slovenia unemployment is about 14–15 per cent. The average rate for the region comes close to the average rate for the EU at around 10 per cent.

This faces us with two serious problems. One is related to structure; in all Central and Eastern European countries there is a geographical concentration of unemployment in depressed areas. In Hungary, with an average of 10–11 per cent, there is 20 per cent in the East and only 6 per cent in the West. There is also a disturbing relationship between geographical concentrations and the growing number of long-term unemployed. These long-term unemployed are those who are likely to be both uneducated and unqualified, and in many countries those belonging to ethnic minority groups; in Hungary and Slovakia these are likely to be gypsies.

These problems are very difficult to tackle without taking into account the context of the economy as a whole and even beyond that, the economy of the region, its economic development and its financing. Financing employment policies takes a great deal of social expenditure, and we live in an age in which the reduction of social expenditure is an absolute necessity – unemployment keeps growing and more and more serious problems are faced in financing. Initially the Eastern European countries had ambitious employment policies based on active measures. A great deal was spent on re-training, now most of the money is spent on funding the employed. However, in terms of the control of inflation, measures appear to be rather more successful. At the beginning of transformation many countries had three-digit inflation – Poland for example had a 685 per cent increase in consumer prices in 1990. The Czech Republic had 56 per cent in 1991, Slovenia 61 per cent and Hungary 35 per cent. By 1995, Poland still had 30 per cent and Hungary 28 per cent; Slovenia slightly more than 10 per cent.

Control of these areas is important in order to have a sound functioning economy, and taken overall the economic strategy, if not wholly successful, has been promising, with strict control over wage growth. The other angle to inflation control is the control of inflationary wage demands in both the private and public sectors and through taxation. The result of such policies has been a considerable decline in real wages. In 1991 in the Czech Republic and Slovenia real wages declined by 24–27 per cent – this represents a very radical reduction. In Hungary the same reduction was experienced but this time it took place in several steps, the Hungarians clearly are more careful! In 1991 there was a 7 per cent reduction, in 1995 a 12 per cent reduction and in 1996 the reduction was about 2 per cent – taken together this amounts to more than 20 per cent. In Poland the reduction was 30 per cent over the same period, but in other countries such as Russia cuts were even more radical. In Russia in 1990 there was a 30 per cent reduction in real wages, in 1991 a 40 per cent reduction, and in 1992 a 60 per cent reduction; one is left to wonder what remained, but in a sense it is often an academic question as in Russia and countries of the former Soviet Union it is common practice for the non-payment of wages – a phenomenon which does not occur in Hungary or its neighbours. As for the reductions – these were beneficial for a number of reasons: economics balances; because the countries concerned became even more attractive to foreign capital; and they helped to control inflation. The question now is whether this strategy can be continued. Some financial experts argue that it is possible to continue to reduce real wages by as much as may be necessary for the sake of the economy. Others have doubts as such policies generate such serious social tensions. These have been managed until now, but the reduction of real wages beyond a certain point also tends to undermine the quality of labour as well.

An important indicator of economic development in the region and one to which little reference is made is productivity – this has been a weakness in the structure of the economy in the past. There has been a decline in GDP; industrial production has declined even more sharply. There has been the decline of employment, and the reduction in employment has not been followed by an improvement in productivity, in fact productivity deteriorated at least in the first years of the transformation. This is despite the other positive aspects of the economy. Following 1992/3 an improvement began in Poland and Hungary. The productivity difference between Eastern Europe and Western Europe is a serious problem. Since 1973 Hungary's level of production was one-third that of the Western European level, now it has fallen to one-quarter. In 1973, Hungary's productivity level was two-thirds that of Spain – this has now reduced to a third. If an attempt is to be made to narrow the difference to keep pace with Western Europe and even the levels of South-East Asia and Japan, there will need to be a radical improvement in the area of productivity. Certainly the success story of South-Eastern Asia and Japan is based on rapid growth in productivity, and that is what Central and Eastern Europe needs to emulate.

Finally, some comment needs to be made about the social dimension of the economic changes in Central and Eastern Europe. This is a very complicated topic and one which is open to much debate. When economic transformation began very little attention was paid to the social dimension. The Central and Eastern European countries were offered ready-made recipes by western politicians and international financial organizations: how to stabilize the economy, how to build-up and reform their institutions, how to develop a market economy. At that time nobody was interested in the social consequences of the economic changes, and in fact they presented very few problems because the political changes taking place in most of the countries produced a kind of euphoria which enveloped at least momentarily the social problems – but in Hungary there was no euphoria! Rather the reverse, it was clear in Hungary that economic transformation would have winners and losers and what is known now is that there have been very few winners and a great many losers. This problem is one that is a great challenge and has to be tackled from a political point of view as all Eastern European countries now have democratic systems rather than military juntas – there are general elections every four years. In Central and Eastern Europe there are only two ways of becoming more efficient. The first has already been done – reducing real wage levels and improving performance through employing fewer people. The second is reform of the welfare system, or, one might say, the demolition of the welfare system. All countries in Central and Eastern Europe have inherited a welfare system which simply cannot be financed. This includes pensions, sickness allowances, family and other benefits. In the previous system all those who received benefits worked in the state sector and almost everybody worked in the state sector. These benefits were rather generous, for example pensions at the level of 60–65 per cent of the current wages in the state sectors. The pensionable age in all countries in the region is 55 years for women and 60 years for men. These costs are currently financed from payroll taxes that amount to about 50 per cent of the payroll and state budget. Practically all countries in the region are faced with this difficulty and there are two problems, the first is that as with western pensions there is a growing dependency ratio due to the declining birth rate. So an ever-smaller proportion of the working population are paying for the pensions and other benefits of those who become retired. Secondly, state revenues including payroll taxes continue to shrink as a result of the decline in real wages. It will be almost impossible to increase taxes as they are already extremely high. In Hungary there is a combination of the Norwegian system – which relies on sales – tax and the Swedish system which is progressive, relying on the rising incomes of taxpayers. As real wages and purchasing power are falling, taxation also falls.

There is also a concern that there is too much concentration of income in the state budget. Today in Hungary, as well as in all the Central and Eastern countries, about 60 per cent of the total income is concentrated in the state budget – this is extremely high. What is required is reform of this very generous and extremely expensive social welfare system and this will be a very painful task that has the risk of leading to social tension. The major challenge facing the region is how to balance the management of tax, macro-economic stabilization and economic restructuring, whilst at the same time maintaining social and political stability.

Part 2

Strategic Implications of Global Change

4 Dinosaurs versus Dragons: Should Strategic Management Theory Redirect its Focus to the East?

Derek F. Channon

Since the late 1970s when the term 'Strategic Management' came into widespread use superseding previous labels such as Business Policy and Corporate Strategy, a plethora of texts have been produced and a field of management created. Much of this activity has originated in the US and as such it has largely reflected US management practice. Moreover, many of the concepts adopted by western corporations have evolved in the USA and have often been introduced in other developed countries by American management consultants.

There is virtually no discussion in these leading texts of management structures and practices adopted by emerging corporations from the countries of the Pacific Rim. This despite the fact that since the 1960s these economies have been exhibiting superior economic performances to those of their western counterparts. As a consequence our theories rest upon a number of US values such as the concept of capitalism within a free enterprise society, conducted without governmental intervention except as a buyer or specifier as in defence procurement, with an objective of profit maximization and an active stockmarket supported both by individuals and institutions.

The question needs therefore to be asked, are our theories appropriate? Moreover, should they be imposed on other countries where values and cultures are different, and where the solutions suggested may not have the consequence of meeting their economic and cultural needs. Further, is it even true to claim the western models are actually best? Consider the following:

- The US is presently the world's largest debtor nation.
- Japan is the largest net creditor, with other oriental economies also enjoying higher growth and substantial balance of trade surpluses.

47

- The yen/dollar exchange rate has moved dramatically in favour of the yen.
- World reserve currencies are moving away from the dollar to include other currencies such as the yen and the Deutschmark.
- Japanese industry has heavily defeated US and European competitors in many important industry sectors such as consumer electronics, machine tools, robotics and automobiles, forcing segment retreat, drastic restructuring and even exit.
- Led by Korea, other little-Dragon economies are also growing rapidly following in most cases a similar strategy to that of Japan.
- The sum of the other Asian economies (excluding Japan) seems likely to exceed US GDP by the millennium.

These factors go virtually unreported and the reasons for them are unexplained in our present theories and teaching of strategic management. The balance of this paper deliberately compares and contrasts a number of differences between western theories and eastern management practices.

FREE MARKET VERSUS STATE INTERVENTION

The US economic model stresses the capitalist system, *laissez-faire*, the survival of the fittest and minimal state intervention. In large part this model has operated in the USA although political intervention has occurred in some industries such as agriculture, energy, defence and the like. Nevertheless, ownership by the state has been minimal. In most European countries where socialist governments have held power some industries such as utilities, coal and transportation have been in public ownership. Others have been highly regulated or protected. Nevertheless, heavy economic direction has generally been avoided.

Contrast this with the experience of the oriental economies. State ownership has been common covering a wide range of industries, with directed investment to specific industries the norm either via state-owned banking systems or via preferential funding for government inspired projects. In Japan, the Ministry for International Trade and Industry has orchestrated the restructuring of the economy three times since World War II. Indeed, those heavy industries which formed the foundation of Japanese postwar economic recovery have now become the scrap sectors of basic shipbuilding and steel, commodity chemicals, refining aluminium and pulp and paper. These low value-added, relatively undifferentiated, high capital-intensity, high energy-consuming and highly polluting industries have given way to high value industries such as automobiles, consumer electronics and machine tools. Further, as these industries themselves become threatened by the other emerging Asian economies, Japan is building its position in new sectors such as robotics, information based industries, new materials and biotechnology.

Similar approaches have also been made by Korea, Taiwan, Thailand, Malaysia and Singapore. As China also begins to grow rapidly a similar pattern seems likely with only Hong Kong seemingly adopting a free market approach. Given the economic success of these countries where government intervention has been high, should we not question the adoption of a western model for countries such as the emerging economies in Eastern Europe?

SHORT-TERM VERSUS LONG-TERM INVESTMENT PERSPECTIVE

There are many who argue that the capitalist system notably in the USA and UK, encourages a short-term investment mentality in corporate management. Certainly in the USA there is greater pressure for short-term economic performance because of the pressures from institutional shareholders. Moreover, the development of the leveraged buyout in the USA, and later in Europe, brought a new type of investor to the market, forcing managements to be continuously beware of corporate raiders. Whilst this pressure reduced in the early 1990s in the face of recession and a shortage of risk capital to finance such bids, the mid-1990s has seen a significant resurgence in bid activity. In addition, the dealing activity in the world's capital markets owes much more to short-term speculation in foreign exchange, futures, options and other new short-term instruments than it does to real economic activity.

By contrast, the major corporations in Asian economies are essentially protected from unwanted bids due to their ownership. In Japan, a substantial percentage of the leading corporations' shares are usually held in friendly hands by fellow members of their industrial groups. In the case of the Korean *chaebol*, family ownership or control via their holding companies similarly ensures they are not subject to stock market pressures. Elsewhere in Asia, state or family ownership is also common. Only in Germany, where banks either hold or can vote large blocks of stock, do companies feel able to take a long view. This position permits Asian companies to undertake long-term investment strategies often in concert with governmental visions of a country's economic future.

FINANCIAL SEPARATION VERSUS FINANCIAL INTEGRATION

In the USA, partially as a result of the Great Crash, the banking industy has maintained an arms-length relationship with its customers. Substantial equity investments in third parties is prohibited, and insurance and banking integration within the USA is also not permitted. A similar pattern of arms-length relationships applies in the UK. In Germany the banks do have significant shareholdings and can also vote shares which they hold as investments on behalf of clients. The result of this perspective is that when companies owing money to banks get into trouble, the banks often take recourse to receivership or administration to recover their money. Many western corporations thus take a negative view of their banks.

By contrast in the East the banking industry tends to be closely integrated into economic development. In Japan the six leading *keiretsu* groups are centred upon the major commercial banks, trust banks and life insurance companies with their lending policies heavily influenced by the Ministry of Finance. Elsewhere in Asia the banking sector is still state owned in large part, or again heavily influenced by government with the exception of Hong Kong. As a result, in the Asian economies government has substantial influence in the direction of available investment capital which is harnessed to support a centralist view of industrial development.

DIVEST NON-CORE ACTIVITIES VERSUS CONTINUOUS DIVERSIFICATION

Since the early 1980s when Peters and Waterman (1989) attempted to identify the sources of corporate excellence, it has become fashionable to 'stick to the knitting' or 'retreat to the core' by divesting activities not seen as essential. This trend has been reinforced by the rapid spread of 'value planning' where businesses within a corporate portfolio are assessed to establish whether or not they add or destroy shareholder value. Those businesses deemed to destroy value are candidates for closure or divestment. Further, corporate raiders have sought to identify target companies where the break-up value was greater than that of corporations as a whole. In the late 1980s the creation of new financial instruments such as high interest or 'junk bonds' encouraged a host of such bids and also caused a number of diversified concerns to dismember themselves to avoid them.

By contrast there has been little such activity amongst large Asian corporate groups or enterprises. The major contributors in the dragon economies are usually highly diversified business groups operating in a range of service and manufacturing activities. In Japan the horizontal *keiretsu* groups contain a microcosm of the industrial economy. In addition each contains one of the leading city commercial banks, a long-term trust bank, life and non-life insurance concerns and one or more *soga shosha* or trading company. These latter concerns are unique to the Japanese and operate as major traders around the world in many thousands of product markets. Far from decreasing their product market scopes, these industrial groups are constantly increasing the diversity of their activities both as groups and within individual group member companies. In addition to the horizontal *keiretsu* there are a number of vertically-integrated *keiretsu* such as the leading automobile producers and in some service sectors. Finally, a number of more recently created companies such as Matsushita and Sony are also highly diversified.

In Korea, the economy is also dominated by a number of major industrial groups, the *chaebol*. These groups too are highly diversified although they have been restricted from developing extensive financial service industry interests, nor have they established major trading companies. Elsewhere in Asia, largely centred on Chinese family managements, other highly diversified groups have developed also containing mixtures of service and manufacturing activities, but with some bias to include property businesses in addition to trading and financial services.

DOWNSIZING VERSUS CONTINUOUS EMPLOYMENT

In recent years many western companies have engaged in 'downsizing', in particular by radically cutting costs in the face of increased competition by lower-cost competitors especially from Asia. In particular, downsizing has resulted in drastic cuts in employment notably in the USA but also in the European economies.

Reengineering has been made fashionable since 1988 when Hammer and Champy (1993) introduced the concept of obliterating work rather than restructuring it. Many corporations have thus sought quantum leaps in productivity, a move to horizontal organizations, and re-designing work around a series of core processes. Most such projects have been introduced by external consultants, but there has been a high failure rate with estimates varying from 30–70 per cent. At the same time there has also been many very successful examples.

By contrast the Asian approach, again pioneered in Japan, has been one of *kaizen* or continuous improvement with changes being incre-mental rather than radical. This process has also been coupled with the expectation of job security, to remove workforce fear and encourage participation in the change process. Employment security is then lar-gely ensured by continued investment for growth and diversification.

To date this system has been perceived to be superior to that of the West, although whether it can withstand adverse foreign exchange movements brought on by economic success only time will tell. While the techniques of reengineering are now filling much management lit-erature, *kaizen* techniques are much less discussed, although (just in time) JIT and (total quality management) TQM are talked about but seldom implemented on a basis which makes them an integral com-ponent of corporate culture.

FEAR VERSUS HARMONY-BASED ORGANIZATIONS

Complementing *kaizen*-based continuous improvement systems is the need to involve all the people in the enterprise. The workforce in such organizations forms a key ingredient in successful improvement. They are a primary source of ideas. Indeed it is normal in some Japanese corporations for the shopfloor to come up with millions of suggestions each year, the great majority of which are implemented by the workers themselves. These organizations seek to eliminate all forms of 'waste' such as unnecessary stocks, jobs, space and the like. This also has the beneficial side effect of drastically reducing capital intensity. The workforce is aware of the company's strategy, and activities are care-fully measured and monitored, not by the accountancy function, but in terms of business operations.

Contrast this with what is often found in western organizations. We tend to build safety stocks, supervision is considered essential, pro-

ductivity decisions often don't involve the workforce, employee suggestions are few, corporate strategies are often not communicated, the
control systems are financially rather than operationally based, and
headcount reductions are sought to achieve productivity gains. This
tends to create an environment of fear versus one of harmony.

COST-PLUS VERSUS TARGET COSTING

It is often the case in western corporations that product pricing
is undertaken on the basis of cost-plus. Products are designed, en-
gineered, manufactured, marketed and sold. Price is determined by
adding all costs and then a required margin is added to this total.
Moreover, product development tends to be sequential, moving from
one function to the next, resulting in extra costs and substantially increasing product development times.

For decades many Japanese companies have operated a system of
target costing, whereby the end price is established first and cost is
then derived by reversing back to the required cost. Moreover, the
process is conducted by integrated functional teams.

Ford, for example, is just introducing on a global basis a system of
target costing with a concept known as Vision 2000. Toyota Motor has
had such a system in place for around 40 years.

OUTSOURCING VERSUS INSOURCING

Many western companies are increasingly turning to outsourcing as
a way of containing or reducing costs. While historically it has usually been the case that non-strategic activities have been given over to
external contractors, the present trend includes handing over critical
activities such as information technology. In addition, in some cases
companies are turning to outside concerns to purchase critical components in order to reduce investment intensity and research and development costs.

This phenomenon is less true amongst Asian companies which tend
to try to retain in-house the production of critical components,
achieving low cost by offering to supply western concerns by badge
engineering products and driving for global standardization. This has

been very noticeable in industries such as office automation, consumer electronics and automobiles. Many Asian corporations also seek to maximize value-added by vertical integration, then using component production as a source of diversification into new businesses. Komatsu, for example, initially produced specialist engineering plastic components, robotics and electronic equipment to service its earth-moving equipment operations. These have all since been developed into new businesses in their own right.

While outsourcing is clearly an alternative in many cases to internal investment, and helps to reduce capital intensity, the strategic make or buy decision may not be as immediately obvious as western literature might suggest.

TRADING UP VERSUS STRATEGIC MINIATURIZATION

From the trade-up strategy introduced by General Motors' Alfred Sloan to compete against Ford, many US corporations have adopted such policies especially in industries where replacement demand has become important. In addition, a substantial contribution to profitability was achieved by servicing or by providing spares and disposables. Examples include such companies as IBM, Caterpillar and Xerox. Products were also sold to specialist buying departments for centralized operations through specialist channels.

By contrast, Asian and especially Japanese producers have tended to deliberately design to minimize products. This has enabled them to expand markets to mass segments not serviced by leading western competitors. This has, in turn, encouraged decentralized activities, different customer buying processes, the use of mass channels, design to eliminate servicing requirements and/or the use of serving specialists, and in particular to open personal markets in addition to business markets.

This strategy has allowed Asian producers to achieve lower overall cost structures than western competitors, despite having low market-share positions in the top market segments. The effect has been dramatic in industries such as imaging, computing, automobiles, motorcycles, earth-moving equipment, telecommunications and robotics. Moreover, western competitors have often initially ignored the impact of such smaller products only waking to the challenge when serious market-share erosion has taken place.

ORGANIZATIONAL VARIANTS

Studies have been undertaken which have attempted to suggest that
the organizational evolution of Asian groups mirrors that of the West,
where firms tend to have evolved from functional structures through
holding companies to multidivisional forms as identified by Chandler
(1962). And that later, strategic business units have been introduced
which are often encourgaged to compete for resources with the introduction of some form of portfolio planning system.

In reality, though, while some of these concepts are present in Asian
structures there are also substantial differences. With the exception of
Japan many Asian industrial groups are still dominated by families
even though professional managers may have been introduced. In Japan, for example, family ownership of the prewar *zaibatsu* groups was
largely eliminated after World War II, although some family managements have emerged in newer enterprises. However, the make up of
highly diversified *keiretsu* groups with their complex cross-holdings is
only mirrored by other Asian groups.

In addition, there are serious differences in the way in which corporations are managed. This can be illustrated in table 4.1 which lists a
series of different variables with western companies tending to the left
of each variable continuum and eastern companies to the right.

Table 4.1   Organization variations between East and West

	← WEST	EAST →
Management type	Specialists	Generalists
Promotion criteria	Meritocracy	Seniority
Management style	Conflict and competition	Cooperation and harmony
Organization	Profit-centred SUBs	X functional integration
Motivation	Money	Loyalty
Job security	Low	High
Salary differentials high	High	Low

STRATEGIC PLANNING VERSUS STRATEGIC VISION

The process of strategic planning has developed extensively since the
mid-1960s when it was introduced. Most corporations in the West
today produce such plans. For many companies they are produced by

specialist planning units, often closely related to the finance function and they tend to be financially driven. Many plans run for three years and are revised annually. The planning cycle may be coupled to the budgeting process but often is not. The pressure for performance also tends to mean that the budget itself often takes precedence over the longer plan views. This may well result in strategic investments and the like being deferred in the search for annual profit performance. Portfolio planning systems have been widely introduced together with strategic business-unit structures which are encouraged to compete for resources during the planning cycle. When businesses are classified as in decline or as cash-cows, management often chooses not to communicate plans for divestment or downsizing to the workforce.

Again there is a contrast to Asian practice. In Japan, for example, formal planning departments are common but the process for setting a plan is very different. Plans normally run for three years and usually start off with a 'vision' by the President. Such a vision is rarely counted in financial terms, will have a name, last at least three years but will often extend well beyond this. For each three-year plan, while financial forecasts are made many operational objectives are expressed in non-financial measures. In many western corporate reorganization projects, new management information systems are introduced installing similar measures known as System Performance Indicators. A difference with western practice, however, is that in Japan the information contained in the system is produced by the workforce and known to all relevant employees. Furthermore, in businesses which are indecline every effort is made to grow out of decline by diversification or re-configuring activities to create new businesses. This may be done through technology fusion, for example, whereby new industries are created by the amalgamation of a number of old technologies. For example the creation of Mitsubishi Materials aims to develop a major new materials business from traditional cement and non-ferrous metals activities. While such revitalization takes place, workers may be assigned to other plants, suppliers and other members of the same industrial group to avoid forced redundancies amongst those employed on the expectation of lifetime employment.

SUMMARY AND CONCLUSIONS

- This chapter has compared and contrasted the differences between a number of concepts in the field of strategic management as espoused in western texts and theories with practices observable in Asian corporations. The differences observed have obviously been shown in relative black and white terms, while most firms will lie somewhere along the continuum of the differences identified. Nevertheless, the presence of so many apparent opposites in the application of many of the concepts suggests that the present theoretical base needs to recognize the differences that exist. It further raises many questions such as:

- Is the free market economy truly a superior economic model?
- Should government be involved directly in industry structure development?
- Do protectectionist policies lead to inefficiency?
- Are hire and fire policies best for productivity?
- Should diversion continue or retreat?
- Should financial service corporations operate at arms length or be integrated with industrial concerns?
- Is the dragon model potentially superior, especially for emerging economies, and should westem economies embrace it?
- How far should we rewrite strategic management theory and adjust business school curricula to make management students aware of eastern management practice?

It is hoped the answers to these and other questions will stimulate and contribute to our understanding of the emergence of eastern global enterprises.

References

1. Thomson, A.A. and Strickland A.J. (1995) *Strategic Management*, 8th edn (Homewood, Ill. Irwin).
2. De Wit, R. and Meyer, R. (1994) *Strategy: An International Perspective* (Minneapolis: West Publishing).
3. Johnson, G. and Scholes, K. (1992) *Exploring Corporate Strategy* (New Jersey: Prentice Hall).
4. Peters, T. and Waterman, R. (1982) *In Search of Excellence* (New York: Harper & Row).
5. Rowe, A. and Mason, R., Dickel, K. and Snyder N. (1989) *Strategic Management* (Reading, Mass.: Addison-Wesley).
6. Channon, D. (1991) 'Le défi Americain ou Le défi japonais: quelle est la différence?', *European Business Journal*, vol. 3. no. 4, p. 18–19.

5 Global Strategy and Repeated Games

Robin Matthews

INTRODUCTION

Deregulation of markets, financial globalization, the diffusion of information technologies, the evolution of flexible organizations, and shorter product cycles,[1] are interrelated stimuli for changes in the dynamics of competition,[2,3] that have taken place, on a global scale, since the early 1980s. Many firms are experiencing the trauma of a supply shock from developing nations. Deregulation of capital markets has made it possible to transfer capital and technology from industrially advanced countries, so developing nations can compete not just in cheap commodity products but in those requiring sophisticated technologies. They have three times as many people of working age as the OECD countries, and the transfer of skills added to their acquiescence in significantly lower wages means that the scope of competition has widened, and there is an international market for labour as well as products. If it was ever true, the maxim[4,5] that firms need to concentrate on either reducing their costs or differentiating their products no longer holds. Rivalry is manifested globally by cooperation through mergers and alliances, fuelled by foreign direct investment, as well by competition. The magnitude of change since the 1980s means that the period is a watershed in business history. Unusual events have become commonplace and widespread experiences. Competitive advantage has to be continually created and recreated, and survival, for many organizations, requires a capacity to learn as well as to reduce costs and to be responsive to customers.[6,7,8]

The constant drive to create and recreate competitive advantage perhaps means that we need to redefine what constitutes normal behaviour in firms, and to recognise change rather than continuity as the norm, the unexpected instead of the usual. Chaos may be an appropriate image. Organizations as well as their environments have become more interdependent. Fordist mass production, standardization and capital intensity which spurred relatively stable oligopolistic structures

58

of the past, has been replaced by flexible production which involves integrated supply chains, simultaneous engineering, continuous incremental innovation, just-in-time production and team work. Interdependence between variables may be simple to describe in isolation, but when large numbers of decisions and variables interact their collective behaviour seems irregular and unpredictable. The relevance of the metaphor of chaos theory to understanding interdependence is that it incorporates abrupt changes in causal processes.

Swings of fashion present credibility problems for corporate strategy at the practical level. Recommendations to diversify on the basis of the product cycle, growth share matrices, conglomerate diversification were succeeded by fashions for core businesses, divestment and outsourcing. Enthusiasm for planning has been followed by disenchantment,[9] commitment and intuition transcends the ultra rationality of planning and controls. In the 1980s, debt briefly replaced equity as an incentive to efficiency,[10] only to be ousted as obligations and bankruptcy escalated: no doubt current and future strategic fads will undergo similar reversals. Many of the problems of alternating fashions in business consultancy result from the inevitable adoption of partial frameworks. The advantage of a general framework is that it enables particular models to be seen in perspective and thus makes reactions to change potentially more effective, precisely because it enables decision-makers who typically have only partial control over variables and limited cognition to view their prospective choices against the background of a broader more holistic perspective.

BACKGROUND

The uncertainty of the competitive environment has introduced a new credo into business orthodoxy. The credo is simplistic: people are seen as vessels who will automatically generate value added if only they are imbued with corporate vision, culture, a sense of mission, or the latest management fad.[11,12] The main point is sound, but unless there is some correspondence between the goals of organizational and their own aspirations, staff can scarcely be expected to respond to corporate objectives with zeal.[13] However, contradictory pressures exist that reduce the sense of commitment among employees below the levels required to achieve a cooperative mission or culture. In response to competition, executives at the top of organizations have been driven to renege upon implicit commitments to staff about security of employment, and conditions of work, in order to reduce costs.[14] For all their advantages, flexible systems are more fragile than the Fordist and Taylorist systems they replace. Interdependence expressed in self-managed teams and integrated supply chains, together with just in time production, the zero buffer principle, quality control, cooperation between designers and producers means that the new flexible organizations are much more vulnerable than their predecessors to human resource problems and breakdowns in communication.

Furthermore, the cost changes associated with flexible post-Fordist production techniques often reflect a shift rather than a reduction. Costs reappear in other forms; for example as unemployment and social security charges, and diminished expectations of work mean that they also surface as health expenditures and crime.[15,16,17] The remodelling of industry in the UK as firms and industries are replaced, in part exemplifies the 'creative destruction' that Schumpeter (1934) described as smokestack industries wither and inefficient firms are supplanted.[18] However, the story may not end at this point because cost-reduction strategies feed back on organizations. Perhaps dynamism in a society requires inequality of wealth as well as insecurity, but as has been hinted[19] the incipient resentment of the dispossessed means that the system itself may be unsustainable unless it generates a reasonable expectation of lifetime employment.

Handling complexity may involve identifying simple relationships that require simple rather than complicated management styles.[20,21] The essence of simplicity is *ceteris paribus* focusing on a few relationships, excluding others. Much of the progress of modern science has been made possible by ignoring interdependence and feedback and instead compartmentalizing problems. The whole is broken down into parts and the parts examined as if they were separate. *Ceteris paribus* is an indispensable assumption in science, but its rationale is to postpone not to neglect the complex considerations of interdependence and change. The division between economics and strategy is one example of a dichotomy that has become too fixed. Seldom do economists relate the growth of unemployment in Europe and poverty at work in the United States directly to the strategic dilemmas of corporations. Moreover, corporate rationalization policies rarely take account of the consequent human and social costs. Discussion of corporate governance is another illustration of the problems of the partial approach. Since their interests have been arbitrarily elevated above other stakeholder groups, the benefits of lean production accrue to shareholders but social costs feed back on organizations in the form of reduced commitment and morale.

Strategic thinking reflects another partition. A dichotomy has been fabricated between analysis and imagination. Seen historically, this is a legacy of the rejection by the romantic poets of enlightenment rationalism and utilitarianism.[22] Earlier writers in the literary cannon[23] would have found the distinction astonishing, but since the middle of the nineteenth century poetry has been seen as the antithesis of rational discourse, and scientific analysis denied the epithet creative. In strategy, the split between analysis and imagination materializes in many different ways including a schism between the rational and the intuitive, between hard and soft management styles, and between planning and crafting strategy.[24,25] One result is that treatment of subjects like mission, intention, culture and learning in organizations, shunning analytical rigour, often reduces to a wish list empty of predictive power and designed to support pre-existing arguments about how companies should change. Meanwhile, executives, under the impression that rationality is divorced from feeling pursue the logic of corporate restructuring myopically, without compassion, and regardless of the long run impact on morale, making it difficult to build up the intangible assets on which creativity is based – commitment, willingness to learn and imagination.

Creativity describes mental processes that can be summarized by the word *cognition*, leading to opportunities that are novel and unique; solutions, ideas, conceptualizations that may be manifested as new products, technologies or artefacts.[26] It also involves *intention* in the sense of a willingness to put creativity on the agenda – and as has been remarked[27] innovation is frequently a question of just this. Rational behaviour is concerned with choosing from a given set of alternatives and realizing them by actions. Cognitive ability is therefore limited, rationality in the form of recognizing alternatives and creativity in the form of creating new ones are impossible to separate in practice. How can we know whether a new artefact represents the creation of new, or the realisation of existing, potential? Rationality and creativity, analysis and imagination, are complementary rather than rival modes of thought or behaviour. This is not to detract from the mystery of creativity. However, creativity is subtly cooperative. The analogy[28] between leadership and the creation of a play which involves an interaction between playwright, cast and audience could be extended to creation of any artefact, an interdependent activity involving people its realization, development, production and dissemination. The analogy mirrors the view[29] of literary creation as an interaction between author, text, social milieu and reader. The metaphor used in this chapter, to illustrate a corresponding process, is a repeated game. In an environment where competition and change are perceived to have intensified, competitive advantage is a potential that has constantly to be created and recreated through a mix of selfish and altruistic behaviour which is mediated by the corporate culture.

Complexity is distinguishable from simplicity in that it requires a longer message to describe it.[30,31] It is a common perception that organizations and their environments are becoming increasingly complex. Simplicity underlies complexity: the approach of research and consultancy in the strategy field is to construct simple, partial frameworks (the value chain, core competencies, or the integration responsiveness framework) which identify key variables and interactions in order to exploit, for competitive advantage, any simple regularities and patterns existing within complexity. Descriptions of interaction between variables in each framework are based on simple models (competition, entry barriers or games for example), whose usefulness depends upon the approximation of their assumptions to reality. However, simple laws can result in behaviour which appears random. Even though they are accurate, if partial, metaphors of reality, the simple relationships described by models and frameworks may be consistent with indeterminacy in the payoff function. Most simple frameworks go through a predictable cycle from infatuation, through disillusion, to rejection, because they are mis-specified or they are necessarily selective and ignore important elements of strategy. So a general framework is useful in so far as it enables partial approaches to be seen as part of a more universal complex system.

The payoff function, including evidential expected utility and symbolic utilities, extends the notion of rationality beyond purely instrumental or causal utility.[32] Decision-taking by S on an evidentially expected basis means that he or she will cooperate because others, $-S$, facing the same circumstances are expected to reciprocate. Symbolic utility implies a care for the significance of actions no matter what immediate effects they cause or produce. In later sections a link is forged between evidential utility and corporate culture, and between symbolic utility and the related notions of mission and intent. In the concluding section, these connections are used in developing the notion of a sustainable organization. The role of preferences and the non deterministic nature of the function is then discussed.

THE MODEL – PAYOFFS IN AN ORGANIZATION

The determinants of expected payoffs, Z, are expressed by the inequality (5.1):

$$Z \leq \{[\theta_s, \theta_{-s}] \text{ all } S \varepsilon N; [N]; [A]; [C]; [H]; [E]; [P]; [\Omega] \qquad (5.1)$$

Payoffs are measured as value added, an economic surplus or rent accruing to stakeholders. So Z represents total payoffs accruing to stakeholders, including owners, staff and the community. It is argued that the distribution of payoffs as well as their absolute and relative value measured in money or utility determines whether organizations are sustainable or not. In equation (5.1), (θ_s describes the choices of decision-maker S. Other variables are of two kinds: the first are the *decision variables* themselves, and the second, *state variables*, determine decisions and their transformation into payoffs and are in turn affected by them.

The *decision variables* are $[N]$, $[A]$ and $[C]$. $[N]$ denotes the number of value adding activities $[A]$, and $[C]$ symbolizes the coalitional structure of an organization. Briefly, $[A]$ is a vector or matrix of activities which add value; $[A]$ corresponds to the elements in the value chain. The number of such activities $[N]$ describes the size and scope of an organization. The way in which basic activities are grouped into divisions or functions is described by the coalitional structure $[C]$.

The *state variables* that affect the impact that S has upon decision variables and upon payoffs; are given by $C\theta_{-s}$, $[H]$, $[P]$, $[E]$ and $[\Omega]$. The variable θ_{-s} describes strategic decisions taken by other decision-makers and coalitions in a particular organization. $[H]$ is an irreversible state variable expressing the effect of an organization's history on its capabilities; $[P]$ denotes the preferences of decision-makers; $[E]$ is the business environment about which rational expectations are held; and $[\Omega]$ is a random variable. Payoffs are the value attached to outcomes by stakeholders. Utility, defined as an index of preferences, is determined by outcomes together with the probability of those outcomes occurring. Payoffs, in turn, are viewed as potential rather than actual values: hence the inequality.

A number of different processes are summarized in inequality (5.1):

1. causal relationships between decisions about $[A]$, $[N]$ and $[C]$ and expected outcomes in terms of payoffs;
2. preferences, which determine strategic choice;

3. [H] reflecting the effect of past changes on present capabilities;
4. the interaction of decision-makers expressed by θ_s and θ_{-s} and
5. a random element [Ω], emphasizing the non-deterministic nature of the function.

The inequality (5.1) is a symbolic way of representing the complexity of strategy. Complexity arises from a number of sources. Interaction between many agents or decision-makers and variables may result in payoffs which are unpredictable. Deterministic relationships between variables, described by differential or difference equation systems, can lead to behaviour that seems to all intents and purposes random. Furthermore, small changes in the initial conditions [H] can have magnified effects upon the path of the system: these effects suggest that one interpretation of (5.1) is in terms of chaos.

CHAOS

The relationship between variables and payoffs, especially the impact of the business environment [E], may well be chaotic. The metaphor of chaos has become fashionable in strategic discourse. The term chaos is rather misleading as it suggests a lack of form and may cause confusion. If a system is in utter disorder and lacks structure nothing much can be said about it scientifically. In the context of expression (5.1) the significance of chaos is that although there is a deterministic relationship implicit in the underlying differential equations, the relationship between decision variables and payoffs may behave in a non-deterministic or random way. Although there is an underlying pattern, it may be hidden, difficult to discover and qualitative in the sense that it springs from preferences expressed in corporate culture or what has come to be termed strategic intent. Outcomes may not turn out to be as expected for a number of reasons; changes in *decision variables* and in *state variables* affected by such changes may produce discontinuous even catastrophic effects on outcomes and payoffs; infinitely small changes in the *state variables* may have dramatic and incalculable effects. Thus the variable [Ω] is a reminder that the pattern we seek in events may have complex fractal patterns, rather than the linear extrapolations that arise in conventional models of planning and forecasting.

RATIONALITY AND PREFERENCES

Rationality, broadly defined, is behaviour which has two characteristics: being consistent and being goal-directed. At one extreme this
can degenerate into utility or profit maximization, narrowly defined;
but this is not necessarily the case. The goal-directed aspect of rationality, for example, can be extended to include non-selfish behaviour. Discussion is developed[33] to consider three types of utility;
(1) *causal*, (2) *evidential*, and (3) *symbolic*.

1. *Causal utilities* relate strategic actions to expected payoffs via a set
    of causal connections in which outcomes are determined by a set of
    causal probabilistic relationships, but not by choice of the action
    itself. Agent S may assess the expected payoffs (or utilities) of
    action A for example entering an alliance with another company to
    cooperate by sharing information in a joint research programme
    (summarized by θ_s), as being causally determined by the (sub-
    jective) probabilities of success of the programme, but not by the
    extent of his or her commitment to cooperation. In other words,
    the likelihood of a partner's cooperation is not seen as dependent
    upon his own demonstrated commitment.
2. *Evidential utilities* spring from one individual's perceptions of an-
    other's decision processes. The impulse for evidential utilities is the
    supposition that others, faced with similar alternatives, will re-
    spond in the same way as oneself. If cooperative action is seen by S
    to result in mutual benefit, S assumes that other decision-makers
    $-S$ will see the situation in the same way and adopt cooperative
    action. Therefore, according to evidential utilities the expected
    payoffs to S are partly determined by the commitment of S to the
    research programme, because S reckons that dedication to sharing
    information is likely to be reciprocated (and lack of dedication
    punished), and hence increases the probability of the alliance's
    success.
3. *Symbolic utilities* arise when a probable outcome of an action is
    associated with another outcome or state to which the individual
    attaches utility. Using the previous example, I may cooperate
    wholeheartedly because I attach utility to having a reputation for
    being a trustworthy partner. For example, producing in a way that
    is perceived to minimalize pollution, or protect endangered spe-
    cies, yields payoffs in terms of a saleable output, while $-S$ may get

utility not just from the output itself but also, symbolically, from being associated with an environmentally-friendly company.

Culture is reflected by the probability that particular decisions θ_s will occur. In unforeseen contingencies, particularly, many decision equilibria are possible and informal principles are needed to deal with them. This issue has been considered to be defined[34] as any clustering of decisions around certain principles as a focal point effect. Other authors link focal points to culture.[35] Since decisions reflect underlying preferences and utilities, the domain of culture is in utility space.

The three types of utility reflect corporate culture, and focal points may be apparent in all of them. However, the argument can be carried further. *Evidential utilities* relate in particular to the cooperative aspects of culture and symbolic utilities to strategic intent.

Evidential utility connects the utility of an action to possible outcomes via conditional probabilities. Decisions taken by S influence the probability of cooperative decisions being made by others $-S$. By his or her decisions S can affect the probability of outcomes occurring which depend on the decisions made by others. Likelihood of mutually advantageous cooperative decisions is increased by corporate cultures that nurture cooperation as the norm, even when it may not be in the short-term interest of *players* to cooperate. The practical implication of this is that culture-change programmes designed to increase cooperation within an organization should target conditional probabilities. The most obvious way of doing this is to establish a history of trust in corporate relationships with stakeholders as a whole.

If mission statements are more than mirages, their purpose is to associate *symbolic utilities* with behaviour patterns which increase corporate payoffs. Whereas culture may be expressed by the utilities themselves and the penchant for cooperation in conditional probabilities, establishing a sense of mission or strategic intent is tantamount to enhancing individual payoffs by linking the outcomes of decisions made within an organization symbolically to other, perhaps personal, goals. Later in the chapter, the importance of *evidential* and *symbolic utilities* is illustrated by the metaphor of a repeated game.

INTERDEPENDENT ACTIVITIES

This section focuses on the interdependence of activities [A], and upon the effect of changes in coalitional structure [C]. Initially payoffs are identified narrowly in monetary terms as K, the difference between revenues and costs accruing to an organization. The section concludes with generalizations of a simple model of interdependence and by considering social cost and changes in size $[N]$ through mergers and alliances. On one interpretation, organizations justify their existence[36] only if they add more value as an interdependent whole, rather than as a set of independent parts linked by markets (by an amount which exceeds the costs of organizing team members). That is, their vindication is conditional upon adding value by cooperation. If production of output uses cooperating inputs, it is difficult to determine the individual contribution of each, to monitor performance, and to understand how value is added.[37] Here, to overcome this problem, organizations are viewed as producing joint outputs, and the value they add is the sum of contributions of activities as stand-alone entities, plus their contribution to related activities.

The term activity corresponds to a discrete set of value chains which can be jointly managed on a more or less independent basis and linked horizontally and vertically to others: their definition as, '*a collection of linked activities that takes one or more input and creates an output of value to the customer*' (my emphasis)[38] is a close approximation. It may be interpreted according to the context as an operating company, or a store in a retail chain, a reporting or profit centre, a functional area or a strategic business unit that coordinates and controls production in a divisionalized corporation.

Consider an organization made up of a set of N activities. Value is added by activities here assumed to be completed by two possible players, S and T: (i) as stand alone entities, A_{ST} ($S = T$); and (ii) by a set of potentially synergistic relationships A_{ST} ($S \neq T$). The problem of interdependence between activities is simplified by treating synergies as separate products (or services). Payoffs in the organization as a whole, K, are the sum of these contributions:

$$K \leq \sum\nolimits_{(S,T\varepsilon_N)} A_{ST} \qquad (5.2)$$

In the sense that it summarizes the dependence of payoffs on value-adding activities, given decisions on the other strategic variables in expression (5.1), a snapshot is a useful interpretation of expression (5.2). It can be represented as a matrix as in Figure 5.1a and b. Consider the payoff matrices in the figure. Diagonal elements ($A_{SS} = 3$ and $A_{TT} = 3$) are payoffs to players S and T when they are viewed as stand-alone entities. Off-diagonal elements ($A_{ST} = 6$ and $A_{TS} = 6$) are the net benefits of cooperation: A_{ST} is the contribution of player S to T and A_{TS} that of player T to S. The matrices set out the potential value of the organization, given other variables in the payoff function.

Figure 5.1   Payoff matrix I

S's minimax payoffs, A_{SS}	Payoffs created by S for T, A_{ST}
Payoffs created by T for S, A_{TS}	T's minimax payoffs, A_{TT}

(a)

3	6
6	3

(b)

Interdependence between activities is essentially a two-way process: one activity potentially creates value in others, and similarly it permits other businesses to create value. This might be described as the yin and yang of business synergy: neither would be possible if the organization were unbundled or partitioned in such a way that businesses were effectively isolated.[39]

MEASURING VALUE-ADDING ACTIVITIES

Payoffs in this section are interpreted as value added,[40] the difference between revenues and costs. Since it encompasses all net cash flows, and includes the weighted average cost of capital (net of tax deductions and adjusted for risk), value added is an economic surplus or rent accruing to shareholders. In part, it corresponds to economic value added (EVA) used by companies like Coca-Cola, AT&T and Quaker Oats.[41,42]

In expression (5.2), K can be interpreted as a present value or as an annual net cash flow. Value added is increased by strategies of reducing costs or achieving differentiation which increases leverage over price. It may also be enhanced by managerial diversification which improves on the risk–return trade-off that could be achieved by shareholders[43] or by exploiting tax shields. As an example, British

Airways valued synergy or off-diagonal benefits of their alliance with
US Air by 1994 at \$15 million, and expected these to rise to \$105
million by 1995: the main areas of value added were revenue en-
hancement at travel agents through sharing codes and reservation
screens. The link between economic value added, defined by K, with Z
in (5.1), is partial because the latter is interpreted here as including
payoffs which may be non-monetary to a wider group of stakeholders
than shareholders alone. It is argued in the concluding section that
sustainability requires payoffs exceeding K.

The value of synergies (off-diagonal elements, in Figure 5.1) can be
expressed as the difference between the value of assets under current
management and the replacement cost of businesses viewed as stand-
alone assets. In Figure 5.1b synergies are valued at 12 (18 − 6). This
way of measuring the value of synergies illustrates the reasoning of
certain authors.[44,45] The widespread pessimism about the usefulness of
accounting data for strategic decisions is misplaced. Deficiencies of
accounting theories and methods have been stressed[46] since they reflect
inadequate interdependence. Consequently, it is argued that they are
of limited use either in value-chain analysis or restructuring. The
problem, however, is not with accounting methods as such, but with
the absence of a framework capable of linking information to strategy.

GENERALIZATIONS

Before expressions (5.1) and (5.2) and the data in Figure 5.1 are
transformed into a repeated game, a variety of possible interpretations
can be illustrated. There are some obvious generalizations. Since the
framework in (5.2) illustrates potential synergies within an organization, it can be extended to alliances between businesses belonging to
different firms. Figure 5.1 can also illustrate the problem of *social cost*.
S may be considered as an ethical producer making environmental
savings represented by A_{ST} that the community, T, can reciprocate by
buying the commodity or service produced represented by A_{TS}. Similarly, suppose business S acts as a good employer by protecting jobs,
and in return employees T can make greater efforts to help the company to acheive its objectives.

The topic of acquisitions may also be examined using this framework. Acquiring managers must recreate existing synergies before they
can begin to add value to new businesses. Thus in Figure 5.1a there is
an upward bias by existing owners of the business that is being

acquired (the reservation value is 15), in comparison to potential acquirers who receive only its stand alone value, 3. They must recreate the difference (15 − 3) to add value, if synergy, created in the former organization, is capitalized into the selling price of the business being acquired. This upward bias may explain overpayment by acquiring companies, and also favour management buyouts since existing managers '*might be expected to have a better idea of the value of businesses and the value of synergies than new companies in turn or Management buy-out financiers*' (my emphasis).[47]

If the market also anticipates synergy gains within the purchasing firm, this increases both the burden of acquiring managers and their temptation to restore their position by cutting the wage bill and reneging on implicit contracts with employees. The breach of trust may result in the longer term in a decline in the profitability of newly-acquired and existing assets because it reduces *evidential utility*, the conditional probability that cooperative behaviour in creating synergies will be reciprocated by commitment on the part of senior managers. Deterioration in profit is consistent with the increase in the value of equity, which results from the transfer of wealth from employees and creditors of the firm to its stockholders.[48]

STRATEGIC GAMES

The narratives of modern capitalism resemble the process of natural selection.[49] Competitive advantage has constantly to be created and recreated. In terms of Figure 5.1a positive value added is a sign of success which attracts competitive pressures magnetically, and is extinguished only to be reilluminated by new sources of competitive advantage. Sustainability and growth is generated within the system as a whole by an algorithm − rationality in the search for competitive advantage which is blind to the fate of a particular organization. The goal of strategic decision-making is to recreate competitive advantage within a given organization.

The concern of this section is an investigation of the role of rational behaviour, encompassing *evidential* and *symbolic utility*, in the realization of payoffs: it is not concerned with their origin. Contemplation of the meaning of creativity and rationality reveals how difficult it is to make a distinction between them in practice. Rational behaviour is goal-directed, and choice is circumscribed by scarcity. Creativity is concerned with creating new potential, extending the boundary of

Figure 5.2 Payoff matrix II

	C	D
C	9,9	3,9
D	9,3	3,3

(a)

	C	D
C	Minimax payoffs plus cooperative gains minus transaction costs $(A_S + b_{TS} - c_S) = A_{SS}$ $(A_T + b_{ST} - c_T) = A_{TT}$	S's minimax payoffs minus S's transaction costs $(A_S - c_S)$ T's minimax payoffs plus cooperative gains from S $(A_T + b_{ST})$
D	S's minimax payoffs plus cooperative gains from T $(A_S + b_{TS})$ T's minimax payoffs minus T's transaction costs $(A_T - c_T)$	Minimax value (A_S) (A_T)

(b)

	C	D
C	9,9	1,11
D	11,1	3,3

(c)

	C	D
C	9,9	$-17,26$
D	$26,-17$	3,3

(d)

possibility. If rationality is bounded by limited cognition, how can we discriminate between recognizing what already exists, but is imperfectly known, from what is novel and could not be known until it is discovered for the first time?

Business literature tends to emphasize procedures for replicating creativity. This is the purpose of techniques such as lateral thinking, brainstorming, visualization and retrospective thinking.[50] A division of labour may be advocated in which entrepreneurs hunt opportunities, senior managers (coaches) select and support their initiatives, and leaders build up mission and intention as the foundations for entrepreneuring and replicating creativity. Rationality's imagination and heuristic procedures are spoken of as being directed at arriving at solutions to problems. But attempts to circumscribe creativity in terms of a comprehensive technique, perhaps, inevitably contradict one another because novel situations are being described. Artists seem to rationalize the creative process, valuing, and perhaps overvaluing, the theoretical discipline which controls intuition; scientists irrationalize it, stressing their indebtedness to unconscious intuitions which guide theorizing.[51] Expression (5.1) contains both determinacy and randomness. Arguably, if systems were completely governed by deterministic laws there would be no creativity separate from laying down the laws in the first place: a certain indeterminacy is needed to admit originality.

The next section is concerned with the realization of potential payoffs, consciously or otherwise within an organization, through co-operative behaviour using the metaphor of a repeated game. Creativity like strategy itself may be an unconscious process, even predominantly so. Applied to strategy, underlying the Darwinian concept of natural selection is that complex adaptations can happen without intelligent design or even cognition of potential by a single individual, but as a manifestation of an underlying algorithm or rule.[52] Here, it is argued, algorithms can take many forms including the qualitative patterns resulting from culture, commitment or intent. The focus is on the co-operative aspect of creativity in realizing potential value added. In terms of Figure 5.2, S may be the *author* of value added for T, but its realization depends upon T for without T, the *reader* there are no gains. In terms of the previous examples, trivially, if there are no customers or employees there are no gains to be had from being either environmentally friendly or a good employer, and there are no synergies from acquisition unless there is an acquisition. The nature of the algorithm provided by culture is that it operates through *evidential utility*, whilst commitment and intent express *symbolic utility*.

REALISING POTENTIAL

Figure 5.2a represents the transformation of the data in Figure 5.1a into a game in which gains from cooperation are expected to accrue equally to each player. In the absence of transaction costs, payoffs illustrated in Figure 5.1a translate into the strategic form game in Figure 5.2a. Joint cooperation (*C,C*) leads to payoffs (9,9); cooperation by just one player (*C,D*) or (*D,C*) leads to payoffs (3,9) and (9,3) respectively; joint failure to do so (*D,D*) to (3,3). The game in Figure 5.2a has no dominant strategy: each player is indifferent between cooperation (C), and non-cooperation (*D*). Non-cooperative outcomes result in inefficiency in the sense of failure to realize potential value added.

Generating gains from cooperation involves transaction costs. In the argument that follows transaction costs are supposed to be borne by the player generating the off-diagonal elements. In Figure 5.2b, A_{SS} and A_{TT} are expressed, in general terms as the difference between benefits (A_S and b_{ST} and b_{ST}) and costs (c_S and c_T). So:

$$A_{ST} = b_{ST} - C_S \tag{5.3}$$

and

$$A_{TS} = b_{TS} - C_T \tag{5.4}$$

It can be seen that the inclusion of transaction costs transforms the game into the prisoner's dilemma form. Transaction costs are assumed like benefits to be symmetrical so $b_{ST} = b_{TS}$, and $c_S = C_T$. In Figure 5.2c transaction costs are 2, still giving payoffs (9,9) = (11 − 2, 11 − 2) to cooperation: but assuming that all costs are associated with the *giver*, non cooperation (*C,D*) = (1,11), and (*D,C*) = (11,1) gives potentially higher payoffs. In Figure 5.2d a more extreme set of costs and benefits is illustrated: $A_S - b_{ST} - c_S = A_{TS} = b_{TS} - c_T = 26 - 20$ Minimax values are unchanged: in the absence of cooperation payoffs are equal to the minimax values (3,3).

REPETITION

If the game in Figure 5.2b and c is played only once on the basis of causal payoffs alone, non-cooperation (*D,D*) is the Nash equilibrium outcome (the best action of decision-maker *S*, given the anticipated actions of others – *S*). However, purely instrumental decision-making may result in cooperative outcomes.

Treating strategy as a repeated game gives insights into how co-operative behaviour might evolve. Consider, first, an infinitely repeated game. If strategy is seen as a repeated game and if the discount rate is 1, any norm of behaviour can be supported as a Nash equilibrium provided that it ensures payoffs at least as great as minimax values. This theorem is demonstrated by introducing strategies which penalize departures from cooperation. Failure by one player to co-operate in order to gain short-term advantage, is expected to be countered with *punishment* by the other in the form of retaliation, lasting until all short-term gains are eliminated. Assume T is the *transgressor*, the gains from breaking the cooperative rules is C_T. There is an incentive to appropriate the gains from cooperation and avoid the cost of creating them for others; the greater the transaction costs, the bigger is the incentive to do so.

Substantial gains from non-cooperation imposes costs on S who has to *punish* T for breaking faith, thereby reducing the credibility of the threat of punishment. If T is the transgressor, the number of cycles required to wipe out are $(b_{ST} - c_T)^{-1} c_T$. Respective losses from punishment are $b_{TS} - c_T$ and $b_{ST} - C_T$. If both players believe in the reality of retribution, a game such as shown in Figure 5.2c and d, that is infinitely repeated has a dominant strategy (C,C), the Nash equilibrium: a one-period punishment of withdrawing cooperation will more than wipe out the gains of a player who deviates: in Figure 5.2d nearly 5 periods are required and costs the punisher the same amount as the transgressor, reducing the credibility of punishment.

Thus rational behaviour on the basis of *causal utilities* alone may be sufficient to realise cooperative outcomes. There are two well-known qualifications to the argument. The first concerns the length of the game, and the second the discount rate. Games played for a finite period may result in non-cooperative solutions (D,D). In the last period of the game it pays each player on the basis of causal utilities not to cooperate, and by backward induction non-cooperation becomes the norm for the duration of the game. If the game is repeated a finite number of times, but so frequently that the final horizon approaches slowly, results are much the same as in the infinite case. The second qualification involves the discount factor. If this is far greater than or less than 1, the results in this section are different. Earlier payoffs are preferred to later ones so short-term gains may be preferred to longer-term gains which, with larger discount rates, would be preferable. A low discount rate may reflect a high cost of capital, or a preference for the welfare of current over future generations in the form of a high social rate of discount. It may be a symptom of mutual distrust; parties to the alliance may consider their partners likely to renege in the future. In the case of social costs, the community in general may consider big companies have a high propensity to lie. In industrial relations, employees may feel that employers are unlikely to reward commitment with job security.

CULTURE AND MISSION

So far, expected payoffs have been interpreted instrumentally as utilities associated with outcomes (measured in money terms) multiplied by the probability of those outcomes occurring. The games illustrated had equilibria in pure strategies with probabilities of cooperation or non-cooperation of zero or one. Probabilities of outcomes were unaffected by decisions themselves. As we saw earlier, *evidential* payoffs are determined by utilities, weighted by the conditional probabilities of outcomes which are seen as partly contingent upon decisions themselves. If a history develops of cooperative action when it is seen to be mutually advantageous, this increases the conditional probability $(A_{SS}|c_S)$, or $(A_{SS}|c_T)$ of cooperative outcomes in the future.

A tradition in the study of corporate culture as a means of achieving competitive success is to consider whether some companies have an inherent advantage over others. The purpose of the enquiry is often to find support for prejudices about how companies should be run. Anglo Saxon companies, for example, are urged to learn from their Japanese rivals.[53,54] If culture is defined as shared assumptions, or norms which govern behaviour, it is reflected in the conditional probabilities of group responses in a range of circumstances. In a cooperative culture there is a relatively high conditional probability of mutual decisions by others, θ_{-S}, given collaborative actions by individual S, θ_S. In the repeated game of Figure 5.2, a cooperative culture is one with a high conditional probability of reciprocal responses if one individual acts cooperatively, or fails to do so.

If the outcomes of decisions are linked symbolically to others which give utility, this again increases overall payoffs. In this case payoffs of decision-makers are increased directly, rather than indirectly via conditional probabilities. The purpose of mission and vision statements is to connect decisions of staff or customers which increase corporate profits, to other outcomes which they may find personally attractive. Linking of one outcome with another can be malignant or benign, so working upon *symbolic* utilities is hazardous. Economic development in Britain has been said to have been fostered by the association of capitalism with the Protestant ethic; the current idealization in the UK of Victorian values, and internationally of market economics embedded in privatization and individual choice has the same purpose. The parallel, at the micro level, is the identification of the goal of individual perfection with the production of quality in production or service, and in visionary companies such as Body Shop, Virgin, Microsoft and GE cultivation of a myth leadership with lifestyles which customers and staff can identify, by faithfully purchasing the product or committing themselves devoutly to corporate interests. It is not difficult to illustrate less benevolent symbolism, overt or subliminal.

CONCLUDING REMARKS

Implications for Sustainable Organization

The implications for the game illustrated in Figure 5.2 are clear. Realization of gains from cooperation, in minimizing social cost, in achieving trust and hence increased productivity in employer–employee relations, and in achieving synergy gains in international mergers and alliances, may depend upon the ability to increase the conditional probabilities that stakeholders attach to decisions which optimize mutual benefit in spite of short-term disadvantages to themselves. Co operative behaviour can also be increased by linking corporate objectives narrowly defined as competitive advantage to those of the stakeholder group as a whole. If the game in Figure 5.2 is seen in terms of the mutual nature of creativity within organizations (techniques, products and activities which generate competitive advantage), survival may depend upon understanding the Bayesian nature of corporate culture and the symbolic nature of strategic intent.

The implicit assumption in current narratives of competition is that the shareholder is the key stakeholder. However, earlier arguments in this chapter suggest that competitive advantage narrowly defined is not sufficient. Rather it depends upon the distribution of payoffs between stakeholders, not simply the absolute level. Four requirements for sustainability are implied: (i) *profitability*, (ii) *superadditivity* so that the whole is worth more than the sum of the parts, (iii) *acceptable tradeoffs* (balance) between different stakeholder interests and (iv) *significance* in the sense of a correspondence between individual values and collective goals.

The conditions of profitability and superadditivity follow the definition of sustainability in terms of narrow competitive advantage. It requires a surplus $K_£$, defined as the difference between receipts $R_£$ and wages and salaries $(W + S)_£$ and other variable costs $M_£$ minus the cost of debt $r_d D_£$, and equity $r_c E_£$:

$$K_£ = R_£ - (W + S)_£ - M_£, - r_d D_£ - r_c E_£ \qquad (5.5)$$

Unless expression (5.5) is zero or positive, the organization destroys rather than creates value. The last term means that shareholders need to be compensated for risk. If the expression progressively falls below zero, first the stockholder as a residual income recipient fails to be compensated for risk, then the company is pushed into bankruptcy as it fails to meet the cost of debt and other contractual expenses.

In addition, competitive advantage requires the whole should be worth more than the parts – *superadditivity*. The organization should be worth more than a subset of coalitions, otherwise value added could be increased by *unbundling*, a term associated with but not invented by Sir James Goldsmith, who valued the constituent businesses of BAT at £17.5 billion, approximately £4 billion more than BAT itself. The larger and more sustained the difference between the actual and potential value of corporate assets, the greater the pressure on existing management teams to increase value added by restructuring, or to succumb to predators. This last consideration was influential in the decision, in 1993, to split ICI into two separate sets of businesses. The search for superadditivity high-return investments has become international. In the 1980s there was a surge in global foreign direct investment. Between 1983 and 1990, United Nations estimates suggest that global flows rose annually by 30 per cent. The largest flows were between the United Kingdom, the United States and Japan, but in recent years there has been an increase in flows to the developing world, mainly in Asia and Latin America.

Shareholders are the recipients of any surplus in equation (5.5). The implicit assumption, in present day narratives of competition is that the shareholder is the key stakeholder. The arguments here suggest otherwise. The concept of *balancing* stakeholder interests reflects the importance of *evidential utilities* and corporate culture for long-run success. Organizations are teams, and realizing potential depends upon cooperative behaviour, which is conditional on cooperative behaviour by others. Many current gains in shareholder wealth are produced by management reneging on implicit contracts signifying a sharp change in organizational history or tradition, and reducing the conditional probabilities of cooperative behaviour being reciprocated, and consequently reducing the weight it carries in decision-making. The result is destruction of the intangible assets on which creativity is based: commitment, willingness to learn and imagination.

COMPLEXITY AND DILEMMAS

Descriptions of the competitive process approximate to the Darwinian notion of evolution through selection and adaptation by an algorithmic process, in this case the operation of markets without the need for an intelligent being in the form of a central planner. In older narratives of competition, the consensus was that trusteeship roles were required of governments. Although the competitive process and the search for profit was the best available means of organizing production, it neglected important trusteeship roles: the provision of public or merit goods, and protection against social costs or degrees of inequality of income and wealth beyond the need to provide incentives. The application of these trusteeship roles, in practice, led at least in the UK and the USA to a brand of corporatism which was rejected in the late 1970s. By then, new motifs were beginning to appear in narratives of competitive advantage: deregulation of financial markets, globalization and regionalization, diffusion of information technologies, the evolution of flexible organizations, and shorter product cycles.

In current narratives, global competition results in increased efficiency and wealth as 'creative destruction' is experienced on an unprecedented scale. Globalization of markets has been accompanied by changes in economic power and the distribution of wealth. Combined with efforts to reduce public spending and make labour markets more flexible, the protection of the welfare state has fallen and inequalities of income have become more pronounced. In the United Kingdom, for example, half of the population lives in households that receive (means tested) benefits.[58] Benefits of economic growth in the United States over the last 15 years have accrued to just 1 per cent of the population. Globalization in its current stage enriches newly-industrializing poor nations, increases insecurity and job losses among the semi-affluent in the richer nations, whilst greatly increasing incomes of those who benefit from the process. The fashion for maximizing the market value of employee skills prevalent in the 1970s is now passé. In expression (5.5), employees feature as a cost. The surplus available to stockholders increases in proportion to the unemployment created by executives, who are driven partly by the pressures of global competition and partly by eagerness to prove that they are au fait with the latest management consultant slogan, reengineering the corporation. Drivers in the United Kingdom and North America also come from the prevalence of stock options as rewards for senior management who are finding themselves incapable of providing for the income expectation of the middle classes.

In modern narratives, survival is contingent upon satisfying stockholder interests, and organizations are subjected to the inexorable processes of global competition. The interests of other stakeholders are subordinate and, in any case, the increases in efficiency and cost reductions brought by globalization ensure greater overall payoffs even though there may be regrettable changes in distribution.

This chapter suggests that the conventional narratives neglect the complexity associated with organizational payoffs. Organizations have the capacity to destroy the basis of their own competitive advantage. The paradox of reengineering and lean production for example is that they seem to be necessary for survival, but the higher payoffs they bring involve redistributions which destroy balance and significance. Perhaps sustainability of particular organizations is a transient state which fades, but with difficulty may be renewed. In this case sustainability becomes an issue for society as a whole. Keynes' intuition was that capitalism may be the best system available and that it depends upon certain inequalities, but if these become too great the system begins to destroy itself.

The trusteeship roles required against the contingencies mentioned earlier have not disappeared, they have merely become submerged by the myth. To repudiate the modern myth of competitive advantage is not to deny it as an important theme, but it has become a rhetoric signifying that society exists not just for the purposes of business, but for a very narrow group of stakeholders. At best the modern myth of global competition is a partial one – a simple story reflecting one aspect of complexity. Perhaps a shift in corporate consciousness may have to await a new Kondratieff upturn, in the form of a demand shock, originating from increased incomes in the formerly poor nations.

Notes

1. J. Womack, D. Jones and D. Roos, *The Machine that Changed the World* (New York: Macmillan, 1990).
2. J. Stopford, 'The Impact of Global Political Economy on Corporate Strategy', paper presented to the Carnegie Bosch Institute's Conference on the Challenge of the Multinational Competition (Stuttgart: May, 1993).
3. C.K. Prahalad and R.A. Bettis, 'The Dominant Logic: A New Link between Diversification and Performance', *Strategic Management Journal*, vol. 7 (1986).
4. M.E. Porter, *Competitive Strategy: Techniques for Analysing Industry and Competitors* (New York: Free Press, 1980).
5. M.E. Porter, *Competitive Advantage: Creating and Sustaining Superior Performance* (London: Collier Macmillan, 1985).
6. C.A. Bartlett and S. Ghoshal, *Managing Across Borders: The Transnational Solution* (Boston: Harvard, 1989).
7. C.A. Bartlett and S. Ghoshal, 'Changing the Role of Top Management: Beyond Strategy to Purpose', *Harvard Business Review* (1994).
8. C.K. Prahalad and G. Hamel, 'The Core Competence of the Corporation', *Harvard Business Review*, May–June (1990).
9. H. Mintzberg, '*The Rise and Fall of Strategic Planning* (New York: Prentice-Hall, 1994).
10. M.C. Jenson, 'The Eclipse of the Public Corporation', *Harvard Business Review*, vol. 67 (1989).
11. C. Hampden-Turner, *Corporate Culture for Competitive Edge* (London: Economist Publications, 1990).
12. A. Campbell, M. Devine and D. Young, *A Sense of Mission* (London: The Economist Publications, 1990).
13. N.M. Tichy and M.A. Devanna, *The Transformational Leader* (New York: John Wiley & Sons, 1986).
14. C.K. Prahalad and G. Hamel, *Competing for the Future* (Boston, Mass: Harvard Business School Press, 1994).
15. E.A. Allen and D.J. Steffensmeier, 'Recent Evidence on US Crime Rates', *American Sociological Review*, vol. 41 (1989).
16. R.J. Sampson and J.D. Woodredge, 'Measuring Qualitative Differences in US Crime', *Journal of Quantitative Criminology*, vol. 22 (1987).
17. D. Downes, 'Why Inquality is Still a Factor', *The Times Literary Supplement*, no. 4842 (1995).
18. J.A. Schumpeter, *Business Cycles* (London: Harrap, 1948).
19. J.M. Keynes, *The General Theory of Employment, Interest and Money* (London: Macmillan, 1973).
20. S. Ghoshal and N. Nohria, 'Horses for Courses: Organisational Forms for Multinational Companies', *Sloan Management Review*, Winter (1993).
21. S. Ghoshal and N. Nohria, 'Internal Differentiation within Multinational Corporations', *Strategic Management Journal*, vol. 10 (1989).
22. T. Eagleton, *Literary Theory: An Introduction* (Oxford: Basil Blackwell, 1983).

23. H. Bloom, *The Western Cannon: The Books and the School of Ages* (London: Macmillan, 1995).
24. H. Mintzberg, *Mintzberg on Management* (New York: Free Press, 1989).
25. H.I. Ansoff, *Corporate Strategy* (London: McGraw-Hill, 1969).
26. G. Morgan, *Imagination: The Art of Creative Management* (London: Sage, 1993).
27. K.J. Arrow, *The Limits of Organizations* (Oxford: Blackwell, 1974).
28. F. Westley and H. Mintzberg, 'Visionary Leadership and Strategic Management', *Strategic Management Journal*, vol. 10, pp. 17–32 (1989).
29. R. Barthes in D. Lodge (ed.), *Modern Criticism and Theory* (London: Longmans, 1968).
30. M. Gell-Mann, *The Quark and the Jaguar* (London: Abacus, 1995).
31. R.D. Stacey, *Strategic Management and Organizational Dynamics* (London: Pitman, 1996).
32. R. Nozick, *The Nature of Reality* (Chichester, UK: Princetown University Press, 1995).
33. T. Schelling, *The Strategy of Conflict* (London: Harvard University Press, 1980).
34. D.M. Kreps, in P.J. Buckley and J. Michie, *Firms, Organizations and Markets* (Oxford: Oxford University Press, 1996).
35. R.A. Coase, 'The Nature of the Firm', *Economica*, IV (1937).
36. A.A. Alchian and H. Demsetz, 'Production, Information Costs and Economic Organization', *American Economic Review*, no. 6 (1972).
37. M. Hammer and J. Champy, *Reengineering the Corporation* (New York: HarperCollins, 1993).
38. R. Matthews, *Managing for Success* (London: Confederation of British Industry, 1985).
39. J. Kay, *Foundations of Corporate Success* (Oxford: Oxford University Press, 1993).
40. R. Matthews, *The Organization Matrix: Core Business and Structure*, The Handbook of Business Disciplines (University of America Press, 1994).
41. R. Matthews, *Corporate Structure as a Cooperative Game: Theory and Applications* (Kingston Business School Series, 1996).
42. A. Campbell and K.S. Luchs, *Strategic Synergy* (Oxford: Butterworth–Heinemann, 1992).
43. G. Wittington, *Inflation Accounting: An Introduction to the Debate* (Cambridge: Cambridge University Press, 1989).
44. J. Edward, J. kay and C. Mayer, *Economic Analysis of Accounting Profitability* (London: Clarendon Press, 1987).
45. R.H. Kilmann, *Beyond the Quick Fix* (London: Jossey Bass, 1986).
46. *Financial Times*, 18 May, 1995.
47. A. Schleifer and L. Summers in A. Auerbach and D. Reihus, *Corporate Takeovers: Causes and Consequences* (Chicago: University of Chicago Press, 1988).
48. D.C. Dennet, *Darwin's Dangerous Idea: Evolution and the Meaning of Life* (New York: Simon & Schuster, 1995).
49. M. Goodman, *Creative Management* (London: Prentice-Hall, 1995).
50. A. Koestler, *The Act of Creation* (London: Pan, 1969).

51. J. Maynard Smith, *Evolution and the Theory of Games* (Cambridge: Cambridge University Press, 1982).
52. R. Pascale and A. Athos, *The Art of Japanese Management* (New York: Simon & Schuster, 1981).
53. F. Fukayama, *The End of History and the Last Man* (London: Penguin, 1992).
54. F. Field, 'Making Welfare Work', *The Economist* (20 May 1995).

References

Alchian, A.A. and Demsetz, H. (1972) 'Production, Information Costs and Economic Organization', *American Economic Review*, 62.
Allen, E.A. and Steffensmeier, D.J. (1989) 'Receny Evidence on US Crime Rates' *American Sociological Review*, vol. 41.
Arrow, K.J. (1969) 'Economic Organization Issues Pertinent to the Choice of Market vs Non-market Allocation', in *Collected Papers of Kenneth Arrow* (Cambridge Mass.: Belknap Press).
Arrow, K.J. and Hahn, F.H. (1971) *General Competitive Analysis* (Edinburgh: Holden-Day).
Arrow, K.J. (1974) *The Limits of Organizations* (Oxford Blackwell).
Auman, R.I. (1985) 'What is Game Theory Trying to Accomplish', in K.J. Arrow and S. Honkapohja (eds), *Frontiers of Economics* (Oxford: Basil Blackwell).
Axelrod, R. (1984) *The Evolution of Co-operation* (New York: Basic Books).
Barthes, R. (1968) 'The Death of the Author', in D. Lodge (ed.) (1988) *Modern Criticism and Theory* (London: Longmans).
Bartlett, C.A. (1986) 'Building and Managing the Transnational: The New Organizational Challenge', in M.E. Poner (ed.), *Competition in Global Industries* (Boston: Harvard Business School Press).
Banien, C.A. and Ghoahal, S. (1989) *Managing Across Borders: The Transnational Solution* (Boston: Harvard Business School Press).
Bloom, H. (1995) *The Western Cannon: The Books and the School of the Ages* (London: Macmillan).
Carmpbell, A., Devine, M. and Young, D. (1990) *A Sense of Mission* (London: Economist Publications).
Chandler, A.D. (1962) *Strategy and Structure: Aspects in the History of the Industrial Enterprise* (Cambridge, Mass.: MIT Press).
Coase, R.A. (1937) 'The Nature of the Firm', *Economica*, IV.
Coase, R.A. (1960) 'The Problem of Social Cost, *Journal of Law and Economics*, 3(1), October.
Datta, D.K. (1991), 'Organizational Fit and Acquisition Performance: Effects of Post Acquisition Integration', *Strategic Management Journal*, vol. 12, pp. 281–297.
Day, R.H. (1975) 'Adaptive Processes and Economic Theory', in R. Day and T. Groves (eds), *Adaptive Economic Models* (New York: Academic Press).
Demsetz, Alchian, A. and H. (1972) 'Production, Information Costs and Economic Organization', *American Economic Review*, 62.
Downes, D. (1995), 'Why Inequality is Still a Factor', *The Times Literary Supplement*, no. 4842, September.

Fudenberg, D. and Tirole J. (l993) *Game Theory* (London: MIT Press)

Gell-Mann, M. (1995) *The Quark and the Jaguar* (London: Abacus).

Georgescu Roegen, N. (1971), *The Entropy Law and the Economic Process* (Cambridge Mass.: Harvard University Press).

Ghemawat, P. (l991), *Commitment: The Dynamic Strategy* (New York: Free Press).

Goodman, M. (l995), *Creative Management* (London: Prentice-Hall).

Goold, M. and Campbell, A. (1987) *Strategies and Styles: The Role of the Center in Diversified Companies* (Oxford: Basil Blackwell).

Hahn, F. (1990) *The Economics of Missing Markets Information and Games* (Oxford: Clarenden Press).

Hayek, F. von (1945) 'The Use of Knowledge in Society', *American Economic Review*, vol. 35.

Hayek, F. von (1973) *Law Legislation and Liberty*, vol. 1 (Chicago: University of Chicago Press).

Jenson, M.C. (1989), 'The Eclipse of the Public Corporation', *Harvard Business Review*, vol. 67.

Jensen, M.C. and Mechlin, W.H. (1979) 'Theory of the Firm Managerial Behaviour, Agency Costs and Ownership Structure', *Journal of Financial Economics*, 3.

Jenson, M.C. and Ruback, R.S. (1983) 'The Market for Corporate Control: The Scientific Evidence', *Journal of Financial Eonomics*, ɪɪ, pp. 5–50.

Jung, C.G. (1968) *The Archetypes and the Collective Unconscious* (London: Routledge).

Kay, J. (1993) *Foundations of Corporate Success* (Oxford: Oxford University Press).

Keynes, J.M. (1936), *The General Theory of Employment, Interest and Money* (London: Macmillan).

Koestle, A. (1969), *The Act of Creation* (London: Pan).

Koopmans, T.C. (ed.) (1951), *Activity Analysis of Production and Allocation* (New York: McGraw-Hill).

Matthews, R. (1994), 'The Organizational Matrix Core: Businesses and Structure', British Academy of Management: proceedings, Lancaster University.

Maynard Smith, J. (1982), *Evolution and the Theory of Games* (Cambridge: Cambridge University Press).

Morgan, G. (1993), *Imagination: The Art of Creative Management* (London: Sage).

Mintzberg, H. (1994) *The Rise and Fall of Strategic Planning* (New York: Prentice-Hall).

Neison, R. and Winter, S. (1978), 'Forces Generating and Limiting Concentration Under Schumpeterian Competition', Bell Journal of Economics, 9 (2).

Nozick, R. (1995),The Nature of Rationality (Chichester, UK: Princeton University Press).

Peters, T.I. and Waterman, R.W. (1982) *In Search of Excellence* (New York: Harper-Collins).

Porter, M. E. (1980), *Competitive Srategy: Techniques for Analysing Industries and Competitors* (New York: Free Press).

Porter, M. E. (1985) *Competitve Advantage: Creating and Sustaining Superior Performance* (London: Collier Macmillan).

Porter, M. E. (1991), 'Towards a Dynamic Theory of Strategy', *Strategic Management Journal*, vol. 12, pp. 95–117.

Radner, R. *Information, Incentives and Economic Mechanisms*, essays in honour of Leonid Nurvvicz (Oxford: Blackwell).

Sampson, R.I. and Wooldredge, I.D. (1987) 'Measuring Qualitative Differences in US Crime', *Journal of Quantitative Criminology*, vol. 22.

Schumpeter, J. (1948) *Business Cycles* (London: Harrap).

Smith, A. (1759) *The Theory of Moral Sentiments* (New York: Liberty Classics, 1969).

Stacey, R.D. (1996), *Strategic Management and Organizational Dynamics*, (London: Pitmon).

Wernerfelt, B. (1984), 'A Resource Based View of the Firm', *Strategic Management Journal*, 5 (2).

Williamson, O. E. *The Economic Institutions of Capitalism: Firms, Markets, Relational Contracting* (New York: The Free Press).

Winter, S. (1964), *Economic Natural Selection and the Theory of the Firm*, Yale Economic Essays, 4.

6 Winners and Losers in the West: Ranking by Adjustment Capacity

Richard Brown

INTRODUCTION

The framework developed in this chapter had its origins some two years ago when I was asked to review the outlook for the European economies as part of the Manchester Business School's annual conference on Prospects for the British Economy. A natural starting point was the forecasts of international bodies such as the IMF (1993) and the OECD (1993). After all, these are prepared by large teams of highly competent economists who have the benefit of close and regular contact with the countries concerned. In the event I quickly became disillusioned with these official forecasts, to the extent that I wrote a piece for the *Observer* (30 October 1994) which appeared with the lurid title of 'Flawed Theology of the IMF High Priests'!

There were two obvious problems. First, the forecast period – some two years – was too short to be of any use for business decision-makers. The IMF did produce some medium-term projections in 1994 but these looked more like wishful thinking as far as the European economies were concerned. For example, German growth over 1995–98 was forecast to average over 3 per cent per annum. This in turn leads to the second main criticism. The forecasting techniques were still too Keynesian in the sense that forecasts for GDP growth were built-up from its demand components. Now this is quite acceptable if you are trying to decide whether, say, French growth next year will be 1.5 per cent or 1.7 per cent. However, the longer the forecast period, and for most business purposes this has to cover at least 5 years, the greater the influence of supply-side factors. In fact at a time when European unemployment stubbornly remains over 10 per cent despite large fiscal deficits, it would appear that supply-side factors are highly relevant in the short term as well. However, forecasting models still lack any systematic way of incorporating these.

There is also a further problem in that the forecasts of the demand components are in part derived from econometric equations estimated over historical periods. In order to use these in forecasts it has to be assumed that no structural changes have occurred. It is of course possible to test for this in the estimation period. However, even if structural breaks were absent in the past it is surely unrealistic to expect them not to be present in the current environment of unprecedented structural change in product, labour and financial markets.

If the emperor has no clothes, how do we go about attiring him? After all the economic outlook in Europe, America and Japan is highly relevant to production and sales decisions. If, for example, Europe is going to remain a low growth area, even within the industrialized world, then other things being equal this strengthens the case for concentrating sales efforts outside this region, at least for products dependent on market growth. The objective of this chapter is to attempt to develop a framework to analyse which countries will succeed, and which won't, in this brave new world.

DIFFERENCES IN ECONOMIC STRUCTURE

An immediate issue, which is particularly relevant to global change, is the extent to which national economic performance is relevant in the current environment. The counter-argument is that increasing globalization will lead to convergence in economic performance. For example, global capital markets can severely limit the ability of a country to pursue macroeconomic polices significantly out of line with those in the major economies. Countries which might otherwise wish to impose punitive tax rates on individuals or corporations now find that these are self-defeating. There does seem to be convergence on market-oriented policies at the micro-level coupled with 'responsible' anti-inflationary policies at the macroeconomic level.

The counter-argument is that significant differences in economic performance still exist among industrial countries. For example, unemployment is relatively low in the USA and Japan but is over 20 per cent of the working population in Spain. During the 1980s, US growth exceeded that of the EU, contrary to catch-up/convergence theory. Swedish living standards are no longer one of the highest in the world. Growth prospects in the EU are currently a matter for concern.

Thus it appears that differences still exist in economic structures among countries which impact on economic performance. In a fundamental sense these differences arise in part because no country practices pure *laissez-faire*, in the sense of the complete absence of government from economic life. This in turn reflects perceived problems outlined below with the unfettered operation of free markets.

- *Economies of scale* – these can lead either to the existence of monopoly (which justifies competition policy) or to the failure of domestic firms to enter an industry because of insufficient capital (which is said to justify nationalized industries or state subsidies).
- *Public goods* – these are goods, for example defence or public parks, which have high fixed costs but whose *marginal* consumption is almost costless. In theory these goods should be made available free of charge, with the costs met through taxes. Left to the market, these goods will be under-provided.
- *Externalities* – for example training, can benefit an economy to an extent well beyond the immediate cost, justifying either subsidy or regulations to encourage it. Wage negotiations are also claimed to involve externalities through the leap-frogging of claims, wage–price spirals and so on. This is said to justify the centralization of such negotiations.
- *Imperfect information* – the free market model tends to assume perfect knowledge. Its absence leads to legislation on consumer protection, health and safety, as well as minimum wage laws and some form of welfare state. Imperfect information is also said to lead to short-termism in financial markets and corporate decision-making, in turn justifying anti-competitive structures in some countries (for example the effective prohibition of hostile take-overs).

Thus in practice the state, either through legislation or more directly, plays an active role in the economies of all western countries. However, the form of intervention varies considerably. It is possible to recognize a number of models, for example the US/UK Anglo-Saxon model is probably closest to the *laissez-faire* paradigm. At the other extreme is the collectivist Scandinavian model, with the German model not far behind. In their different ways these models all claim to tackle the problems of pure *laissez-faire*. And yet it is surely not unreasonable to suppose that their success in doing so will depend in part on the environment in which they are operating.

ADJUSTMENT CAPACITY

So what sort of environment are firms going to be operating in? This is, and will be, one of considerable change. In recent years we have seen the collapse of communism, the take-off of growth in an increasing number of developing countries, and the explosion of technology. This in turn is transforming exactly which products and markets will be high growth and high value-added.

This suggests that a successful firm or economy will have a high degree of adaptability to change or adjustment capacity. The annex to this paper defines four key criteria which contribute to adjustment capacity. These, together with their underlying components, are summariszed in Table 6.1.

Table 6.1   Adjustment capacity – the criteria

Market and Product Orientation	• Share of exports to developing countries • Comparative advantage in services and high value-added manufactures
Corporate Efficiency	• High profitability • Low non-wage costs • High R&D • High international direct investment
Labour Market Efficiency	• Decentralized labour market • Well-trained labour force • Low unemployment
Macroeconomic Stability	• Low fiscal deficit • Low interest rates • Stable growth pattern

The annex contains a detailed rationale for choosing these criteria for assessing adjustment capacity. A summary of the characteristics of a high adjustment is given below:

- *Market and product orientation* – involves high exports to fast growing developing countries together will have a comparative advantage in high value-added manufactures and services and a comparative disadvantage in low value-added, labour intensive, manufactures.
- *Corporate efficiency* – means having an efficient corporate sector which is profitable, has small non-wage costs (permitting greater flexibility in remuneration), high R&D and large international in-

vestment flows (both inward and outward, thereby increasing exposure to best practice and competition).
- *Labour market efficiency* – requires an efficient labour market, defined as having a flexible, decentralized wage-bargaining system, good training and low unemployment.
- *Macroeconomic stability* – includes a stable macroeconomic environment, which is associated with low fiscal deficits and interest rates and a history of stable growth.

Underlying these criteria is a paradigm with a few key elements. First, causality running from access/openness to competition, to efficiency, to high productivity and hence to high wages and living standards. Second, a stress on flexibility, decentralisztion and speed of response. Third, the belief that the traditional arguments for corporatism and intervention, that is market failure such as economies of scale, externalities and imperfect information have been weakened by recent and prospective developments in the world economy; at the same time the latter have highlighted the likelihood of government failure, in particular the slow speed of response to rent-seeking behaviour.

In the annex, 10 countries are assessed against these criteria (essentially the Group of 10 less Canada and Sweden plus Spain and Denmark). This gives us countries representing 96 per cent of EU GDP, plus the USA and Japan as comparators. Under each of the four criteria countries are ranked from 1 to 10. For example, Japan has the smallest fiscal deficit and is ranked 1, Italy has the largest and is ranked 10. Within each criterion the various component rankings are averaged, producing an overall ranking for that criterion. The rankings for the four criteria are then averaged to produce an overall ranking of adjustment capacity.

Table 6.2 lists the countries in order of their overall standing on adjustment capacity. Before discussing this a few comments are made on the individual criteria.

With respect to *market and product orientation*, Japan and the USA stand out as having over 40 per cent of their exports to developing countries. The highest European country is Italy with just over 20 per cent. Japan's comparative advantage looks good, with a large and growing comparative advantage in high-technology manufactures. At the other extreme we have Italy with a large and growing comparative advantage in labour-intensive manufactures.

As for *corporate efficiency*, Italy scores very badly on all components. Belgium and France are almost as bad except on international

Table 6.2   Adjustment capacity – the results

Country	Market/ product orientation	Corporate efficiency	Labour efficiency	Macro-economic stability	Total
Japan	1	1	1	1	4
USA	2	2	2	3	9
Germany	5	5	4	2	16
UK	3	3	3	7	16
France	4	8	5	5	22
Netherlands	8	4	6	4	22
Denmark	10	6	9	6	31
Italy	7	10	7	8	32
Spain	6	7	10	10	33
Belgium	9	9	8	9	35

Note: 1 is best, 10 worst.
Sources: see annex.

direct investment where they score well. Japan and the USA are in the top three on all components except international direct investment (this is expressed as a proportion of GDP which may disadvantage the larger economies).

Turning to *labour markets*, Italy manages a mid-table position thanks to its relatively decentralized labour market. On this criterion Germany scores very badly. However Belgium, Denmark and Spain perform badly overall, with Japan and the USA once again ahead of the pack.

With respect to *macroeconomic stability*, not surprisingly the UK does badly here, the only consolation being that Belgium and Spain do worse. Again, not surprisingly, Germany does very well.

Turning to the overall results, one possible outcome is that countries could all be huddled together in the middle, doing well on some criteria but not on others. It must be emphasized that this is not the case here. By and large the same countries tend to do well, and the same badly. In fact the sample can be divided into four groups:

1.   First come *Japan* and the *USA*, and by a long margin. Japan comes first under all four criteria, the USA second in three and third in the other (Germany pips it for macroeconomic stability). According to the criteria adopted these countries have far and away the greatest adjustment capacity.

2.   *Germany* and the *UK* are in the 'good European' category. It is difficult to separate these two, the order changing according to the

data series used. Germany is held back by its labour market in-efficiency, and the UK by its macroeconomic instability.
3. The *Netherlands*, is held back by its poor market and product or-ientation, and *France*, is held back by its inefficient corporate sector.
4. Finally the 'poor European' group of *Italy, Denmark, Belgium* and *Spain*. All these countries perform below average in all of the four criteria. There are one or two glimmers of hope – Italian labour market flexibility, Danish corporate efficiency and Spanish com-parative advantage are not too bad, for example, but overall on these criteria the outlook here is dire.

CONCLUSIONS

Pulling the various strands together, a number of conclusions emerge:

1. The results are consistent with the EU remaining a low growth area compared with the USA and Japan. The USA in particular, with its high adjustment capacity and low adjustment need looks well-placed. Japan has to make the transition to being a consumer society (partly its own and others' services), and to enjoy being a rentier as an increasing proportion of its manufactured output is produced elsewhere. However, its very high adjustment capacity bodes well.
2. Within the EU the prospects look much more heterogeneous than the forecasts indicate. In particular, Belgium, Spain and Italy combine low adjustment capacity with high adjustment need. Gi-ven the expected global economic environment and the above criteria, their outlook is bleak. Germany is particularly interesting – the greatest adjustment need but better placed than many in Europe to achieve it.
3. In this framework the UK looks relatively good because it has a low adjustment need and by European standards quite good ad-justment capacity. The UKs problems are poor macroeconomic stability and a poor market orientation. However, the UK has fi-nally succeeded in concentrating its export effort on Europe just when this is a low growth area of the world economy!

Some implications for EMU can be inferred from this ranking of EU member states. The Maastricht timetable for EMU looks hopelessly optimistic. Fulfilment of the convergence criteria is not the major problem, given that intra-European fiscal transfers are so small – under these conditions strict macroeconomic convergence is needed to minimize the costs of the loss of national exchange rate and monetary policy. However, quite a few countries are a very long way from satisfying these criteria. Nevertheless, the case for a two-speed monetary Europe may be strong. Indeed, something like this seems to be going ahead as the ERM has been reinvented by stealth for some countries. The composition of this group (Germany, France, Belgium, Denmark and the Netherlands) is presumably based on trade links with Germany and the need for monetary credibility. However, these countries have very different adjustment capabilities – Belgium in particular looks unsuited to such an arrangement. Finally, the case for EMU itself can be questioned. The economic case for it has gone along the lines that there are benefits and costs but over time the benefits have risen as intra-European trade has increased (augmented by the 1992 process) while the costs have fallen because of macroeconomic convergence.

However I would argue two points:

1. If countries start to switch their export efforts to benefit from the strongly growing markets in the developing countries, then the trend towards higher intra-European trade may be reversed.
2. The costs associated with the loss of exchange rate and monetary policy will rise, in particular, for those countries with low adjustment capacity.

This suggests that the formal EMU process should be put on hold with those who wish to be free to continue their informal linking arrangements with the DM.

ANNEX

Market and Product Orientation

With respect to market orientation the key distinction made is between developed and developing countries. Most medium to long-term forecasts have growth in the industrialized countries, as a bloc, at around 2.5–3 per cent per annum; for the developing bloc as a whole the figure is about double at some 5–6 per cent per annum. Furthermore, the tendency for exchange rates in developing countries to appreciate over time (that is, to close the gap on their purchasing power parity exchange rates) means that the growth of real disposable incomes in these countries will exceed their already high growth rates. This means that the fast growing markets will be found in the developing world. Hence the industrialized countries are ranked according to the importance of *exports to developing countries in that country's total exports* (see Table 6.3).

There are at least two qualifications. First, it makes the assumption that those best placed to exploit the faster growth expected in developing countries are those who already have a strong export orientation there. Second, it does not attempt to take into account differential growth rates among developing countries. While these are undoubtedly present in the past, they narrow in most forecasts as the Southeast Asian model is copied elsewhere, notably in South America.

With respect to *product orientation*, countries are assessed according to the extent of their comparative advantage in producing the goods and services likely to be the most profitable in the future. These include high value-added and customized manufactured goods and services. At the other extreme are the more standardized, low-technology, labour-intensive goods which the developing countries have a comparative advantage in producing. Of course assessing comparative

Table 6.3   Market and product orientation

Country	Share of exports to developing countries	Comparative advantage in high value-added manufactures	Total	Rank
USA	40.6 (2)	14 (2)	4	2
Japan	45.6 (1)	235 (1)	2	1
Germany	18.1 (6)	−118 (6)	12	5
France	19.8 (4)	−99 (4)	8	4
Italy	21.6 (3)	−392 (10)	13	7
UK	19.1 (5)	−39 (3)	8	3
Belgium	12.5 (9)	−268 (8)	17	9
Denmark	13.4 (8)	−269 (9)	17	10
Netherlands	10.6 (10)	−154 (7)	17	8
Spain	16.5 (7)	−108 (5)	12	6

Sources: Export shares – IMP *Direction of Trade* yearbook, 1993; Comparative advantage – 'Industrial Policy in OECD Countries', OECD, 1992.

Table 6.4   Revealed comparative advantage

	Shares in USA manufactured exports			
	High-tech	Medium-tech	Low-tech	Labour-intensive
1970	159	110	67	58
1990	161	89	74	63

Source: OECD, 1992.

advantage here is notoriously controversial. Table 6.4 provides a cal-
culated revealed comparative advantage in manufactured exports for
the USA by comparing the importance of various categories of goods
in the exports of the USA.

Thus we begin by computing *the excess of the high-tech share over
the combination of the low-tech and labour intensive shares* – for the US
in 1990 this comes to 24 percentage points. However, some countries
have seen dramatic changes in the importance of different categories of
goods over time. We give equal weight to these by computing changes
in shares from 1970 to 1990. The US figure here is $-10 = (161 - 159) -
(74 - 67) - (63 - 58)$. Thus the final US figure is $14 = (24 - 10)$.

Corporate Efficiency

A total of five measures have been used to assess corporate efficiency
(see Table 6.5). The first two are estimates of *profitability* on the
grounds that in open economies profitability denotes efficiency. The
UNIDO measure is an estimate of the gross surplus (per \$100 of
output) of the manufacturing sector in 1990; the OECD data are an
estimate of the rate of return in the business sector for 1994. Both these
estimates have the advantage of being available for a wide range of
countries. There is a reasonable correlation between the two for most
of the 10 countries with the exception of Denmark, the Netherlands
and Spain.

The next measure is an estimate of *non-wage cuts*, specifically employers' social security costs as a proportion of average earnings. The
argument here is that in the fast-changing environment of the late
1990s, remuneration should be as flexible as possible so that it can
cope with, for example, changes in product demand and innovation,
shifts in skills requirements and availability, regional disparities and so
forth. Non-wage costs tend to be inflexible, hence the lower the better.

Table 6.5   Corporate efficiency

Country	Profitability		Non-wage costs	R&D	IDI
	UNIDO	OECD			
USA	25.7	18.4	7.7	2.7	8.3
Japan	26.6	15.1	7.6	2.9	7.5
Germany	24.7	12.8	18.2	2.8	7.2
France	15.3	14.1	43.8	2.3	11.8
Italy	14.2	11.7	50.1	1.2	5.1
UK	23.0	11.3	10.4	2.3	31.2
Belgium	17.5	12.4	41.9	1.7	27.5
Denmark	20.6	10.7	0.00	1.4	10.1
Netherlands	11.1	15.1	10.8	2.3	29.1
Spain	15.9	19.6	30.2	0.6	10.5

	Ranking					Total	Rank
USA	2	2	3	3	7	17	2
Japan	1	3	2	1	8	15	1
Germany	3	6	6	2	9	26	5
France	8	5	9	5	4	31	8
Italy	9	8	10	9	10	46	10
UK	4	9	4	6	1	24	3
Belgium	6	7	8	7	3	31	9
Denmark	5	10	1	8	6	30	6
Netherlands	10	4	5	4	2	25	4
Spain	7	1	7	10	5	30	7

Finally, we have *R&D expenditure* (as a proportion of GDP) as a proxy for product innovation and cumulative flows of both inward and outward *international direct investment* (again as a proportion of GDP). Product innovation is clearly vital for those corporations continuing to produce in high-cost countries because it should help develop the more technically advanced, differentiated, high value-added products. International direct investment exposes a country's corporate sector to best practice abroad. The McKinsey Global Institute Report, for example, noted that foreign direct investment has been far more important than trade as a force for improving productivity.

Labour Market Efficiency

Three measures are used here. The first attempts to capture the *degree of centralization of the wage bargaining process* – the argument is the

Table 6.6　　Labour market efficiency

	Centralization	Graduates	Unemployment	Total	Rank
US	1	2	2	5	2
Japan	2	1	1	4	1
Germany	9	3	5	17	4
France	5	4	9	18	5
Italy	3	9	8	20	7
UK	4	5	3	12	3
Belgium	6	8	6	20	8
Denmark	10	7	7	24	9
Netherlands	8	6	4	18	6
Spain	7(E)	10	10	27	10

Sources:　Centralization – L. Calmfors and J. Driffill, 'Bargaining Structure, Corporatism and Macroeconomic Performance', *Economic Policy*, vol. 6, 1988 (Schmitter study excluded, rank for Spain estimated); graduates/unemployment – OECD *Economic Outlook*.

more decentralized the better, in view of the rapid product and market changes taking place (this reverses what was once conventional wisdom). We make use of the Calmfors/Driffill study which reports the results from four studies which rank countries according to the degree of centralization. These results are averaged to produce a ranking for this category. Next we take the proportion of *graduates in the labour force* as an (imperfect) indicator of the quality of the labour force. Finally, we rank countries according to unemployment rates as a direct measure of whether the labour market is working or not (see Table 6.6).

Macroeconomic Stability

The need for more stable or 'better' macroeconomic policy is often claimed to be one of the ways by which governments can help industry. Exactly what is meant here tends to vary from shopping list to shopping list but the key end-products relate to growth and inflation. In particular it is often argued that:

- growth should be sustainable, avoiding the destabilizing boom and bust cycle; a volatile economic cycle increases uncertainty which in turn dampens investment and harms the productive potential of the economy; negative growth is said to be particularly harmful, often forcing otherwise viable enterprises to go to the wall; and

- inflation should be as low as possible; high inflation (which also tends to be erratic) distorts the price mechanism and harms efficiency; it also raises interest rates thereby hitting cash flow.

Of course no economy experiences stable non-inflationary growth for any period of time – external shocks come along, and consumer and business confidence can be very fickle. Meanwhile faulty and out-of-date statistics, uncertainty about how the economy works, and delays in changing economic policy can all limit the ability of governments to minimize the cycle. All this said, however, some governments would appear to be much better than others in conducting macroeconomic policy.

In Table 6.7 we assess governments against three criteria:

1. *Fiscal deficits* – all European Union members currently (1996) exceed the Maastricht criteria (a fiscal deficit of less than 3 per cent of GDP and a net government debt to GDP ratio of under 60 per cent); while fiscal retrenchment will have to take place, the greater this is the more problems it poses for other elements of the

Table 6.7 Macroeconomic stability

Country	Fiscal	Monetary	Stability	Total	Rank
USA	3.0 (2)	6.34 (2)	0.72 (6)	10	3
Japan	0.3 (1)	3.15 (1)	0.89 (3)	5	1
Germany	3.5 (3)	6.49 (3)	0.92 (2)	8	2
France	5.9 (7)	6.70 (5)	0.85 (5)	17	5
Italy	9.2 (10)	10.45 (10)	0.94 (1)	21	8
UK	7.4 (9)	8 10 (8)	0.89 (4)	21	7
Belgium	5.6 (6)	7.30 (6)	0.63 (9)	21	9
Denmark	4.2 (5)	7.67 (7)	0.65 (8)	19	6
Netherlands	3.9 (4)	6.51 (4)	0.55 (10)	16	4
Spain	7.1 (8)	10.01 (9)		27	10

Notes: Fiscal deficit – general government balance as a proportion of GDP, IMF estimates for 1994; *source – World Economic Outlook*. Monetary credibility – yield on 10-year benchmark government bonds; *source – Financial Times* 15 March 1996. Growth stability – R2 from linear growth trend equations estimated over 1972–91; *source –* 'Long Term Economic Growth and Growth Stability – An Enquiry', M. Foster, MBA dissertation, 1993 (note that the UK is ranked below Japan because of more years of negative growth). With respect to the overall ranking, the UK has been placed above Belgium on account of its lower debt to GDP ratio.

adjustment process – hence countries are ranked in descending order of the size of their fiscal deficits.
2. *Monetary credibility* – this is measured by the size of interest rates on 10-year government bonds; on the assumption that in a global capital market real rates of interest are equalized among countries, high medium to long-term interest rates reflect either risk premia or high expected inflation rates – the greater these are the more costly is medium-term corporate finance.
3. *Stability of growth* – a direct measure of the volatility of the cycle.

References

Calmfors, L. and Driffill, J. (1988) 'Bargaining Structure, Corporatism and Macroeconomic Performance', *Economic Policy*, vol. 6.

Foster, M. (1993) 'Long Term Economic Growth and Growth Stability – An Enquiry', MBA dissertation, Manchester Business School.

International Monetary Fund (1993) *IMF Direction of Trade Yearbook* (New York: IMF).

International Monetary Fund (1993) *World Economic Outlook* (New York: IMF).

Organization for Economic Cooperation and Development (1993) *Industrial Policy in OECD Countries* (Paris: OECD).

Organization for Economic Cooperation and Development (1993) *OECD Economic Outlook* (Paris: OECD).

The Financial Times, 15 March 1996.

7 Restructuring Strategies: Global Pressures, Local Responses

Ian Taplin and Jonathan Winterton

Globalization, coupled with deregulation, with the ending of the Multi-Fibre Arrangement (MFA) has presented clothing manufacturers in the high-wage countries with intensified competition from enterprises in the low-wage economies. The globalization of economic activity (Taylor and Thrift, 1986) revealed the vulnerability of labour-intensive mass production industries to imports from low-wage economies, since Taylorist production is easily replicated in newly-industrialized countries (Dicken, 1992). Clothing manufacture in the high-wage economies, often viewed as a 'sunset industry', is undergoing rapid restructuring through factory closures and company downsizing, while enterprises in the newly-industrialized low-wage countries are attracted to garment manufacture by the relatively low barriers to entry. While the outcome is an intensification of the new international division of labour, the local responses to the changes in the global clothing marketplace involve a range of restructuring processes within the clothing industries in high-wage economies.

This chapter outlines an heuristic model of restructuring, drawing upon existing meta-theories, and uses the model as a framework of analysis of contemporary change in the clothing industries of high-wage economies. The empirical evidence draws upon research completed over the past five years into the restructuring of clothing industries in the USA (Taplin and Winterton, 1995), the UK (Barlow and Winterton, 1995; Taplin and Winterton, 1996), and in a comparative study of the UK, USA, Finland, Italy, Germany and Japan (Taplin and Winterton, 1997).

AN HEURISTIC MODEL OF RESTRUCTURING

The model developed here represents an attempt to elaborate and to systematize the dimensions of restructuring within a framework which will serve as an heuristic device for analysing contemporary change in the clothing industries. Restructuring can be seen as an inherent part of capitalist development and the process of capital accumulation, which permits the continual expansion of profit accumulation (Bradbury, 1985) through the conscious and planned response of firms (Hilowitz, 1987) to regenerate the prevailing regime of accumulation, by modernizing and raising efficiency and to develop new capacity in growth sectors (Tailby and Whitson, 1989). While noting that restructuring is a continuous process, it is also important to acknowledge the episodic nature of rapid phases of restructuring, and in particular the acceleration of restructuring during the 1980s following the oil shocks of 1973 and 1979, and the associated crises of the 1970s (Thrift, 1988).

The crises, manifest in economic terms as a crisis of profitability (Lipietz, 1982), in production terms as a crisis of Fordism (Piore and Sabel, 1984), and in institutional terms as a crisis of corporatism (Monks and Minow, 1995), form the starting point of meta-theories seeking to explain the reasons for, and consequences of, the fragmentation of markets, paradigm shifts in production relations and quantum leaps in technological infrastructure.

Restructuring can be viewed as a multi-dimensional, multi-layered set of processes, entailing three distinct stages: sources, responses and outcomes. The relationship between the stages and the different dimensions are shown graphically in Figure 7.1. The sources may act as imperatives, factors which enterprises ignore at their peril, or as options, factors which are discretionary. Imperatives and options include: political factors, such as restrictions on trade or their removal; economic factors, including changes in product and labour markets; social factors, including consumer tastes and demographic trends; and technological factors, like microprocessor based innovations. The imperatives may operate as impulses promoting restructuring, as when product markets are liberalized, or as constraints which restrain restructuring, for example through subsidies for an indigenous industry or trade tariffs on imports.

Options may represent opportunities for change, favourable situations of which the parties may take advantage, and facilitators, the adoption of which makes some aspect of restructuring easier. The widespread adoption of a facilitator such as a new production technique by major competitors may operate as an impulse upon enterprises which have not yet adopted the development. The sources attributable to state policies may form part of a coherent strategy, as

101

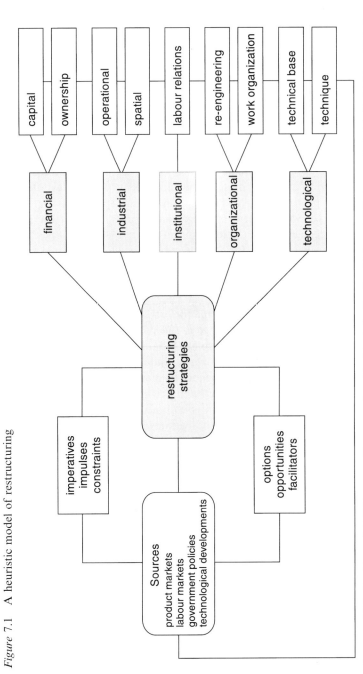

Figure 7.1   A heuristic model of restructuring

Source: I.M. Taplin and J. Winterton 'Restructuring Clothing', in Taplin, I.M. and Winterton, J. (eds) *Rethinking Global Production: A Comparative Analysis of Restructuring in the Clothing Industry* (Aldershot: Avebury, 1997).

with initiatives to weaken trade unions allied with other moves to liberalize labour markets, or they may entail contradictory policies such as deregulation to promote entrepreneurial activity and intervention to maintain employment standards.

Changes in product markets are seen as major sources of restructuring in several influential meta-theories. The saturation of mass markets due to overproduction, and the fragmentation of markets for standardized products are central to the flexible specialization thesis (for example Sabel, 1982; Piore and Sabel, 1984). It is argued that the development of new segmented markets has demanded 'flexible forms of organization which permitted rapid shifts in output' (Sabel, 1989, p. 18). Firms producing high-quality, low-volume products for niche markets have evolved new organizational forms, centred on much smaller specialized production units than their mass production forerunners. However, the saturation of mass markets is assumed rather than demonstrated, and the stable replacement demand of consumer goods, which sustains much mass production, is ignored (Williams *et al.*, 1987, p. 426).

The development of flexible microelectronics-based innovations is seen as the driving force of change in several meta-theories (Womack, Jones and Roos, 1990, for example). Although as a production paradigm, flexible specialization is formally independent of any particular technology, increased responsiveness to market changes through the adoption of microelectronics is seen to facilitate its development. Moreover, flexible specialization is assumed to lead to enskilling or reskilling, because 'the computer restores human control over the production process, machinery is again subordinated to the operator' (Piore and Sabel, 1984, p. 261), and the new forms of work organization could mark 'the end of the division of labour' (Kern and Schuman, 1987, p. 163).

The responses to these sources are a set of managerial actions, the objectives of which are to effect restructuring in at least one of the five dimensions distinguished: financial; industrial; institutional; technological; and organizational. These managerial 'strategies' are not necessarily coherent consistent policies put into practice in full knowledge that they will have the desired objectives of achieving critical success factors. Restructuring strategies are invariably modified in the light of changes in the external environment and are mediated through the operation of vested management interests, and through the institutions of worker resistance. The resultant emergent strategies may be no more than a series of proactive and reactive actions, and *ad hoc* responses to immediate crises. Actions include decisions on new capital issues, mergers and acquisitions, product diversification, plant closures and relocation, investments in new technologies and strategies to raise productivity or quality. The responses play a pivotal role in the restructuring process, since they demonstrate that the agency of individuals is necessary for sources to be translated into restructuring strategies. It is to be expected that the specific restructuring strategies adopted will vary between countries, sectors and enterprises, according to specific local imperatives, options and traditions.

Restructuring outcomes are visible when the actions implemented in pursuit of the emergent restructuring strategies take effect. The analytical distinction between the five dimensions of restructuring strategies can be maintained and elaborated further in the case of restructuring outcomes.

Since the early 1980s there has been extensive financial restructuring of enterprises in response to the globalization and fragmentation of product markets, and as a result of government initiatives such as privatization and measures to promote employee share ownership. The UK privatization programme has been one of the major examples of capital restructuring (Beesley, 1992) which is being emulated extensively elsewhere, while across the European Union the development of the single market has stimulated a pan-European merger boom. Capital restructuring is reflected in changes in ownership, company acquisitions and disposals, and investment decisions which in turn affect industrial and technological restructuring. While ownership appears to have become more concentrated at the retail end, in garment production there has been extensive new capital formation involving small and medium-sized enterrises (SMEs).

Industrial restructuring refers to both inter- and intra-industrial changes in the distribution of capital, labour, enterprises and establishments. The decline of manufacturing and heavy basic industries, coupled with the expansion of the service sector, is common to all developed economies. Within particular industries or enterprises, industrial restructuring is manifest as a restructuring of operations, through such processes as rationalization and redundancy. Operational restructuring has spatial consequences because plant closures, relocation and new establishments are uneven in their distribution across regions.

Institutional restructuring includes a variety of attempts either to reconstruct or to deconstruct industrial relations. Reconstruction may seek to build new high-trust relationships and collaborative arrangements underpinned by employee-centred enskilling and empowerment, or may seek to individualize pay structures and relate reward more closely to performance. Deconstruction extends from limiting collective bargaining to discontinuing existing agreements and withdrawing recognition from the representative institutions. In the recently-privatized enterprises in the UK, for example, corporatist relations and highly-regulated pluralist structures have been replaced with more commercially-oriented, unitarist approaches to the management of human resources (Pendleton and Winterton, 1993).

At the organizational level, restructuring includes comprehensive business process re-engineering, where an organization is restructured around business units, and de-layering, where an organization is redesigned into a 'flatter' structure to promote efficiency. In terms of work organization, cross-functional teams may be established, or initiatives such as total quality management (TQM) or team working introduced. The restructuring of work organization results in changes in the labour process, reflected in the skill required and autonomy afforded to individuals, and the division of labour between different categories of workers. For some years the trade press has publicized teamworking and related initiatives to enhance productivity and quality, which may have been adopted by the more dynamic enterprises.

Technological restructuring may involve changes in the material technical base (hardware or instruments of labour) or the technique of production, or both. Technological changes in turn influence and constrain (and are influenced and constrained by) changes in work organization, as reflected in the division of labour between people and machines, skill and job autonomy. The development of the microprocessor in the mid-1970s led to a widespread adoption of microprocessor-based innovations which have transformed automation, monitoring and control of production.

The analytical distinction which has been made between the different restructuring outcomes is rarely clear in practice, as different outcomes may represent diverse strategies in response to several causes or to a common cause, or they may be different facets of a single strategy. Industrial and technological restructuring are often complementary outcomes of a capital restructuring programme. The privatization of public enterprises in the UK, similarly, prompted significant operational restructuring and a transformation of labour relations. Some restructuring outcomes are designed to support parallel restructuring objectives; restructuring labour relations, for example, may be a prelude to operational or organizational change, which might otherwise have been resisted by the unions.

Restructuring outcomes may also have a feedback effect, acting as sources of further restructuring in the same industry or in a sector with which it interfaces. Operational, spatial and institutional restructuring impacts upon the labour market and may be intended, for example, to contribute to labour market flexibility, a goal shared by the governments of most high-wage economies despite the very different approaches to achieving flexibility. Inevitably, restructuring is uneven in its impact upon different economies, industries, enterprises, establishments and classes of workers.

In the remainder of this chapter, the heuristic model developed above is employed as a framework of analysis to explore restructuring in the clothing industries of high-wage economies, dealing in turn with the sources of restructuring and the restructuring strategies adopted by enterprises. It is clear that clothing in all the countries considered is undergoing profound and rapid restructuring, and that there are elements of commonality and diversity between the countries. By way of conclusion, therefore, explanations are offered for the patterns of restructuring, and their relevance to global change in clothing is assessed.

SOURCES OF RESTRUCTURING

The model summarized in Figure 7.1 identifies four sources of change (product and labour markets, government policies and technological developments) which can operate as imperatives (impulses or constraints) or as options (opportunities or facilitators).

In the clothing industries of the high-wage economies studied, two primary global sources might be expected to have acted as imperatives to restructuring: product market changes and political initiatives. Fashion changes in product markets over the past two decades have involved an expansion of casual and fashion wear in place of formal clothing, a revival of formal clothing associated with design, quality and exclusivity, and the introduction of more seasonal changes. This market segmentation and fragmentation has reduced the size of production runs as well as the time available for manufacturers to respond to product demand. While these market changes have created a crisis for mass production in clothing, as in other manufacturing industries, it is important to recognize the limitations of mass production techniques in the clothing industry (Rainnie, 1991, p. 47). The smaller units and bespoke tailoring have always involved unit or very small-scale production, while the bulk of clothing manufacture, employing specialized sewing machines on a production line, provides a classic example of Taylorist work, but not of Fordist mass production since it was organized as batch production.

Emprirical investigation confirms that product market fragmentation has been a major impulse to restructure the clothing industries in all six countries studied. The high quality, designer label end of the market demonstrates the extent to which the clothing market is becoming increasingly global, while market segmentation is apparent both in niche markets and in more frequent seasonal changes. Horizontal market segmentation is a major driver of industrial restructuring, and has been associated with the vertical segmentation of production whereby small establishments sub-contract a limited range of operations in the overall production cycle. Vertical segmentation of production in the USA and the UK, for example, has been characterized by major manufacturers or retailers retaining control over design and quality, with garment assembly being sub-contracted to smaller 'cut, make and trim' (CMT) establishments (Taplin and Winterton, 1995).

Political initiatives at the supra-national level have in the past been important in constraining the rate of restructuring of clothing industries in high-wage economies through the regulation of imports under the Multi-Fibre Arrangement (MFA) (Jones, 1984; Silberston, 1993). The MFA was designed to allow the textile and garment industries of developed countries 'time to restructure in order to better withstand the consequences of a trading system free of quotas' (NEDO, 1990, p. 4). The MFA, first agreed in 1974, was renewed and extended several times, but under the 1994 GATT agreement, the textiles and clothing import controls are to be phased out completely by just after the end of the millennium (Jones, 1994; Khanna, 1994).

The removal of the MFA following the globalization of clothing markets (OECD, 1994) constitutes a liberalization of clothing product markets which was expected to act as an impulse to accelerate the restructuring of garment manufacture in high wage economies (Jones, 1996), and phasing out the MFA was cited as a major impulse to restructuring of clothing in all the countries studied. Other forms of deregulation were also expected to operate as facilitators of restructuring, promoting an increase in small-scale clothing enterprises which can compete with imports by replicating the employment conditions of low-wage economies. In some countries, further deregulation has exacerbated the effect of relaxing the MFA; liberalization under Item 807 in the US (Taplin, 1997) and the reduced role of Ministry of Industry and Trade (MITI) as a regulatory agency in Japan (Garanto, 1997), for example.

Increased import penetration, representing the third major impulse to restructuring, is seen as a consequence of market fragmentation and deregulation. Clothing imports from low-wage economies have intensified cost competition on a global scale and added to the pressure for shorter lead times arising from market segmentation. Despite the low wages of clothing workers relative to workers in other manufacturing industries in high-wage economies, differential labour costs are the major impetus for increased imports from low-wage countries because of the labour intensity of garment manufacture (Scheffer, 1994, p. 112). Outsourcing production to low-wage economies offers one possible route for clothing manufacturers in high-wage economies to retain market share (Anson, 1992).

In the countries with the highest pay rates, Finland, Germany and Japan, import competition has been exacerbated by contracting clothing markets (Kasvio, 1997; Adler and Brietenacher, 1997; Garanto, 1997). In Germany and Japan, falling demand reflects reduced household expenditure on clothing products, while in Finland and Germany traditional markets have been lost with the disintegration of the Soviet Union. Labour market conditions have also acted as an impulse to restructuring in these countries because the relatively low wage rates in clothing present employers with the problem of retaining labour while remaining cost-competitive. The problem has also been manifest in some parts of the UK, owing to local labour shortages (Winterton and Winterton, 1997a), and has acted as a stimulus to spatial relocation in the US (Taplin, 1997).

Other factors have provided new opportunities or facilitated the adoption of new strategies, thereby influencing restructuring strategies. Market fragmentation has presented clothing enterprises with the opportunity to develop focused differentiation and niche marketing strategies, concentrating on high value-added production. Such strategies have been pursued most effectively in Italy (Belussi, 1997), followed by Germany, Japan and, to a lesser extent, the UK and Finland. Trends in the UK, Germany and Japan, however, suggest that importers will adopt similar strategies, moving away from low-cost mass markets into quality branded and designer label goods.

Clothing enterprises have the opportunity of meeting import competition where labour market conditions are conducive to using ethnic
minority workers and homeworkers to reduce unit labour costs, as in
the UK and US. Wage depressing tactics have been facilitated by
permissive deregulatory environments created by policies to foster
entrepreneurial activity in the UK and by anti-union state legislation
in the US. Two of the very high-wage economies, Finland and Japan,
have also introduced a degree of labour market deregulation in an
effort to constrain labour costs, but Italy and Germany maintain
minimum wage regulation.

Even where there is a relatively high degree of labour market regulation, as in France and Germany, a significant section of the garment industry draws upon the secondary labour market, using ethnic
minorities, migrant workers and homeworkers. Much of the growth in
small clothing firms in France, Germany and the UK is in inner city
areas, and disproportionately involves ethnic minority workers and
entrepreneurs (Hoel, 1982; Mitter, 1986; Phizacklea, 1987; 1990; Ram,
1994; 1996).

It was assumed that new technological developments might have
acted as facilitators of contemporary change in the clothing industries
of high-wage economies. Technological innovations such as computer-
aided design (CAD), computer-controlled cutting (CCC) and computerized production monitoring systems have become more widely
available over the past two decades, enabling innovations at the design
and cutting stages, in the transport of garments between machines, and
in the overall monitoring and control of production operations as well
as through *ad hoc* modifications to existing machinery (Rush and
Soete, 1984). Less technological innovation has been designed in
make-up or garment assembly because of the technical difficulties of
fabric handling and because relatively low labour rates act as a dis-
incentive to technological substitution.

While technological innovations are available globally, clothing industries are characterized by a slow rate of adoption of new technology. Leading enterprises have introduced new production technologies
in all the countries studied, and this is being actively promoted in Japan by MITI. Innovation is normally concentrated in the larger enterprises (Hoffman and Rush, 1985), but piecemeal technological
changes have had a significant impact upon work organization (Barlow and Winterton, 1996). Moreover, the low-tech clothing companies
are no less profitable than those which have invested in new equipment
(Groves and Hamblin, 1989; Winterton and Barlow, 1996).

RESTRUCTURING STRATEGIES

The imperatives and options identified as sources of change have led clothing enterprises to respond with a range of restructuring strategies, as well as marketing strategies devised to cope with product market fragmentation.

There has been relatively little financial restructuring of clothing industries in recent years, and unlike the vertical integration of the previous decade the supply chain became disintegrated during the 1980s. The upstream and downstream linkages with clothing manufacture, textiles and retail, however, continued to become more concentrated. Clothing enterprises now have to contend with more powerful monopoly suppliers and monopsony buyers, increasing the pressure for greater efficiencies to maintain shrinking profit margins. There has been some horizontal concentration in Italy, through mergers and acquisitions, and this is associated with some increase in capital intensity. In the UK and Finland, however, ownership has become more fragmented as a result of substantial SME growth, and these enterprises are generally under-capitalized. In Japan, ownership restructuring has been less important than patent agreements which are at the heart of the differentiation strategy.

There has been profound industrial restructuring in all six countries, involving both operational and spatial changes. Operational restructuring has entailed a substantial contraction of clothing employment in the UK, Finland, Italy and Germany, where large firms have declined in number and the remainder have downsized operations. Large firm contraction has been accompanied by SME growth in the UK, Finland and Italy. In Japan, however, where SME networks have always been important, clothing industry output and employment has remained relatively stable.

In all countries clothing manufacture has become more vertically segmented, and subcontracting has become more prevalent, involving SMEs (UK, Finland and Italy), ethnic minority workers (UK, US and Germany) and homeworkers (UK and Finland). Increased subcontracting is designed to improve cost competitiveness, defending market share against imports when expenditure on clothing is in many cases declining. Secondly, sub-contracting facilitates faster delivery in response to the shorter lead times demanded by market fragmentation and import penetration. Thirdly, outsourcing assists a marketing strategy of focused differentiation by devolving responsibility for quality to the sub-contractors.

The spatial dimension to the restructuring of clothing industries common to all six countries is the increased adoption of outward processing trade (OPT), sub-contracting production to enterprises in low-wage economies in order to compete with imports on cost and delivery time, while retaining value added in the home country. Blyth (1996) has shown that off-shore outsourcing decisions require a consideration of infrastructure, service and delivery as well as material and labour costs, including overhead and social costs. Exchange rate fluctuations also need to be taken into account. Even taking all these costs into account, the magnitude of the labour cost gap (in $ per standard minute) between the high-wage and low-wage economies is so great that clothing manufacturing costs in the UK (towards the bottom of the high-wage range) are about 40 per cent higher than the comparable costs in Turkey (towards the top of the low-wage economies), and 200 per cent higher than China (towards the bottom of the low-wage economies).

In the UK, OPT mainly involves sourcing from the Far East, especially Hong Kong and, increasingly, China. In the US, offshore production mainly involves Mexico and the Far East. The former Soviet Union (FSU) has become increasingly important in OPT for the UK (Romania), Germany (Hungary) and Finland (the Baltic states). Japan's OPT strategy, which developed relatively late, has predominantly involved China for garment production, rather than Taiwan, Vietnam and Korea which represent the major sources of imports. Significantly, whereas design operations are normally retained in the high-wage country, Japanese enterprises are also relocating design to Europe because of the global dominance of European designers.

Some indigenous clothing industries have also experienced internal spatial restructuring. In the UK, the growth of SMEs has been predominantly in inner city areas having a relatively high proportion of ethnic minority workers (London, Leicester, Bradford). Similarly, relocation strategies in the US have been away from the unionized, high-wage north-east towards the non-union, low-wage southern states and the west coast. In Italy, and to a lesser extent Japan, relocation has centred on the creation of industrial districts and SME networks.

Institutional restructuring has been relatively unimportant in most of the high-wage countries studied because labour relations in clothing industries is traditionally harmonious. Where clothing workers are unionized at all, their bargaining power is low and there is no tradition of militancy. Nevertheless, wage-depressing tactics have been adopted in some areas to compete on cost with imports from low-wage countries, and the failure to establish effective trade unionism in the North Carolina garment industry, for example, has maintained employer domination and kept wages low (Taplin, 1994, p. 329). Similarly, the growth of SMEs coupled with deregulation in the UK and Finland has been conducive to wage depression and work intensification which may have been resisted more effectively in the larger, organized clothing plants.

Organizational restructuring has involved both process re-engineering and changes in work organization. The external response to shorter lead times led to the vertical segmentation of production (operational restructuring), while in all six countries, an equivalent internal response has involved process re-engineering based on just in time (JIT) and quality review (QR) techniques, at least in leading edge companies. In Japan, where *kaizen* (continuous improvement) permeates all manufacturing industry, further forms of business process re-engineering have been used to support innovation strategies, and to a degree this is also true of Germany although there the improvements have been limited by outmoded organization.

The adoption of JIT and QR in order to meet shorter lead times, coupled with focused differentiation based on design and product quality, has been associated in all cases with restructuring of work organization. Teamworking and multiskilling have been introduced in the UK and US, but there is little evidence of a departure from Taylorist principles of job design and the emphasis is on work intensification, although the new forms of work organization are generally preferred by work teams (Winterton and Winterton, 1997b). There has been a similar transformation of work methods in a significant number of enterprises in Italy and Germany, where the emphasis is on building competence through vocational training, an approach which is widely perceived as evidence of an emergent flexible specialization strategy. In Finland and Japan, there is more ambiguity concerning this restructuring of work organization, which may conform in specific factories with either the Anglo-American or European approaches. Where the emphasis is on productivity, the process is mostly one of work intensification, whereas an emphasis on flexibility through employee development can be construed as a potential flexible specialization strategy.

New technologies and techniques of production have been globally available for many years but, as noted earlier, clothing manufacturers have been slow to innovate. Technological restructuring has, nevertheless, occurred in all countries in modern companies with access to adequate capital. New technologies have primarily been introduced at the design and cutting stages (CAD and CCC), which has been associated with materials savings and some deskilling. In all countries there are examples of new production techniques, such as modular manufacturing, which are often associated with JIT and QR initiatives as well as with teamworking. Paradoxically, in Italy and Germany where flexible specialization is most widely discussed as a survival strategy, the clothing industry is viewed as having a low innovation potential and investment is inadequate. The most extensive adoption of new technology is in Japan, where a major automation programme supported by MITI is transforming production methods in line with the innovation strategy.

PATTERNS OF RESTRUCTURING

It remains to offer explanations for the similarities and differences identified in the restructuring strategies adopted by clothing enterprises in the six countries. From the similarities of the experiences analysed it is possible to develop the general heuristic model into a specific model of restructuring of the clothing industries in high-wage economies. The refined model demonstrates the relationships between sources and strategies, and illustrates how different restructuring strategies are inter-related. In the new model shown in Figure 7.2, the sources of restructuring are represented as a range of external environmental influences acting upon clothing enterprises. The restructuring strategies are identified as responses to key imperatives deriving from specific challenges of the external environment, and the outcomes are shown.

The revised model reveals two apparently contradictory trajectories, represented by the tendencies towards enskilling on the one hand and deskilling on the other. While one or other approach predominates in some countries, for the most part both exist in parallel partly because different enterprises pursue different strategies, and partly because some strategies contain internal contradictions. Significant details and differences must be explored in comparing the experiences of the countries before attempting explanations.

The fragmentation of clothing markets and their deregulation with the ending of the MFA, are global phenomena which have led to increased import penetration from low-wage countries to each of the high-wage countries studied. Increased imports have universally

Figure 7.2   A model of restructuring of the clothing industries of high-wage economies

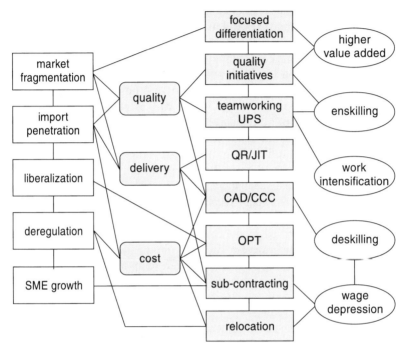

Source: I.M. Taplin and J. Winterton 'Making Sense of Strategies for Survival: Clothing in High Wage Economies', in Taplin, I.M. and Winterton, J. (eds), *Rethinking Global Production: A Comparative Analysis of Restructuring in the Clothing Industry* (Aldershot: Avebury, 1997).

intensified competition on costs and delivery times. In response to market fragmentation, clothing enterprises have developed strategies of focused differentiation and niche marketing, especially in Italy, Germany and Japan and, to a lesser extent, in the UK and Finland. In Italy the strategy is associated with design, and in Germany and Japan with quality and status. A similar strategy has been adopted in the UK by producers of labels like Burberry, and in Finland by Luhkta, and is being copied by low-cost producers of imports to the UK, Germany and Japan.

In the three highest wage countries, Finland, Germany and Japan, the situation is exacerbated by market contraction. External market

Restructuring Strategies

contraction in Finland and Germany has been the result of their sensitivity to the collapse of markets in the FSU, while internal market contraction in Germany and Japan is explained by changing patterns of consumer expenditure. Relatively high labour rates in all three countries present enterprises with special difficulties in retaining labour and remaining cost-competitive. In Finland and Japan labour market deregulation has been designed to ease the problems, while in the UK and US the purpose has been to stimulate entrepreneurial activity. The German clothing industry, with a greater product market contraction and a more regulated labour market, has been forced to divest capacity more rapidly.

Market fragmentation introduced two imperatives: a focus on quality, and shorter lead times. Import penetration, stimulated by the removal of the MFA, also increased the importance of cost and reinforced the delivery imperative. The intensification of competition is therefore reflected in three imperatives: quality, delivery and cost, and the strategies identified in the countries considered contribute to the pursuit of these imperatives. The remaining task is to consider why different strategic responses have been emphasised in particular countries.

The pursuit of quality under a focused differentiation marketing strategy might be assumed to lead automatically to total quality initiatives. In fact, the TQM influence is only apparent in those UK and Japanese enterprises which have pursued niche marketing, along with some US firms which have not. This suggests that the TQM approach reflects culture and tradition more than specific market imperatives.

The delivery imperative caused by shorter lead times is more clearly associated with both internal and external restructuring strategies. Internally, enterprises have adopted QR and JIT techniques in all six countries, while externally production has become vertically segmented leading to increased sub-contracting. The internal strategies have been most prevalent in the UK, US and Japanese enterprises, and sub-contracting has also increased. In Finland, Italy and Germany, sub-contracting has been more important, but internal strategies have also been adopted. These experiences suggest that internal and external restructuring strategies are complementary rather than alternatives.

Differences in emphasis between sub-contracting to indigenous SMEs and outsourcing in the form of outward processing trade (OPT) are apparent in this context of increased sub-contracting. In the UK, Finland, Italy and Japan, the SME sector has been most important because the environments are conducive to SME development. Government policies have encouraged SME growth in the UK and Finland, while in Italy and Japan SMEs are thriving in the industrial districts fostered by policy initiatives. Foreign sub-contracting, or OPT, is common to all the countries considered except for Italy, and the form of OPT is affected by location and tradition. In the UK and US, OPT involves mainly enterprises in countries which are traditional sources of imported garments, while Finland and Germany are outsourcing to the FSU because of their tradition of serving FSU markets and their geographic proximity. Japan's OPT is also influenced by location, although as a longer-term strategy, Japanese enterprises are substituting China for the traditional far-eastern production sources of imports.

New forms of work organization are clearly associated with the adoption of QR and JIT techniques in all countries, and especially in the more advanced enterprises. The impact of teamworking, modular systems and UPS varies significantly between countries, with productivity and work intensification emphasised in the UK and US, compared with competence building and enskilling in Italy and Germany. The difference reflects the dominance of Taylorism in the Anglo-American approach, in contrast with the new European production norm based on a high wage, high value-added approach. There are different ambiguities in the cases of Finland and Japan. In Finland there is a tension between the economic crisis, prompting efforts to intensify work, and the traditions of Scandinavian progressive work organization. In Japan the dominant mode of production is not purely Taylorist, but seeks to harness workers' tacit skills and knowledge to intensify work.

Where new technology has been adopted in response to quality, delivery and cost imperatives, it is associated with the larger enterprises in the UK, US and Finland which have better access to capital. The adoption of new technologies is more limited in SMEs, which in part accounts for the low innovation potential of Italian clothing enterprises. In the case of Germany, however, the limited adoption of new technology reflects the industry's crisis and rapid contraction. The more extensive technological innovation in Japanese clothing enterprises, including SMEs, is a direct consequence of the role of MITI and the longer-term perspective of the Japanese finance industry.

New technologies such as CAD and CCC are openly acknowledged as deskilling work by clothing industry management, and while this may be a less important motive than quality and containment of material costs, the effect is to depress wages. Sub-contracting and relocation also have wage depressing effects and the specific focus which these take depends upon the country environment and prevailing labour market conditions. Thus in the deregulated environment of the UK, sub-contracting to SMEs reduces labour costs more than in the relatively regulated Italian environment. Wage depression based on ethnic minority exploitation is a feature of clothing in the UK, US and Germany because ethnic minority workers are concentrated in local labour markets in these countries. Similarly, relocation has a major impact on labour costs in the US because labour markets are subject to local state, rather than federal, regulation (or deregulation).

The differences between the patterns of restructuring of clothing in the high-wage economies are, therefore, more of degree and emphasis than of fundamental principle. Clothing enterprises in all of the high-wage economies face common challenges and the need to address the same imperatives. The restructuring strategies have much in common and the diverse combinations reflect variations in the opportunities, constraints and traditions of the different country contexts. While some enterprises in some countries provide some evidence of the emergence of a new production paradigm, for the most part the restructuring of clothing in high-wage economies represents merely a reconfiguration of Taylorist production.

References

Adler, U. and Brietenacher, M. (1997) 'Production, Technological Change, Organization and Vocational Standards: The German Clothing Industry and International Competition', in I.M.Taplin and J.Winterton (eds), *Rethinking Global Production* (Aldershot: Avebury).

Anson, R. (1992) 'Demise of the MFA', *Manufacturing Clothier*, vol. 73, March, pp. 16–19.

Barlow, A. and Winterton, J. (1995) 'Restructuring Strategies: An Analysis of Changes Implemented by UK Clothing Companies', *Journal of Clothing Technology and Management*, vol. 12, no. 3, pp. 19–34.

Barlow, A. and Winterton, J. (1996) 'Work Organization and the Restructuring of Clothing Production', in I.M. Taplin and J. Winterton (eds), *Restructuring within a Labour Intensive Industry* (Aldershot: Avebury), pp. 176–98.

Beesley, M. (1992) *Privatization, Regulation and Competition* (London: Routledge).

Belussi, F. (1997) 'Dwarfs and Giants Maintaining Competitive Edge: The Italian Textile Clothing Industry in the 1990s', in I.M. Taplin and J. Winterton (eds), *Rethinking Global Production* (Aldershot: Avebury).

Blyth, R. (1996) 'Sourcing: The Implementation of Global Strategy through Informed Choice', in I.M. Taplin and J. Winterton (eds), *Restructuring within a Labour Intensive Industry* (Aldershot: Avebury), pp. 112–41.

Bradbury, J.M. (1985) 'Regional and Industrial Restructuring Processes in the New International Division of Labour', *Progress in Human Geography*, vol. 19, pp. 38–63.

Dicken, P. (1992) *Global Shift: The Internationalization of Economic Activity*, 2nd edn (London: Paul Chapman Publishing).

Garanto, A. (1997) 'In Search of Competitive Advantage: Contemporary Change in the Japanese Apparel Industry', in I.M. Taplin and J. Winterton (eds), *Rethinking Global Production* (Aldershot: Avebury).

Groves, G. and Hamblin, D. (1989) 'The Effectiveness of AMT Investment in UK Clothing Manufacture', Cranfield Institute of Technology (mimeo).

Hilowitz, J. (1987) *Education and Training Policies and Programmes to Support Industrial Restructuring in the Republics of Korea, Japan, Singapore and the United States*, Training Policies Discussion Paper no. 18 (Geneva: International Labour Office).

Hoel, B. (1982) 'Contemporary Clothing 'sweatshops': Asian Female Labour and Collective Organization', in J. West (ed.), *Work, Women and the Labour Market* (London: Routledge and Kegan Paul).

Hoffman, K. and Rush, M. (1985) 'From Needles and Pins to Microelectronics: The Impact of Technological Change in the Garment Industry', in S. Jacobson and J. Sigmundson (eds), *Technological Trends and Challenges in Electronics* (Sweden: University of Lund).

Jones, R.M. (1984) 'The Multi-Fibre Arrangement', *Hollings Apparel Industry Review*, vol. 1, no. 2, pp. 21–65.

Jones, R.M. (1994) 'The GATT Agreement 1994', *Journal of Clothing Technology and Management*, Spring, pp. 46–69.

Jones, R.M. (1996) 'Changes in Regional Employment in the UK Clothing Industry, 1971–1991', in I.M. Taplin and J. Winterton (eds), *Restructuring within a Labour Intensive Industry* (Aldershot: Avebury), pp. 61–111.

Kasvio, A. (1997) 'A Difficult Path to Recovery: New Strategies for the Finnish Clothing Industry', in I.M. Taplin and J. Winterton (eds), *Rethinking Global Production* (Aldershot: Avebury).

Kern, H. and Schumann, M. (1987) 'Limits of the Division of Labour: New Production Concepts in West German Industry', *Economic and Industrial Democracy* vol. 8, no. 2, pp. 151–70.

Khanna, S.R. (1994) 'The New GATT Agreement', *Textile Outlook International*, no. 52, March, pp. 10–37.

Lipietz, A. (1982) 'Towards Global Fordism?', *New Left Review*, no. 132, pp. 33–47.

Mitter, S. (1986) 'Industrial Restructuring and Manufacturing Homework: Immigrant Women in the UK Clothing Industry', *Capital and Class*, no. 27, pp. 37–80.

Monks, R.A.G. and Minow, N. (1995) *Corporate Governance* (Oxford: Blackwell).

National Economic Development Office (1990) *The State of the Clothing Industry* (London: NEDC).

Organization for Economic Cooperation and Development (1986) *Globalisation of Industrial Activities: A Case Study of the Clothing Industry* (Paris: OECD).

Pendleton, A. and Winterton, J. (eds) (1993) *Public Enterprise in Transition: Industrial Relations in State and Privatized Corporations* (London: Routledge).

Phizacklea, A. (1987) 'Minority Women and Economic Restructuring: The Case of Britain and the Federal Republic of Germany', *Work, Employment and Society*, vol. 1, no. 3, pp. 309–25.

Phizacklea, A. (1990) *Unpacking the Fashion Industry: Gender, Racism and Class in Production* (London: Routledge).

Piore, M., and Sabel, C. (1984) *The Second Industrial Divide* (New York: Basic Books).

Rainnie, A. (1991) 'Flexible Specialisation: New Times or Old Hat?', in P. Blyton and J. Morris (eds), *A Flexible Future? Prospects for Employment and Organization* (Berlin: Walter de Gruyter), pp. 43–61

Ram, M. (1994) *Managing to Survive: Working Lives in Small Firms* (Oxford: Blackwell).

Ram, M. (1996) 'Unravelling the Hidden Clothing Industry: Managing the Ethnic Minority Garment Sector', in I. Taplin and J. Winterton (eds), *Restructuring within a Labour Intensive Industry* pp. 158–75.

Rush, H. and Soete, L. (1984) 'Clothing', in K. Guy (ed.), *Technological Trends and Employment: Vol. 1 Basic Consumer Goods* (London: Gower), pp. 174–222.

Sabel, C. (1982) *Work and Politics* (Cambridge: Cambridge University Press).

Sabel, C. (1989) 'Flexible Specialisation and the Re-emergence of Regional Economies', in P. Hirst and J. Zeitlin (eds), *Reversing Industrial Decline?* (Oxford: Berg), pp. 17–70.

Scheffer, M.R. (1994) 'Internationalisation of Production by EC Textile and Clothing Manufacturers', *Textile Outlook International*, January, pp. 101–23.

Silberston, Z.A. (1993) *The Future of the Multifibre Arrangement: Implications for the UK Economy* (London: Pinter).

Tailby, S. and Whitson, C. (eds) (1989) *Manufacturing Change: Industrial Relations and Restructuring* (Oxford: Blackwell).

Taplin, I.M. (1994) 'Recent Manufacturing Changes in the US Apparel Industry: The Case of North Carolina', in E. Bonacich and P. Ong (eds), *The Globalization of the Apparel Industry in the Pacific Rim* (Philadelphia: Temple University Press), pp. 328–44.

Taplin, I.M. (1997) 'Backwards into the Future: New Technologies and Old Work Organization in the US Clothing Industry', in I.M. Taplin and J. Winterton (eds), *Rethinking Global Production* (Aldershot: Avebury).

Taplin, I.M. and Winterton, J. (1995) 'New Clothes from Old Techniques: Restructuring and Flexibility in the US and UK Clothing Industries', *Industrial and Corporate Change*, vol. 4, no. 3, pp. 615–38.

Taplin, I.M. and Winterton, J. (eds) (1996) *Restructuring within a Labour Intensive Industry: the UK Clothing Industry in Transition* (Aldershot: Avebury).

Taplin, I.M. and Winterton, R. (1997) *Re-thinking Global Production: A Comparative Analysis of Restructuring in the Clothing Industry* (London: Avebury).

Taylor, M.J. and Thrift, N.J. (eds) (1986) *Multinationals and the Restructuring of the World Economy* (London: Croom Helm).

Thrift, N.J. (1988) 'The Geography of International Economic Disorder', in D. Massey and J. Allen (eds) *Uneven Redevelopment* (London: Hodder and Stroughton), pp. 6–46.

Williams, K., Cutler, T., Williams, J. and Haslam, C. (1987) 'The End of Mass Production?', *Economy and Society*, vol. 16, pp. 405–39.

Winterton, J. and Winterton, R. (1997a) 'De-regulation, Division and Decline: The UK Clothing Industry in Transition', in I.M. Taplin and J. Winterton (eds), *Rethinking Global Production* (Aldershot: Avebury).

Winterton, J. and Winterton, R. (1997b) 'Training Strategies for Restructuring, Transition and Reconstruction: The Role of Adult Education in En-skilling and Empowerment', in M. Amutabi *et al.* (eds), *Globalization: Rethinking Adult Education and Training* (London: Zed Books).

Winterton, R. and Barlow, A. (1996) 'Economic Restructuring', in I.M. Taplin and J. Winterton (eds), *Restructuring within a Labour Intensive Industry*, pp. 25–60.

Womack, J.P., Jones, D.T. and Roos, D. (1990) *The Machine that Changed the World* (New York: Harper).

Part 3

Technological Change and Global Change

8 Setting Standards: Strategies for Building Global Business Systems

Roland Kaye and Stephen Little

There has been much discussion of global integration of business activity which has been facilitated in part by information and communication technologies (ICTs). The process of globalization is complex
and its implications are not fully understood. While its outcomes are
debated from social, political and economic perspectives, the role of
ICTs is treated largely as neutral and facilitative. This chapter argues
that far from being neutral the technologies of ICT embody culture
and hence are carriers of social, economic and political change.

The chapter presents three case studies to illustrate the implications
of technological innovation for cultural aspects of the firm. These case
studies raise the issue of how far technology should be responsive to
the local culture as opposed to being a force for cultural change. The
chapter then explores the role of standards as a way of neutralizing
and enabling adoption of technology through the processes of *de facto*
and *official* standards. Standardization allows the commodification
of technology which arguably overcomes incompatibilities between
sourcing and usage cultures. This technological rationality has been
the basis of office automation and a major feature of globalization.
However, the chapter also argues, based on evidence from North East
Asia, that there is strong evidence of cultural resistance to many of
these technological innovations. These resistances are reflected in some
characteristics of the case studies adding weight to the view that technology is not rational and neutral.

Finally the chapter reflects on the problem of diffusion which is
implied in both globalization of business practice and the diffusion of
technology, a process which implies generation of diversity rather than
consistency. It is this diversity which is beneficial to new innovation
and cultural adoption but at the same time it conflicts with current
models of standard setting and the rationalistic model of technology.

GLOBAL BUSINESS ENVIRONMENTS

Global economic integration is growing rapidly, facilitated in part by information and communication technologies (ICTs). An increasing number of organizations span national and regional cultures which then become intraorganizational differences. Standards, whether for hardware, software or procedures, have long been regarded as the appropriate means of achieving the inter operability demanded by increasing globalization. Standards are intended to achieve economy and inter-operability, however a number of significant players in the world economy are operating in a technical context and to sets of standards, official and de facto, which have been shaped by outside cultural assumptions. Such standards reflect established technical and institutional frameworks which may differ from those of later adopters.

Heenan and Perlmutter (1979) present the characteristics of four different approaches to internationalization: ethnocentrism, polycentrism, regiocentrism and geocentrism. The approaches themselves are presented as representing progressive stages of internationalization. Evans, Taylor and Holzman (1985) present five stages in the development of corporations from strictly domestic to multinational. However, it has been argued that across the components of a large transnational corporation there might be practices associated with several of these stages. Hu (1992) presents six criteria by which to judge the nationality or inter-nationality of transnational corporations, which suggest that truly stateless enterprises are yet to emerge. The geographical spread and scope of corporations still favours the country of origin, although a number of prominent corporations might be termed 'bi-national'. Hu suggests that corporations based in relatively small economies might locate the majority of their resources externally.

However, ownership and control are likely to demonstrate which are the 'home' locations. With few exceptions the majority of employment is in the home country, and foreigners are unlikely to be represented on the main boards. The frameworks for legal nationality and tax domicile likewise are not geared to 'stateless' operations. For example, Nobes and Parker (1985) present a range of taxonomies of variation in accounting practice across the globe, which relate zones of influence both to the initial development of modern accounting in Scotland and England, its subsequent spread though other Anglophone cultures, and the effect of alternative models on the emergence of spheres of influence. Their own attempt at classification presents UK and US influenced alternatives as well as tax-based and law-based approaches. Evans, Taylor and Holzman (1985) report that the first professional discussion of the harmonization of accounting practices took place in 1904, and that these objectives are still being pursued actively (see *Economist*; 1995).

Effective inter-operability in globalized, transcultural systems requires a new understanding of both the standards incorporated into systems and the criteria by which their performance is judged. The concept of 'standards' must be extended beyond the organization's technical infrastructure to user-characteristics and cultural dimensions. However, for this to happen the dynamics involved in the creation of both officially sanctioned standards and emergent defacto standards must be considered. Both have been used as mechanisms for defining, bounding and segmenting the marketplace. Any standard implies an acceptance of some common denominator across a range of circumstances. For officially determined standards, these denominators must be the lowest and most inclusive available. In fast developing fields of technology this may mean abandoning the cutting edge and closing the boundary of the decision space available to users of the technology.

Ohmae (1990) presents an optimistic scenario of a global and borderless economy at variance with the account of bifurcation into core and periphery within organizations and between organizations given by Burris (1993). Both views assume a key role for inter and intra-organizational communication systems supported by information technology. However, both pessimistic and optimistic scenarios may be accused of assuming a relatively unproblematic deployment of such systems, but from both perspectives there remain practical obstacles to borderless interoperability.

Task Environments and Institutional Environments

In western economies established models of technical development have drawn on a technocratic framework, with an essentially positivistic linear view of both technical and social development. More recently identification of institutional constraints on technical action has led to the evaluation of qualitative and participative methods of entry into organizational activity. The successful development and diffusion of complex systems requires at least some reconciliation of the very different dynamics operating at institutional levels and at the levels at which detailed technical design decisions must be made. If technical considerations dominate this process, a technocratic rationality is likely to hold sway; if institutional concerns dominate, then the technical limitations of complex systems are likely to be ignored. These apparently contradictory rationalities are accommodated by organizational actors on a daily basis so that even organizations demonstrating a highly developed formal approach to technical development may contain bodies of myth and anecdote which function to supplement or subvert the content of their formal systems.

Scott (1987) distinguishes between the task environment of organizations and their institutional environment, and points out that the latter is a relatively recent concern of organization theorists and requires very different responses from the better understood task environment. The two principle concerns of task-environment management are the protection of the central work processes, principally through *buffering* strategies, and the management of the relationship with the task environment as a social and political system, dealt with through *bridging* strategies. The task-oriented view sees the environment as a source of inputs, markets for outputs, competition and regulation. Institutional theory is currently gaining interest among organization researchers since it addresses very different concerns from the task-oriented views commonly incorporated into management science. The institutional orientation seeks to build bridges into the environment by conforming to expected categories of staff and structure. Scott argues that organizations exchange elements with their technical environments, but are constituted by elements from their institutional environments. These elements are not transformed by the organization as are technical elements and inputs. Instead they are made visible to outsiders with their distinctive features remaining intact. The purpose is to legitimize the organization and to reassure clients by bridging to the institutional environment. Isomorphism within business and industrial sectors is the result; organizations become more alike over time as they draw upon a common institutional framework.

DiMaggio and Powell (1991) identify three mechanisms which lead to isomorphism: *coercive* isomorphism associated with political influence and legitimacy, *mimetic* isomorphism stemming from standard responses to uncertainty, and *normative* isomorphism associated with professionalisation. Cross-cultural technical initiatives must acknowledge the coexistence of technical and institutional dimensions in organizations. A 'metatechnical' approach implies that managerial and institutional concerns are also technical, and therefore any framework embracing both design and its organizational context is *meta*-technical. It presupposes a systems view of design and its place in the organization, but not a consensual one.

CASE STUDIES

Open systems theory argues that explanatory variables must be as varied as the phenomena they seek to explain. The contingency approach to organization theory argues that organizations whose internal features best match the demands of their technologies or their task environments can be expected to be most effective. However, contingency models can overlook the issue of equifinality: different conditions and causes may give rise to the same outcomes. Nevertheless, little is said about real interests of participants and groups. There may be real benefits for actors in promoting sub-optimizing decisions which otherwise appear to limit efficiency and effectiveness. Clegg (1987) makes an important distinction between the established view of uncertainty as a contingency, and the use of uncertainty in support of the exercise of power, illustrating the point with the ambiguity evident in the interpretation of building contracts by the actors involved in the construction process. It may be argued that the former understanding is apparent in a task orientation, the latter in an institutional orientation. Organizational culture can therefore be seen to be as closely associated with institutional choices as with technical choices and task environments.

   Power relations in organizations may be well-entrenched and difficult to counter, extending to the institutional level of cognition. Douglas (1987) argues that the high triumph of institutional thinking is to make the institutions appear invisible and this invisibility can compound the difficulty of getting an expanded context accepted within any established institutional and organizational framework. The following case studies furnish some insight into the cultural and institutional constraints on technical development in complex organizations. Each examines the relationship between technical development and innovation and concurrent attempts to re-institutionalize an organization in the face of a new political and institutional environment. Awareness of the nature of the simultaneous institutional shifts is a key to the outcomes of these technical initiatives.

Buildco: Technical Innovation in Construction

Little (1987, 1988) describes the extended development cycle of a
sophisticated computer-aided architectural design (CAAD) system
serving a company (Buildco) which was established by the British
government in 1937 to provide housing in support of the relief of
economically depressed regions. Recourse to technical innovation has
been made at several points during Buildco's history. The locus of this
innovation shifted from methods of production towards those of
housing management as the focus of activity moved from the production to the management and disposal of housing stock, in response to
changing concerns of central government.

Around 1960 growing concerns with lack of detailed technical control of design standards displaced the immediate postwar concern with
output. A high degree of integration was possible because the company's building department was handling some 50 percet of the construction workload. Where external consultant designers were used
their contribution was guided by the framework of a standard house
type range, to which they frequently contributed, and by standardization of specification and details. During the 1970s an ambitious
CAAD development commenced, in conjunction with a university-
based research group. However, during the late 1970s both the size and
character of Buildco's workload underwent rapid change. With the
increasing age of the postwar stock, capital resources were increasingly
required for modernization to current standards of amenity and performance to maintain its viability. At the same time an increasing
concern for the general condition of housing in inner-city areas led to
the re-allocation of New Town resources to an extensive inner-city
renewal programme. Following IMF intervention in the UK economy,
much closer cost control through the introduction of annual cash
limits meant that the relative priorities of projects had to be more
carefully assessed, with some attention paid to the relative patterns of
spending implied, as well as total expenditure.

As a consequence, new construction projects were frequently concerned with redevelopment sites and the CAAD system could address
only a proportion of new-build work, itself a declining proportion of
capital expenditure. Further expenditure on the development of the
system became difficult to justify. Although some work was carried
out to assess the feasibility of using the system on comprehensive
modernization schemes, the design content of this work was also declining as a result of changing government policies.

As the computing industry as a whole became more mature, the development of sophisticated software for individual users was becoming prohibitively expensive in relation to increasingly available general commercial packages. The close relationship between Buildco and the CAAD research group, involving interchange of staff and refinement of the software at the company, restricted the general commercial appeal of the system. The relatively uncommon hardware on which the system was mounted also caused difficulties. It frustrated attempts to support development costs through income from sales and made transfer to more modern and economical platforms impractical.

Railco: a Failed Innovation

Railco is a transport undertaking formed by the merger of a federal government agency with two state-based organizations. The innovation in question was the pilot implementation of an expert system which, while achieving some technical success, was not implemented by the organization. In 1987 the vendors of the organization's mainframe computer demonstrated an expert systems development shell at its User's Conference, and in 1988 the organization was successful with its proposal to act as a trial site for the development of an expert system application against competition from other organizations in the same state capital. The computer vendor provided hardware, software and personnel support for the company.

Expert systems represent a sub-set of knowledge-based computer applications which have developed from a number of strands of interest within artificial intelligence research from the 1950's to the 1970's. The simplest definition of an expert system is as a computer program which does what an expert does, and they have been advanced as a direct replacement for human cognition.

Railco's successful proposal was for an expert system for the rostering of operations staff, but this was changed to locomotive rostering. Utilizing a rapid prototyping methodology developed by the vendor, an initial demonstration prototype for mainline locomotives was completed and presented after some eight weeks of work. However, over a year of development for operational systems followed. The overheads of familiarization with both a novel software environment and a novel development task supporting a sophisticated process meant that this first component took longer than expected. In addition, during development working practices were altered in ways that reduced the scale of the rostering task itself, with branch workings reducing, and shunt workings being re-allocated to mainline locomotives.

The size of the development team varied between one and four workers, but the development method required a considerable input from the domain expert who was not available for normal duties during that time, although the first module to be trialed did provide him with more time. Early in 1989 the development was abandoned.

Steelco: Successful Innovation and Diffusion

Steelco is the steel-making division of a multidivisional company. Here the consequences of a pilot application similar to Railco's led to further development work, although the nature and intent of expert systems were adjusted in the light of institutional dynamics.

Several laboratories are operated by the company. Individual plants retain their own technical development staff for operational development, but longer-term issues which may be common to a number of sites are dealt with by the appropriate research laboratory. One of these also provides research and innovation support for information systems and technology. The data-processing departments of the entire organization were merged in 1990 to form an information technology (IT) division, providing a rechargeable service to other divisions, and offering external consultancy services. However, innovative IT applications remained the responsibility of research laboratories which are able to evaluate new technology and offer it to potential user-divisions on a trial basis.

Between 1984 and 1985 a pilot expert system was developed in conjunction with the chief operator of the sinter plant at one of the company's steel making locations. The plant prepared material for feeding into blast furnaces for iron production. A pilot expert system was developed to capture the skill of an expert who was due to retire.

This initial development was seen by laboratory staff as a way of demonstrating the capabilities within the steel-making process, prior to negotiating projects for the more central and critical blast-furnace processes. Although equivalent operations were carried out at a number of sites operated by different product divisions (for example sheet and coil, rod and bar), differing practices and different ages of plant within and between sites meant that transfer of systems between sites was not a trivial undertaking.

This application led to the development of a number of process-control and scheduling applications; however, the diffusion of total quality management (TQM) approaches during the development of the pilot also led to a marked change in emphasis in the use of expert systems, and for subsequent initiatives. Instead of mimicking the best available expert, in the classic expert systems sense, they were directed to the provision of 'electronic standard practices' in conjunction with the introduction of the TQM approach to production units. These applications were developed as 'operator guidance' or decision support systems, rather than replacements for human expertise.

By the time a second sinter system was under development at a second production site, TQM practices were in place. Instead of knowledge-acquisition interviews with an expert, written standard operating procedures were used to build the knowledge base for the system. User-reaction to the pilot expert system meant that a greater emphasis was placed on the commitment of end-users to the project, and the communal development of a knowledge base through the establishment of standard practices.

STANDARDS: SECURITY THROUGH COMPROMISE

Standards, whether for hardware, software or procedures, have long been regarded as the appropriate means of achieving inter-operability among organizations and are one obvious response to increasing globalization. The key to success and failure in the case studies outlined above revolved around the issue of standards.

With the advent of TQM in Steelco, or the excessive overheads of a non-standard software development environment at Railco, the standards involved pertain to the organization itself. They may also erupt from the organization's environment to undermine previously secure decisions, as with the competition from relatively unsophisticated de facto standards for the CAD systems painstakingly developed by Buildco.

Official and Defacto Standards

Official standards may be about market definition and closure, as in the case of television broadcast standards, and subject to national and international governmental agreement. The defacto standards which arise from among industry players are different in nature and in intent. They are about capture and maintenance of market share. They may use official standards as a starting point, but will incorporate a more

open aspect to allow further technical developments to be incorporated within a changing envelope and a developing decision
space.

Developers of technology must choose between attempting to establish a de facto standard within a market, or simply following such a
standard created by another player. The cost of following is always to
be reacting to an emerging standard, the prize for leading is to be able
to shape the development of the market itself. The key, however, is the
capture of sufficient market share to make a standard both viable and
plausible to potential adopters. In order to achieve this, individual
developers have formed alliances to promote an agreed approach.
However, achievement of market share is no guarantee of continued
success. Many de facto software standards have been leapfrogged by
continued rapid growth in the market itself and have ultimately failed.
Okot-Uma (1988) presents a matrix to represent the varying levels of
capability in information technology that exists between developing
countries within the British Commonwealth. Such a model, reflecting
Nolan's earlier work (Nolan, 1979), demonstrates the need for suppliers to address the capabilities of users. If advanced technologies are
prematurely deployed they will fail. A 'backfrogging' option, related to
concepts of 'appropriate technology', becomes as necessary in such
situations as leapfrogging over the competition elsewhere.

A compromise between consensus and cutting-edge capability is
involved in the agreement of any standards. Swann (1995) elegantly
demonstrates that officially agreed standards in a maturing technology
will always lag behind state-of-the-art capability through the delay
inevitable in reaching and communicating consensus. The employment
of standards also presents users and suppliers with a set of trade-offs,
as indicated by Figure 8.1.

Both de facto and official standards have been used as mechanisms
for defining, bounding and segmenting the marketplace. Any standard
implies an acceptance of some common denominator across a range of
circumstances. For officially determined standards these denominators
must be the lowest and most inclusive available. In fast developing
fields of technology this may mean abandoning the cutting edge and
closing the boundary of the decision space available to users of the
technology. In terms of the Open System Interconnection (OSI)
layered model of computer communication, discussed below, such
official standards have impacted at the lowest levels where the least
design discretion exists. De facto standards begin to dominate at the
higher levels where greater elaboration and differentiation is possible.

Figure 8.1   Positive and negative incentives for development of standards: users and suppliers

User	Inter-operability; management of choice of supply	Cost of adoption (transaction cost) Greater responsibility for matching system
Supplier	Level playing field for competition (cf. deregulation)	Removal of barriers to entry for competitors

Technical versus Cultural Foci for Standards

Figure 8.1 contasts the concerns of developers of standards with those of adopters. Adopters seek functionality and certainty. Developers must capture early adopters through technical excellence while providing access for late adopters if market share is to grow. Competitors will be using similar access paths to attract customers, so a standard must develop to match emerging features and functionality, even if these are not demanded by established customers. The gain to any customer from moving to a rival must always be kept below the cost of abandoning the adopted standard. Thus de facto standards are in constant flux as additional functionality is brought to established products, undermining the certainty sought by users. The middle strategy for smaller developers of establishing niche markets for specialized standards is also under constant threat as increasing functionality in mainstream products such as word processors and spreadsheets reduces the space for specialized desktop publishing or simulation software.

However, standards themselves cannot solve the problems confronting information managers, whether they are established users of office automation or more recent adopters of these technologies. The standards currently promoted reflect an established view of office automation as the transformation of the technical infrastructure of the workplace, the 'office' rather than the facilitation of the activities and relationships of 'office-holders'. This established, technocratic approach is linear and convergent, focusing on hardware issues. Explicit and implicit learning through the development of both computerized and manual information systems produces a legacy of understanding within organizations which is not captured by this approach. Instead it is seen as 'lag' or 'resistance to change'. There is a degree of cultural appreciation at the technical level of information systems design, as evidenced by research in to computer supported collaborative work (CSCW) (for example Ishii, 1993), but integration with the organizational level of the host culture would require the more social view of human computer interaction promoted by Suchman (1986).

Standards are intended to achieve economy and inter-operability. The notion of inter-operability can be applied to each level of interaction within and between organizations. The OSI model of layers of communication offer a paradigm which is useful in the context of office automation in a globalizing economy in its structure of progressive levels. Each must be matched between systems, but with increasing latitude at higher levels. Effective inter-operability in globalized, transcultural systems requires a new understanding of both the standards incorporated into systems and the criteria by which their performance is judged. The concept of 'standards' must be extended beyond the technical infrastructure of such systems to their user-characteristics and cultural dimensions. Similarly, the established concepts of life-cycle and cost must be extended beyond the physical components of the systems in question, and beyond the costs of training direct users to assess the broader impact of both the introduction and the withdrawal of a system on its organizational setting.

Commodification of Information Technology

The emergence of a market for end-user-oriented software packages is an aspect of the shift from mainframe technology to desk-top provision of computing resources within user-organizations. This involved a cultural change from centralized control of complex software mediated by a technocracy, to direct user-contact with the technology producing a new generation of end-users which is placing different demands upon developers. The indeterminate nature of emergent, de facto standards means that users have some leverage though the feedback they have provided to developers. Implicit knowledge developed by users may produce insights into products which were not available to the developers. At the crudest level this implicit knowledge may convert a 'bug' into a 'feature' which is then documented, but at higher levels of sophistication concepts such as user-defined style sheets may evolve from the pattern of use emerging among the developer's clientele. However, the focus remains technical, with the layering or wrapping of cultural concerns around a technical core. This means that a technical dynamic still dominates development. While users can develop their own market advantage through their own organizational standards, they are still constrained by a technical momentum which leads them to scavenge the margins of functionality for peripheral features suited to their requirements, just as minority user groups must utilize marginal aspects of mainstream applications to their advantage. A focus on the cultural requirements and the differences between organizational and cultural contexts is needed to bring the double advantage of both user-focused development and an awareness of the strengths and weaknesses of particular traditions and approaches.

ACHIEVING GLOBAL ORGANIZATION

Burris (1993) plots the emergence of a technocratic frame in western development from the enlightenment, through the industrial revolution to Taylorist scientific management, to Veblen's 'soviet of technicians'. She argues that the technocratic rationality is the dominant paradigm for workplace organization, polarising the internal labour market and favouring abstract diagnostic and technical activities. This paradigm carries with it a range of implicit cultural assumptions, which imply that the global diffusion of western technology is a substantively rational and inevitable process.

The technocratic perspective sees cultural variation as either irrational or insignificant and not as a resource. Technocracy is gender and culture-blind and incapable of acknowledging cultural differences, understanding of which is critical to smooth interoperability. Instead a technocratic perspective sees a smooth migration of older techniques to less-industrialized countries, while the core economies refine advanced technologies. There is already considerable evidence against such a simplistic view and Burris suggests that Reich (1993) demonstrates a better recognition of global implications for core economies, although still exhibiting a bias towards the expert sector. This bias allows optimistic interpretations of the impact of technologies by focusing on the beneficiaries within the workforce, rather than the affected workforce as a whole.

Rational Systems and Beyond

Despite the claims of technocracy there is a popular appreciation that systemic problems occur within complex organizations, and there are widespread expectations of dysfunction, particularly at large and impersonal scales of organization. Typically, Peter (1986) talks of growth in levels of bureaucratic control as 'proliferating pathology'. The concept of organizational pathology has also been used by several organization theorists to account for unintended outcomes and outputs from organizations. References to underlying concepts can be identified in works ranging from Parkinson's Law via *Up the Organization* to Brooks' 'mythical man-month' (Brooks, 1975).

Achieving a single rationality across any complex organizational setting remains problematic. Brubaker (1984) points out that Max Weber utilizes no fewer than 16 apparent meanings of 'rational' in his writings (see Weber, 1947). There is, nevertheless, a central concern with the irreconcilable tension between formal and substantive rationality. According to Weber, the modern economy has a double rationality: *subjectively* rational and thus purely instrumental market transactions, guided by *objectively* rational and thus purely quantitative calculations. *Formal* rationality is concerned with calculability of means and procedures and ultimately with *efficiency*. *Substantive* rationality addresses the value of ends and results and is ultimately concerned with *effectiveness*.

Non-western Cultures and Globalization

Global economic integration is growing rapidly, although the precise implications of this growth are subject to debate. The acceleration of this growth has been facilitated in part by information and communication technologies which are supporting organizations that span national and regional cultures. These cultural differences then become intra-organizational differences, and as a consequence information systems reflecting different cultural assumptions must interact effect-ively.

Beyond the core of western technical development and diffusion lie a number of economies of growing significance subject to a parallel development, modified by successive inward infusions of technology from the West. In North East Asia a number of economies have been relatively late adopters of many facets of office automation because of a range of cultural differences, not least their use of non-Roman characters. Haywood (1995) outlines the complexity of the develop-ment of the western alphabets and Shepard (1993), writing from direct experience, sets out the technical complexities of networking in an environment that must move beyond the ASCII standard. The situ-ation is in some ways comparable to the technical handicap suffered by Western Europe before the adoption of Arabic numerals. Littleton and Yamsey (1978) emphasize the role of Arabic numerals in facil-itating the emergence of the basis for western accounting practices during the fifteenth century. In conjunction with secular literacy, this technical innovation allowed a range of economic developments such as credit, capital and property rights to find expression in the devel-opment of written accounts.

In North East Asia, computer support for numerical and scientific tasks may have reached levels comparable with the West, but the lack of support for non-Roman text so reduced any advantages over es-tablished manual systems that office automation has been selective and partial. Such countries have made extensive and effective use of a subset of office automation technologies such as fax and telephone that do not incorporate the requirement of a specific alphabet. Castells and Hall (1994) argue that the development of the fax was driven by a Japanese desire to promote a technology which did not disadvantage them over western users.

The sophisticated bit-mapping technology able to deal with ideo-graphic text has emerged relatively late in the process of global dif-fusion of desktop computing. This means that these increasingly significant players in the world economy are operating in a technical context and to sets of standards, official and de facto, which have been shaped by outside cultural assumptions.

Regional, National and Industrial Cultures

Stinchcombe (1965) argues that the industry to which an organization belongs is a strong determinant of organizational structure and culture.

Comparison of the age of an industry with its technological base suggests a related argument that core technologies reflect the age of an industry rather than that of any individual enterprise within it. This technically determined line of argument would suggest in turn that an emergent isomorphism should characterize the successive diffusion of the current generation of information technologies across separate industries. Indeed, notions of networked and post-modern organizations imply such an isomorphism. However, a cultural orientation would imply an expectation that inherently different outcomes would accompany the diffusion of the same technology to different regional settings. Orru, Biggart and Hamilton (1991) reveal strikingly different forms of intra-societal isomorphism among the relatively new industries of Japan, Taiwan and South Korea. Martinez, Quelch and Ganitsky (1992) similarly demonstrate that the notion of 'Latin America' conflates a range of distinctive cultural and economic conditions which will provide a different ranking of attractiveness to outside investors, depending upon which criteria are compared. Kagami (1992) identifies a technology gap between centre and periphery as responsible for the inability of peripheral economies to absorb surplus agricultural labour, thereby creating low wage conditions conducive to less capital-intensive production that at the centre.

The tendency to conflate intra-regional complexity into concepts such as 'Latin America' or 'NE Asian Tigers' reflects the process of imperial, technical and more recently information colonization by the more technically developed nations. Haywood (1995) draws attention to the pervasive nature and potentially destabilizing presence of mass communications from the industrialized core in the most remote communities. Such colonization is a potent vehicle for the diffusion of practices from the centre to the periphery, as indicated by Haywood's mapping of the continued dominance of English, Spanish and Portuguese as both mother tongues and official languages in areas of former colonization. However, one legacy of this primarily European colonization is an overlay of differing cultures in already diverse regions such as Africa and South America.

Culture and Organization

There is a cultural dimension to the established practice and expectations within organizations which imparts its own dynamic to the process of change and development. The case studies show that longitudinal observation offers access to this dynamic. However, a complex issue has been further confused by the variety of ways in which culture has been formulated by different writers on organizations. One conception of organizational culture has been used to explain the relative success of individual organizations and entrepreneurs (Peters and Waterman, 1982). Other writers refer to culture in terms of national differences in social and economic organization. Latin, Anglo-Saxon and traditional cultures are reflected in distinctive organizational types identified in studies examined by Lammers and Hickson (1979).

Turner (1971) describes industrial subcultures which can be identified across individual organizations, and are distinctive from the larger society. Eldridge and Crombie (1974) define organizational culture as characteristic for individual organizations, while Strauss *et al.* (1973) describe a range of cultures within a single organization. Thompson (1967) utilized the concept of an organizational constituency capable of entering into coalition with other constituencies in order to promote its interest. Such a conception allows the formal elements of an organization to be related to the informal communication and negotiation which often modifies, or in extreme cases frustrates, the intentions of management. It also allows consideration of intra-organizational variations in culture arising from these differences of interest and experience.

Similarly, differences in institutional culture can be identified at national levels. Johnson (1983) defines a 'market rationality' as seen in the US where the state is interested in maintaining, through regulation, the mechanisms of competition in order to maximize efficiency. He contrasts this with a 'plan rationality' as seen in Japan where a close working relationship exists between industrial sectors and government departments such as the Ministry of International Trade and Industry in order to pursue common goals with maximum effectiveness. He argues that this essentially different view of the role of public institutions in the economic arena accounts for a great deal of misunderstanding between these trading partners as to what constitutes 'fair trade'.

INSTITUTIONAL AND TECHNICAL DYNAMICS OF DIFFUSION

The case studies demonstrate the necessity of an institutional perspective on technical strategy. All organizations conducted significant

technical innovation against a background of institutional re-align-
ment as political conditions and consequently resources shifted. The
life cycle of organizational myths proposed by Boje *et al.* (1982) can be
seen to be derived from changes in their explanatory power within the
organization and its environment. Changes in Buildco's policy can be
related to postwar changes in the development and construction industry in the UK and elsewhere. Russell (1983) indicates a range of
pressures behind the move to increase both industrialization and
capitalization in the building industries of the East and West in this
period. The factory environment was seen as free from the natural,
seasonal variation and disruption of the building site. A technocratic
underpinning for designers and architects had been laid in the 1920s
and 1930s, within the Modern Movement theorists. The ideology was
already available when economic and political conditions became favourable. To combine Boje *et al.*'s (1982) and Rosenberg and Frischtak's (1984) terms, the myth was in place awaiting the favourable
macroeconomic conditions of postwar reconstruction. This particular
myth incorporated a belief in forms of architectural determinism
which minimized the significance of exogenous political and cultural
conditions.

However, when resources again became scarce a shift in focus took
place in Buildco. Development and construction was replaced by
management and ultimately disposal of housing stock. The technical
focus shifted from the production methods used in the construction of
housing, through the rationalization of control over technical standards, to a concern with management information systems, and the
coordination of the resources required to maintain this existing housing stock. Delays caused by technical control led to extensive short-
circuiting of the formal reporting processes intended to capture and
respond to feedback from the construction process. Problems were
communicated through anecdote instead of formal memoranda.

The core technologies involved were changing out of synchroniza-
tion with their environment, CAAD technology was not fully available
until the conditions it was intended to address had changed. By this
time the CAAD developers were perceived as a remote technocratic
priesthood. Delays in delivery of promised improvements in software
led some-user groups to develop a great enthusiasm for micro-
computers as soon as these were available. After considerable resistance, the technical staff agreed a standard based on an 8-bit
Computer Program Management (CPM) based machine, shortly before the release of the 16-bit IBM personal computer in the UK which

quickly established MS-DOS as the de facto standard for business applications.

The Railco pilot was intended to make a substantial contribution to a core activity, but continuing rationalization of operations impacted directly on the operations targeted by this pilot, revised operating and maintenance procedures reduced or removed the task of rostering locomotives for shunt and local trip workings. This change was a symptom of a substantial re-institutionalization of the organization (Jepperson, 1991), connected to a Federal government national freight strategy which was to transform the organization over the three years following initial contact with the organization. The technical constituency was dominated by a traditional view of railways and their social role in national development, the operating division was already aligning with world best practice anticipating the forthcoming changes and promoting a cultural shift to a streamlined and focused bulk transportation service. In such an environment a technical project based on established and traditional practices was doomed. Despite the withdrawal of support for further expert system development, however, experience of the prototyping approach to software development influenced subsequent IT projects.

In Steelco, the adoption of TQM practices created an opportunity for expert systems to be repackaged as 'electronic standard practices'. While the pilot implementation had been chosen with a view to gaining access to the more central steel-making processes, the goals of the system were revised from a classic expert system replacing human expertise to one of decision support. This allowed the link to TQM practice offering the required consistency of performance, but at the cost of a simplification of the original technical objectives. In effect expert systems were re-innovated at a less-ambitious, more familiar level of technology, utilizing an operator-assistance paradigm within the TQM context. Reduction of variance became the selling point for expert systems technology. In contrast, the task addressed by the pilot project in Railco remained the classic expert system strategy applied to a task which became increasingly marginalized. The development team remained strongly committed to the innovative technology following their success against strong competition for vendor support. Unfortunately their adherence to sound but conservative risk minimization practices allowed further scope for their marginalization, while a higher risk strategy aimed directly at a key functional area could have delivered a more critical function more quickly. Resources were redirected before development could be completed and the functionality of delivered material was the subject of disagreement between technical and operational staff. Arguably a high profile innovation supporting functions perceived by the operating division to be anachronistic was seen as a challenge to the process of re-institutionalization at Railco. Significantly, by the end of the three-year period of observation all the technical staff involved in the pilot scheme had exited the organization, as was observed earlier in Buildco.

Drives to Diffusion

The case studies reveal the difficulty in reconciling a technically focused innovation process with the changing institutional environments of organizations. The very framework for the definition of appropriate or adequate performance is liable to change, creating an insoluble problem of defining appropriate measures for shifting performance criteria. The organizations described in the case studies had all been influenced by developments and practices in comparable organizations in other countries. Buildco imported Scandinavian construction techniques to the UK before World War II. In Australia the federal government has pursued a particularly aggressive policy of tariff reduction and exposure of manufacturing industries to direct competition in order to promote regional and global competitiveness. Railco paid attention to North American rail undertakings in particular in its bid to match 'world best practice', and Steelco frequently referred to DuPont as an appropriate benchmark for their organization as a whole. Such relationships between organizations seeking technical innovation have long been noted in the literature on the diffusion of technology, however in a globalizing economy even medium national players are seeking international comparisons.

Both institutional and technical aspects of diffusion of technology between organizations are subsumed in the S-Curve representation discussed by Rogers (1983). Strang and Meyer (1994) distinguish between diffusion – 'flows among formally autonomous units', and implementation – 'flows among hierarchically placed units'. Complex organizations, such as Steelco, must manage internal diffusion. Organizations which seek to diffuse centrally developed systems must either accommodate intra-organizational cultural differences, or demand that end-user groups adapt to the technology. In particular, organizations which have developed through the acquisition and merger of a variety of extant systems must achieve more than purely technical interenvironment operability. As has been argued above, technical systems reflecting different cultural assumptions must interact effectively.

Figure 8.2 presents two dynamics of diffusion. In the first, an initial adopter, organization A undertakes a technical development on the basis of the needs of the organization at time T1. This technology is deployed in the organization at time T2 at which point the organization itself has developed institutionally through interaction with its environment. In order for the technology, based on a snapshot of the organization at T1 to be usefully developed, the organization must enter into a period of adjustment between the delivered system and the changed needs. We have seen that in Steelco institutional development in the organization led to a major reassessment of the innovative technology, in Railco to its abandonment. Sauer (1993) suggests that such processes of adjustment of both function and performance criteria need to be continuous through the development and life of a system for it to retain the support of its users. The complex technical systems examined by Sauer do not achieve the final routinization or institutionalization described by Rogers (1983)

Organization A reaches the beginning of its payback period on the innovation at T3. Organization B, having observed A's process of

Figure 8.2   Under the S-curve: technical and institutional drives to diffusion of innovations between organizations

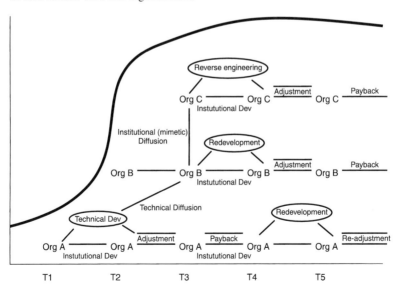

deployment initiates its own development of the new technology at T3. In order to adapt the technology to their own needs they pursue a process of redevelopment, followed by their own process of adjustment, so that payback for organization B begins at T5.

Organization C pursues a more adventurous strategy, however, by deciding to adopt the technology as soon as it is aware of organization B's adoption decision. In this stage of diffusion, however, organization C is faced with a task of reverse-engineering rather than redeveloping the technology since it does not have the example of B to follow. The benefit of the higher risk comes in the earlier arrival at the payback period, however, since C has not waited for B, its model, to achieve a deployable technology. Meanwhile, organization A has already embarked upon its own process of redevelopment following continued change within its requirements.

DiMaggio and Powell (1991) suggest that mimetic adoption is used in situations where means–ends links in a new technology are unclear. A higher risk is involved for the adopter, since reverse-engineering is required rather than the reinvention of a more orderly transfer of technology. Examples of both forms of diffusion are contained in Morris-Suzuki's (1994) review of Japanese technical development. During the nineteenth century some innovation decisions were made on little more knowledge of the technology in question than that of its existence and efficacy in western industry. More recently such decisions have been made with a high level of direct assistance from overseas. In the contemporary situation some of the risks of mimetic innovation can be reduced through the adoption or development of standards.

CONCLUSION

With growing global economic integration, increasingly disparate national and regional cultures are interacting within networked and globalized organizations. Meanwhile information technologies are reducing transaction costs and altering the relative advantages and economies of scale. A complex process of layering of labour markets, both internal and external, at several levels of skill and remuneration can be observed. Some smaller companies have leveraged their position through their ability to absorb technology more quickly and completely than larger enterprises. Granovetter (1973) argues that the least used connections in a social network provide the most valuable information; Kelly (1994) argues that robust responses to complex changing environments require organizational heterogeneity which can be derived from the peripheral and marginal players. For enterprises of every size, however, successful exploitation of the opportunities arising in such conditions will require careful attention to standards for interoperability at technical and cultural levels.

Imperfections in globalization offer the same potential advantages to actors as imperfections in other markets. Okimoto (1989) argues that the ability of Japanese companies to develop their activities through networks of independent subsidiaries rather than through direct expansion of the core business allows flexibility through the persistence of a dual economy. Morris-Suzuki (1994) notes an increasing tendency for sub-contractors to upgrade their skills and technology, with the manufacture of more basic components shifting off-shore. 'Glocalisation', as practised by Japanese corporations adapts global approaches to local situations (Morris, 1991). However, although the origination of the term 'office automation' has been attributed to the Japanese company Ricoh in 1975 (Ohnoe, 1996), the adoption of the technologies involved has lagged behind the West in both Japan and NE Asia generally. The growing volume of inward investment from this region to both North America and Europe indicates that this is not an issue of cost but of compatibility with established office routines. It is clear that key innovations in office automation technology have succeeded where they were mapped on to existing cultural frameworks. Thus the spreadsheet could readily mimic the 20-column analysis paper already in use. Word processors could offer a flexibly automated form of the standard correspondence already developed by many enterprises. Database applications, on the other hand, have remained a technocratic innovation.

Sproull and Kiesler (1991) demonstrate that a process of organizational learning is needed to move beyond the technical effects of direct substitution of information technology for manual processes. The transformative gains in effectiveness represented by Zuboff's (1988) 'informated organization' will come about only through an understanding of the meaning of cultural interoperability at both pre-competitive and competitive stages of development. Such understanding is more likely to arise from the learning process accompanying institutional or mimetic adoption than through a purely technically-driven diffusion process.

Figure 8.2 represents the difference in diffusion trajectories produced by organizational variations in risk-perception and management.

Variations in strategy reflect the institutional and cultural nexus of organizations, both at the micro-level of the individual organization, the meso-level of its sector or industry, and the macro-level of national or regional context. In the globalizing economy, effective interaction among increasingly networked organizations will require the accommodation of such variety through the pursuit of cultural inter-operability within constantly developing standards.

References

Boje, D.M., Fedor, D.B. and Rowland, K.M. (1982) 'Mythmaking: A Qualitative Step in OD Interventions', *Applied Behavioral Sciences*, vol. 18, no. 1, pp. 17–28.

Brooks R. (1975) *The Mythical Man-month* (Reading Mass.: Addison-Wesley).

Brubaker R. (1984) *The Limits of Rationality: An Essay on the Social and Moral Thought of Max Weber* (London: George Allen and Unwin).

Burris, B. (1993) *Technocracy at Work* (Albany: State University of New York Press).

Castells, M. and Hall, P. (1994) *Technopoles of the World: The Making of 21st Century Industrial Complexes* (London: Routledge).

Clegg, S.R. (1987) 'The Language of Power and the Power of Language', *Organisation Studies*, vol. 8, no. 1, January 1987, pp. 61–70.

DiMaggio, P.J. and Powell, W.W. (1991) 'The Iron Cage Revisited: Institutional Isomorphism and Collective Rationality in Organizational Fields', in Powell, W.W. and DiMaggio, P.J. (eds), *The New Institutionalism in Organisational Analysis* (Chicago: University of Chicago Press).

Douglas, M. (1987) *How Institutions Think* (London: Routledge and Kegan Paul).

Economist, The (1995) 'Bean Counters, Unite!', *The Economist*, 10 June 1995, pp. 95–6.

Eldridge, J.E.T. and Crombie, A.D. (1974) *A Sociology of Organisations* (London: Allen and Unwin).

Evans, T. G., Taylor, M.E. and Holzman, O. (1985) *International Accounting and Reporting* (NewYork: Macmillan).

Gouldner, A. (1955) 'Metaphysical Pathos and the Theory of Bureaucracy', *American Political Science Review*, vol. 49, p. 504.

Granovetter, M. (1973) 'The Strength of Weak Ties', *American Journal of Sociology*, vol. 78, no. 6, pp. 1360–80.

Haywood, T. (1995) *Info-Rich Info-Poor: Access and Exchange in the Global Information Society* (London: Bowker-Saur).

Heenan, D.A. and Perlmutter, H.V. (1979) *Multinational Organization Development* (Reading, Mass.: Addison-Wesley).

Hu, Y-S. (1992) 'Global or Stateless Firms are National Firms with International Operations', *California Management Review* (Winter).

Ishii, H. (1993) Cross-cultural Communication and CSCW', in Harasim, L.M. (ed.), *Global Networks: Computers and International Communication* (Cambridge, Mass.: MIT Press).

Jepperson, R.L. (1991) 'Institutions, Institutional Effects and Institutionalism', in Powell, W.W. and DiMaggio, P.J. (eds), *The New Institutionalism in Organisational Analysis* (Chicago: University of Chicago Press).

Johnson, C. (1983) *MITI and the Japanese Miracle: The Growth of Industrial Policy 1925–1975* (Stanford Ca.: Stanford University Press).

Kagami, M. (1992) 'Latin America: Economic Development Theories and their Policies', in *Development Strategies for the 21st Century*, Institute of Development Economics.

Kelly, K. (1994) *Out of Control: The Rise of Neo-Biological Civilization* (Reading Mass.: Addison-Wesley).

Lammers, C.J. and Hickson, D.J. (1979) 'A Cross-national and Cross-institutional Typology of Organisations', in Lammers, C.J. and Hickson, D.J. (eds), *Organisations Alike and Unlike: International and Inter-institutional Studies in the Sociology of Organisations* (London: Routledge & Kegan Paul).

Little, S.E. (1987) 'The Role of Time-frames in Design Decision-making', *Design Studies*, vol. 8 no. 3 pp. 170–82, July 1987.

Little, S.E. (1988) *The Organisational Implications of Computing Technology for Professional Work* (Aldershot: Avebury).

Littleton, A.C. and Yamsey, B.S (1978) *Studies in the History of Accounting* (New York: Arno Press).

Martinez, J.I., Quelch, J.A. and Ganitsky, J. (1992) 'Don't Forget Latin America', *Sloan Management Review*, vol. 33, no. 2, Winter.

Morris, J. (ed.) (1991) *Japan and the Global Economy: Issues and Trends in the 1990s* (London: Routledge).

Morris-Suzuki, T. (1994) *The Technological Transformation of Japan: From the Seventeenth to the Twenty-first Century* (Cambridge: Cambridge University Press).

Nobes, C.W. and Parker, R.H. (1985) *Comparative International Accounting*, 2nd edn (Deddington: Phillip Allan).

Nolan, R.L. (1979) 'Managing the Crisis in Data Processing', *Harvard Business Review*, vol. 52 no. 2 March–April.

Ohmae, K. (1990) *The Borderless World* (London: Collins).

Ohnoe, M. (1996) 'Office Automation and Beyond', *Proceedings of 2nd International Conference on OA and Information Management*, Chiba, November 1996, pp. 25–27

Ohsumi, H. (1991) 'Differences in Business Culture between Japanese and Americans: The Experiences of a Japanese Businessman', mimeo, Kobe, Japan.

Okimoto, D.I. (1998) *Inside The Japanese System* (Stanford: Stanford University Press).

Okot-Uma, R. W'O (1988) *A Synthesis Perspective of Information Technology Capability of Commonwealth Countries*, Science and Technology News, Special Issue on I.T., Commonwealth Science Council, March.

Orru, M., Biggart, N.W. and Hamilton, G. (1991) 'Organizational Isomorphism in East Asia', in Powell, W.W. and DiMaggio, P.J. (eds), *The New Institutionalism in Organisational Analysis* (Chicago: University of Chicago Press).

Peter, L.J. (1986) *The Peter Pyramid* (London: Unwin).

Peters, T.J. and Waterman, R.H. Jr (1982) *In Search of Excellence* (New York: Warner).

Reich, R. (1993) *The Work of Nations* (New York: Vintage).

Rogers, E.M. (1983) *Diffusion of Innovations*, 3rd edn (New York: Free Press).

Rosenberg, N. and Frischtak, C. (1984) 'Technical Innovation and Long Waves', in Freeman, C. (ed.) *Design, Innovation and Long Cycles in Economic Development*, Design Research Publications, London.

Russell, B. (1983) *Building Systems, Industrialization and Architecture* (Chichester: Wiley).

Sauer, C. (1993) *Why Information Systems Fail: A Case Study Approach* (Henley on Thames: Alfred Waller).

Scott, W.R. (1987) *Organisations, Natural, Rational and Open Systems*, 2nd edn (New Jersey: Prentice-Hall).

Shepard, J. (1993) 'Islands in the (Data)Stream: Language, Character Codes, and Electronic Isolation in Japan', in Harasim, L.M. (ed.), *Global Networks: Computers and International Communication* (Cambridge, Mass.: MIT Press).

Sproull, L. and Kiesler, S. (1991) *Connections: New Ways of Working in the Networked Organization* (Cambridge, Mass.: MIT Press).

Stinchcombe, A. (1965) 'Social Structure and Organisations', in March J.G. (ed.), *Handbook of Organisations* (Chicago: Rand-McNally).

Strang, D. and Meyer, J.W. (1994) 'Institutional conditions for Diffusion', in Scott, W.R. and Meyer, J.W. (eds), *Institutional Environments and Organizations: Structural Complexity and Individualism* (Thousand Oaks, Ca.: Sage).

Strauss, A.L., Schatzman, L., Ehrlich, D., Buchner, B. and Shabshin, M. (1973) 'The Hospital and its Negotiated Order', in Salaman, G. and Thompson, K. (eds), *People and Organisations* (London: Longman).

Suchman, L. (1986) *Plans and Situated Action* (Cambridge: Cambridge University Press).

Swann, P. (1995) 'Strategy for Standards Institutions', Presentation to PICT Conference, *The Social and Economic Implications of ICTs*, Queen Elizabeth Conference Hall, Westminster, UK, May 1995.

Thompson, J.D. (1967) *Organisations in Action* (New Jersey: McGraw-Hill).

Turner, G. (1971) *Exploring the Industrial Subculture* (London: Macmillan).

Weber, M. (1947) *From Max Weber*, (eds) Gerth, H.H. and Mills, C.W. (London: Oxford University Press).

Zuboff, S. (1988) *In the Age of the Smart Machine* (New York: Basic Books).

9 The Appropriate Policies for a Successful International Technology Transfer (ITT) to Less-Developed Countries (LDCs)

Reza Salami and Lawrence P. Reavill

INTRODUCTION

This chapter examines the key elements of the effective policies and strategies of technology transfer which contribute to the economic and industrial development of the less-developed countries (LDCs). Firstly, some of the most important and relevant conceptual issues of technology transfer in LDCs will be analysed. The empirical and practical experiences of some East Asian newly industrialized Countries (NICs) will also be studied. Finally, a framework of an appropriate policy and strategy for international technology transfer to LDCs will be proposed.

It is widely believed that international technology transfer (the transfer of technology across national borders) has played an important role in the economic and industrial development of most nations. The successful experience of some NICs, for example those of East Asia and Latin America, has showed that access to advanced technology has enabled them to increase their productivity through the introduction of higher levels of knowledge and skill which have already been developed and understood in the developed country. The acquisition of foreign technology has also led to the more efficient utilization of their natural resources.

It appears therefore that the adoption and adaptation of imported technology together with the improvement of domestic technological capability can be an essential process of economic and industrial development of both LDCs and NICs. In order to take most advantage

149

from global technological change, these countries have used the acquisition of foreign technology as a means of providing a base for the strengthening of their technological capability. However, despite realising the great importance of technology for their development and industrialization, it seems that most LDCs are not able to employ effective strategies and policies for successful transfer of technology. Many developing countries do not appear to have established the necessary procedures to choose the effective technology transfer policy needed for successful industrialization. Therefore, they have to adopt and develop an appropriate strategy for effective transfer and utilization of imported technology.

TECHNOLOGY TRANSFER AND ITS DEFINITIONS

The literature offers several definitions of technology transfer. (see for example Gee, 1981, p. 9; Kanayak, 1985, p. 155; Chesnais, 1986; Stewart and Nihei, 1987, p. 2). The wide variations in the definition of technology transfer indicate the various perspectives that are possible. Technology transfer has been generally defined as the process whereby technology is moved from one physical or geographic location to another for the purpose of application towards an end product (Perlmutter and Saghafi-nejad, 1988). This transfer can take place either domestically, from one sector or firm to another, or it can take place across national boundaries, from one country to another, which is generally accepted as international technology transfer (ITT).

This definition, which can also be called horizontal transfer, is adopted here for our future discussion. However, the term technology transfer was first used as the transformation of the R&D results in the basic sciences into commercial technologies. This definition, which is called vertical transfer, refers to the transfer of technical information from basic research to applied research, from applied research to development, and from development to production.

THE TECHNOLOGY TRANSFER MECHANISM

Technology transfer among nations or international technology transfer (ITT) can take place through a number of different channels and mechanisms that may in some cases exist independently of other channels. There are various classifications for different modes of technology transfer. For example, Cooper and Sercovich (1971) distinguished between direct and indirect, Buckley (1985) refers to the internal and external mechanisms, Erdilek and Rapoport (1985) mention the formal and informal channels, and a study by the United Nations Centre on Transitional Corporations (UNCTC) identifies commercial and non-commercial methods, Karake (1990) specifies packaged and unpackaged, Olukoshi (1990) categorizes between embodied and disembodied, Kim (1991) classifies market and non-market mediated, and Lall (1993) analyses the modes of technology transfer by distinguishing between two broad categories; internalized and externalized forms of technology transfer.

However, different mechanisms of ITT can be summarized in categories such as foreign direct investment; licensing; joint ventures; technical assistant contracts; turnkey agreements; international subcontracting; franchising; reverse engineering; exchange of scientific and technical personnel; conferences; flow of books; journals and other published materials; trade shows and exhibitions; import of machinery; and industrial espionage. The effectiveness of each channel depends on the nature of the technology that is being acquired and the ability and capacity of the recipient country to learn and absorb technological know-how. Thus, the various methods of transfer can be determined by some important factors such as the transferee's and transferor's goals and objectives, the level of technological and managerial capacity in the recipient country, and the industrial policy and strategy of the recipient nation (Choi and Mok, 1986). Therefore, the policy-makers in the recipient country should note that effectiveness of technology importation is significantly affected by the forms and mechanisms of technology transfer. It is thought useful here to explain briefly some of the most important methods of technology transfer to examine their applications according to different situations and circumstances.

FOREIGN DIRECT INVESTMENT

It is believed that foreign direct investment (FDI) is one of the most important channels of technology transfer (Marton, 1986). The transfer of technology through FDI usually occurs when a multinational company (MNC) is involved in the flow of capital, technical, managerial and marketing skills through its affiliates in a foreign country of which the MNC can have the whole, majority or minority of ownership. Since technology is highly concentrated within MNCs, their direct investment plays an important role in transferring technology to developing countries (Prasad, 1981). However, MNCs have sometimes been criticized for not transferring the appropriate technology and the knowhow needed for adapting the foreign technology to the LDCs' local conditions.

It is argued that FDI has flowed more to the countries which have characteristics such as a relatively cheap and skilled labour and abundant natural resources (Zahid, 1994). The importance of FDI to less-developed countries (LDCs) has been increasing over the years. The aggregate flow of FDI to all developing countries exceeded $38 billion in 1992, and $80 billion in 1993, an increase of over 50 per cent over the previous two years and a 400 per cent increase since the mid-1980s (World Bank, 1993). While developing countries in Latin America have attracted more FDI in comparison to those countries in Asia in the 1970s, there has been a slight shift from Latin America to Asia as a major recipient of FDI since the 1980s. As Table 9.1 shows, the average share of Asia in the top ten recipients of FDI increased from 5 per

Table 9.1   Top 10 annual flows of FDI to less-developed countries ($ billion)

Recipients	Total FDI flow to LDCs 1970–1979 20.6	Recipients	Total FDI flow to LDCs 1980–1990 18.7	Recipients	Total FDI flow to LDCs 1988–1992 630*
Brazil	11.3	Singapore	2.3	China	25.6
Mexico	0.6	Mexico	1.9	Singapore	21.7
Egypt	0.3	Brazil	1.8	Mexico	18.4
Malaysia	0.3	China	1.7	Malaysia	13.2
Nigeria	0.3	Malaysia	1.1	Argentina	10.6
Singapore	0.3	Hong Kong	1.1	Thailand	9.5
Indonesia	0.2	Egypt	0.9	Hong Kong	7.9
Hong Kong	0.1	Argentina	0.7	Brazil	7.6
Iran	0.1	Thailand	0.7	Taiwan	6.0
Uruguay	0.1	Taiwan	0.5	Indonesia	5.6
Share of flow to top 10 (%)	66	Share of flow to top 10 (%)	68	Share of flow to top 10 (%)	75*

Sources: Columns 1– 4, UN, *World Investment Report* 1992; columns 5–6 *The Economist*, 1–7 October 1994, p. 29; * estimated figures.

cent to 58 per cent. It also shows that the top slot switched from Brazil in the 1970s to Singapore in the 1980s, and has recently moved to China in the early 1990s.

The importance of the FDI as a main channel of acquiring foreign technology for LDCs will be discussed further in the case studies survey.

JOINT VENTURES

A joint venture can be defined as a collaboration or new investment involving shared ownership between a local firm in the host country and its foreign partner (Adeoba, 1990). The main difference between a joint venture and FDI is that in the former both parties share in the decision-making, control and the benefits of the operation. It is argued that transfer of technology through joint ventures enables the recipient country to share in the use of technologies which they could never explore alone.

However, it should be noted that even a majority shareholding of the recipient firm can not secure its effective control. This is because the foreign supplier of technology usually dominates the operation by a powerful executive management team. As a result, the effectiveness of successful technology transfer through a joint venture to a large degree relies on the degree of association and the participation of both parties in some important areas such as procurement of goods and services, research and development, quality control, and organizational arrangement. Moreover, the willingness and joint efforts of both parties in reducing of costs and increasing their benefits can also account for their success. Therefore, it seems that the joint venture is the preferred channel of technology transfer when the supplier's and recipient's goals and objectives are compatible.

LICENSING AGREEMENTS

Licensing refers to the sale of manufacturing technology by a licenser (supplier) to a licensee (recipient) for a specified duration and certain payments, usually royalties (Telesio, 1984). The major difference between licence agreements and joint ventures is that in the former there is no sharing of equity by the firms involved. The licenser agrees to

provide the required technology through the complete capital investment by the licensee. Moreover, licensing is generally a cheaper source
of technology and also stimulates technological self-reliance in the
recipient country (Prasad, 1981).

It is argued that the countries with a better capability to absorb
foreign technology use licensing agreements as an alternative channel
of technology transfer. For instance, some developed and newly-
developed countries such as Japan and Korea tended to use licensing
rather than foreign equity participation, mainly because of the increased competition among suppliers of technology and the resulting
need to sell existing technology to be able to finance their research and
development. It is also believed that these countries are able to make
full use of licensed technology with little technical assistance from the
transferor (Tsang, 1994).

It should also be noted that the ability of the recipient (licensee) to
absorb and improve licensed technology depends largely on its ability
to understand and control both embedded and embodied technology.
Therefore, the recipient may need to ask the licenser to provide technical training as well as managerial expertise for the acquisition and
assimilation of licensed technology embodied in the modern machinery and equipment (Vakil and Brahmanda, 1990).

THE TECHNOLOGY TRANSFER PROCESS

Various writers have identified three major stages in the process of
international technology transfer: acquisition, adaptation, and improvement of technology (see for example Nelson and Winter, 1997).
However, it would be better to consider a more elaborate sequence of
activities that constitute the process of technology transfer using a
systematic approach, and such an approach is illustrated in Figure 9.1.

The belief is that developing a systematic framework for a technology transfer process can assist policy-makers and planners in less-
developed countries (LDCs) to a successful acquisition of imported
technology. This approach has broken down the process of technology
transfer into a sequence of interrelated stages in order to analyse both
the transferor's and the transferee's goals and objectives through
technology transfer.

In the first stage policy-makers in the LDCs make their decisions for
selecting technology by identifying the needs and objectives that they

Figure 9.1 A systematic model for the technology transfer process

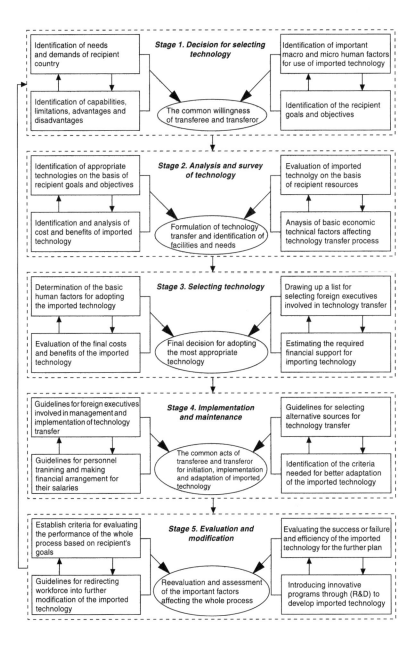

intend to achieve through technology transfer. The country's weaknesses and capabilities are also taken into account at this stage. These may include access to the country's natural and human resources as a potential strength, or lack of adequate infrastructure which limits the country's ability to absorb foreign technology.

Once the country's needs and objectives are identified, the next stage focuses on various technology alternatives in order to choose the appropriate technology based on the country's standards and constraints. The appropriate technology can be selected by ranking priorities for different technologies based on the decision-maker's judgement. The establishment of input–output relationships between different technologies can be a useful method for efficient allocation of resources in terms of identified priorities (Madu, 1988). For example, an output from the oil industry can be used as an input for the petrochemical industry, or an output from the steel industry can be used as an input for the automobile industry. In the third stage, the decision-makers in the country make their final decision for selecting the most appropriate technology. They also determine an appropriate transferor, considering different criteria such as quality of technology, cost of technology, and trade relationships. They also evaluate the financial support needed for importing technology through their final cost and benefit analysis.

In the implementation and maintenance stage, some important criteria needed for better adaptation and assimilation of imported technology are identified through the common acts of transferor and transferee. These criteria differ for each country and depend mainly on the socio-economic and cultural factors in the recipient country. For example, the existence of a relatively skilled labour force may increase the rate of assimilation and absorption of foreign technology in the recipient country. Therefore, it may be necessary for both transferor and transferee to make efforts to design specific training programmes for the labour force in the recipient country to enable them to adapt the imported technology for local use.

Finally, in the evaluation and modification stage, some of the most important success and failure factors affecting the whole process of technology transfer are assessed and evaluated. The policy-makers re-evaluate the previous goals and objectives that the country intended to achieve through technology transfer in order to ensure that all of them are being satisfied. It may be realised that some innovative research and development programmes are needed for further improvement and updating of the existing technologies.

FORMULATION OF THE TECHNOLOGY TRANSFER PROCESS

In order to assess the technological transfer process the following assumptions are used, where subscript 1 refers to the domestic country and subscript 2 to the foreign country.

We represent the existing know-how within the domestic country by A_1, and the foreign know-how which must be imported by A_2. We suppose machinery and equipment B_1 required for production of goods exists in the domestic country, but if there is not enough the required machinery and equipment B_2 must be imported from the foreign country. We represent the local expertise needed for using machinery by C_1, and if there is not enough local expertise then the foreign expertise needed for using the machinery is C_2. The technology transfer process can now be shown in the following matrix of Figure 9.2.

The cell (1,1) shows that the recipient country is fully dependent on foreign technology, because all the technology, machinery, technicians and expertise is imported from a foreign country. In cell (1,2) the R&D institutes in the recipient country have attempted to prepare know-how for the imported technology. In the cell (2,2), the recipient country has attempted to do research and development for copying the

Figure 9.2   Technology transfer process matrix

Stage 1	Stage 2	Stage 3	Stage 4
$A_2 B_2 C_2$	$A_1 B_2 C_2$	$A_1 B_1 C_2$	$A_1 B_1 C_1$
(1,1)	(1,2)	(1,3)	(1,4)
	$A_2 B_1 C_2$	$A_1 B_2 C_1$	
(2,1)	(2,2)	(2,3)	(2,4)
	$A_2 B_2 C_1$	$A_2 B_1 C_1$	
(3,1)	(3,2)	(3,3)	(3,4)

machinery, but must still employ foreign expertise. While the first stage has a large degree of costs and dependency, there is less dependency and costs as the fourth stage is approached. Each recipient country can be located in one of these four stages.

In every stage, there is an effort to change one of the previous factors which were imported from abroad, such as foreign know-how A_2 and technical support C_2, to indigenous know-how A_1 and technical support C_1. In the fourth stage, C_2 changes to C_1, and we can show the step-by-step progression as follows:

$$A_2 B_2 C_2 \rightarrow A_1 B_2 C_2 \rightarrow A_1 B_1 C_2 \rightarrow A_1 B_1 C_1$$

This progression seems to be the most appropriate direction in which to coordinate the industrial and economic policies of the recipient country. Although it is possible to go directly from the first stage to stage 4, the limiting factor will be the local technological capabilities of the recipient country.

THE EXPERIENCE OF INDUSTRIALIZATION AND TECHNOLOGICAL DEVELOPMENT IN SOME SELECTED COUNTRIES

It is believed that the successful experience of industrial and technological development in some East Asian NICs may have many valuable lessons for other developing countries. The importance of the East Asian countries as a model can be attributed to their remarkable performance and their successful experience of development over the past three decades. These countries, which include the first-tier NICs known as tigers or dragons, namely Korea, Taiwan, Singapore and Hong Kong, along with the second generation of NICs, Thailand, Malaysia and Indonesia, have experienced an average growth rate of GNP per capita of near 7 per cent during the period 1965–90 and have also obtained 73.5 per cent of developing countries' manufactured exports in 1990 (World Bank, 1993).

The diversity of these countries in some overall economic indicators such as per capita income, natural resources, and the process of their industrialization, can be helpful for other developing countries with different characteristics in pursuing their own development strategies. Although there are some differences in the stage of development, size of economy and resource endowment, the industrial and technological development experiences of these countries has been of interest to most less-developed countries (LDCs), in particular those which attempt to promote their technological capability through the same pattern of rapid industrialization. The critical success factors of these countries which have led to their rapid industrial and technological development will now be analysed. Singapore and Hong Kong are excluded in this survey primarily because their small size as city states distinguishes them from other East Asian NICs.

Republic of Korea

The remarkable success of South Korea in its very rapid growth rate and industrialization, known as 'the Han-river miracle', has been one of the outstanding success stories of international development. One can generally refer to some factors such as the Confucian ethics (Song, 1990), US aid in the late 1950s and early 1960s (Edwards, 1992; Haliday, 1987), the effective and supportive role of the state (Amsden, 1989; Wade, 1992; Westphal, 1990; Choi, 1994), and a set of appropriate industrial and technological policies (Pilat, 1994; Chang, 1993; Kuznets, 1994).

This includes an early transition to export promotion policies from previous import substitution policies, and also policies which encouraged and facilitated the importation of modern technologies and strengthened its local technological capability. Moreover, Korea's human resource development policy has also played a significant role in providing the high-skilled labour force needed for the absorption and assimilation of foreign technologies. One can also add Korea's efficient macro-economic policies which enabled this country to have the relatively stable economic situation required for successful development. However, one should say that the Korean success is not only the result of a single factor, but a combination of these factors and supportive government policies.

It is argued that the adoption of a strong export-orientation policy facilitated the rapid acquisition of technological capability in Korea in at least two ways. Firstly, the adoption of an outward-looking and export-expansion policy encouraged Korean industrial firms to invest more in technology in order to be able to compete in the world market. Moreover, expansion of exports also accelerated the process of catching-up technologically by allowing imports of goods embodying new technology. The export-promotion policy also assisted Korean enterprises in acquiring the necessary technological capability through informal technical assistance offered by foreign buyers to ensure that Korean-made products met their technical specifications. Therefore, pursuing an outward-oriented and export promotion industrialization policy can be viewed generally as an effective incentive that accelerates the accumulation of human capital and foreign technology (Dollar and Sokoloff, 1994).

Despite the significant effect of export expansion in the rapid industrialization of Korea, this strategy has been criticized by some authors who identified it as a cause of technological dependency (Wu, 1987). They believed that the emphasis on export-oriented production often led to the importation of a substantial amount of foreign inputs needed for producing intermediate goods. In 1990, 22.4 per cent of goods manufactured in Korea were based on foreign technology (foreign parts and inputs needed to produce manufactured goods), compared to 6.2 per cent in Japan, and 1.6 per cent in the US. Of Korea's total exports in 1990, 55 per cent were based on foreign technology (Kim, 1993).

However, as indicated earlier, importing foreign technology has been of great importance in Korea's rapid industrial and technological development. The massive introduction and acquisition of foreign technologies during different stages of its industrialization process enabled Korea to upgrade and develop the existing labour-intensive industries and new technology-intensive industries. Much of the foreign technology has been transferred to Korea through importing capital goods. Although some other methods such as turnkey agreements and reverse-engineering have also been used in the early stages of Korea's industrialization, the importation of technology embodied in machinery and equipment remained the major channel at about 21 times that of other means of technology transfer in terms of value during the period between 1962–1986 (Kim, 1990).

As indicated earlier, the adoption of a set of effective and appropriate industrial and technological policies has been among the most important factors of Korean success. The technological development strategy pursued by Korea in the process of its industrialization has been the introduction of appropriate technology from developed countries for assimilation and improvement, while simultaneously promoting the development of a domestic technological capability. Therefore, the Korean government planned an intensive programme emphasizing expansion of education and training of the labour force in order to promote their capability of absorbing and assimilating foreign technology. The Korean government has also supported institutional

R&D through a number of government assisted organizations in order to promote the country's indigenous technological development. The government has also formulated a long-range plan known as 'Science and Technology Toward the 2000s'. The main objectives of the plan are specializing R&D activities in some high-technology industries such as informatics, bio-technology and new materials, where the country can establish comparative advantage by the year 2000. It is also hoped that the dependency of Korea's industry on foreign technology will be substantially reduced with the successful implementation of the plan.

In summary, Korea's industrial and technological policies can offer useful implications for policy-makers in other developing countries. However, it seems difficult for other developing countries to replicate the Korean model. One should note that some of Korea's institutional capabilities which were vital for its success, such as its high level of education, a well-developed infrastructure, and organisational structure, may not exist in most developing countries. As Lucas (1993) says, simply advising a society to follow the Korean model is like asking an aspiring basketball player to follow the Michael Jordan model.

Taiwan

The successful experience of industrial and technological development in Taiwan, as another first-tier East Asian NIC, has shared several common features with South Korea. Both Taiwan and South Korea followed similar industrialization policies such as an early transition to export-promotion, a heavy and chemical industrialization (HCI) drive, and intensive human resource and liberalization policies. However, there have been slight differences in some aspects such as the methods of technology transfer, the role of the state, and the scale of their industrial enterprises. As indicated earlier, South Korea pursued restrictive policies towards foreign direct investment at an early stage of its industrialization, and relied more on the importation of capital goods and foreign borrowing as a major channel for the transfer of technology. Taiwan, on the other hand, encouraged the flow of FDI through the open-door policies and introduction of various incentives for foreign investors. Taiwan has also employed licensing agreements, imitation and international subcontracting as a major means to acquire technology.

Moreover, while government intervention in both countries has played a significant role in developing adequate infrastructure needed

for strengthening their rapid industrial and technological development, it is argued that the government in Taiwan has been less interventionist and more moderate compared with the Korean government.
The government in Taiwan has also more actively encouraged the
decentralization of industrial activities, which has enabled Taiwan to
maintain a more labour-intensive growth pattern than Korea, achieving higher employment rates and a more equal distribution of income
(Hong, 1993). The state in Taiwan also seemed to manage the processes of foreign technology acquisition in such a way as to maximize
the impact of this technology on the local economy (Simon, 1992).
Moreover, while in South Korea the government has tended to enforce
its policies on larger-sized enterprises, the Taiwanese state exercized
less direct control over private firms and has intervened in key industrial sectors through a large number of small-scale firms.

Having surveyed the overall success factors of Taiwan's rapid industrialization, one can refer to some general factors such as US and
Japanese aid in the period 1950–1965 (Tsai, 1995), the Confucianist
ethic (Brick, 1992), the relatively well-developed infrastructure established during the Japanese colonial period (Brick, 1992; Tsai, 1995),
the effective and supportive role of government (Pang, 1992; Tsai,
1993), the appropriate industrial policy including an early switch to an
export-promotion policy (Kuo, 1983; Chou, 1985; Lin, 1994), and the
intensive human resource development policies (Lin, 1994; Dollar and
Sokoloff, 1994). As mentioned earlier in the case of Korea, it is not
only a specific factor which led to their success, but a combination of
the above factors that resulted in their significant prosperity.

However, various authors have emphasized one particular factor as
most effective and important for the rapid industrialization of Taiwan.
For example, in a survey of industrial policy, productivity growth, and
structural change in manufacturing industries in both Taiwan and
South Korea, Dollar and Sokoloff (1994) believe that a rapid accumulation of physical capital, human capital and technology has been
the key element of their success. Tsai (1995) also refers to the effective
development and utilization of human resources as the most significant factor of Taiwan's success. Kuo (1983), on the other hand, refers
to the adoption of an export promotion policy as a major contribution
to the rapid development of Taiwan.

It is argued that the export expansion strategy has been instrumental
in Taiwan's success. Since adopting an export-oriented policy in the
late 1950s, Taiwan's gross national product (GNP) and industrial
manufacturing has grown by average annual rates of 8.9 per cent and

13.4 per cent respectively. The share of manufactured products in total exports increased from 28 per cent in 1960 to 77 per cent in 1970, and reached 95.9 per cent by 1993 (Dollar and Sokoloff, 1994). As discussed in the case of Korea, the rapid expansion of manufacturing exports in Taiwan acted as a focusing device for technology investments. The export-oriented policy also encouraged the expansion of industries with a comparative advantage by concentrating resources in the country's most productive industries such as electronics, garments and textiles. The establishment of export processing zones (EPZs) since the early 1960s, along with the introduction of various export incentives such as tax exemption, low-interest export loans and so on, accelerated the flow of foreign investment and technology to Taiwan.

In terms of technological development, a number of effective industrial and technological policies have been implemented with the objectives of the acquisition and assimilation of foreign technologies and promotion of indigenous technological capability. The reduction of taxes on importing technology and encouraging FDI through various measures have led to a massive flow of foreign technologies to Taiwan. The development of research and development activity, and extensive investment in infrastructure and human resources have been among Taiwan's policies for strengthening domestic technological capability. The government in Taiwan also built an approximately 35 square mile industrial park to assist the development and growth of hig-tech industries, in particular computers and electronics.

In conclusion, the successful development experience of Taiwan showed that a society with limited resources, and a dense population, would be able to achieve significant results in the industrialization process through long-term planning and concerted effort. Other developing countries can also learn from Taiwan's experience that the adoption of set of appropriate policies including heavy investment in the development of human resources, promotion of export industries, and strengthening the technological capability through transferring technology can be among the most vital policies for their technological development.

Malaysia

Although Malaysia is classified in the second-tier NICs along with Thailand and Indonesia, some of its recent economic and industrial indicators, such as an annual average growth rate of GNP near 9 per cent, the share of manufacturing in GDP of 31.5 per cent, and the share of manufacturing exports of total exports of 74 per cent, indicate that Malaysia should be re-classified in the first-tier NICs (Tsai, 1995). The rapid economic and industrial development of Malaysia during the last 25 years can be attributed to the implementation of some specific industrial policies and plans.

Malaysia adopted an import-substitution policy in the early stage of its industrialization, which mostly involved assembly, packaging and final processing of finished goods previously imported from abroad. Although the import substitution policy assisted Malaysia in building its industrial infrastructure and to some extent contributed to growth, because of a limited domestic market and the introduction of the investment incentives act in 1968 the emphasis of industrial policy in Malaysia shifted to an export promotion policy in the early 1970s. This shift was accompanied by the announcement of a new economic policy (NEP) in 1971, and was followed by the Industrial Co-ordination Act (ICA) of 1975, which resulted in a significant increase in the country's economic and industrial growth. For instance, one can refer to the increase in the share of manufacturing in GDP from 12.2 per cent in 1970 to 14.4 per cent in 1975 (Kuo, 1983).

In the early 1980s, the implementation of the heavy industrialization drive led to the expansion of heavy and chemical industries such as integrated steel mills, the petrochemical complex and the automobile industry, and a shift from labour-intensive to capital and technology-intensive industries. It is also argued that Malaysia followed the Japanese and Korean model of industrial and technological development through the adoption of its 'look East' policies in the early 1980s. This has been more because Japan and Korea suggested development paths less threatening to traditional Malay culture. It is also believed that adoption of an industrial culture which increased productivity, hard work and financial discipline has been a necessary precondition for successful industrialization in Malaysia (Yu, 1995). The highest share of Japan as a major supplier of technology in Malaysia can also be attributed to Malaysia's look East policy. Malaysia has been able to adapt, assimilate and absorb technologies transferred by Japan and other East Asian NICs.

Technology transfer to Malaysia has accelerated the growth rate of economic and industrial development through government policies for the assimilation and absorption of foreign technologies, and promotion of its domestic technological capability. It should be noted that most technologies have been transferred to Malaysia through imports of capital equipment and machinery and complete plants or turnkey projects. Moreover, Malaysian firms have recently obtained their required technologies by entering into joint ventures or licensing agreements with foreign partners. However, as mentioned earlier in the case of Korea and Taiwan, due to its heavy dependence on foreign parts and components, the technological dependency has been even higher in Malaysia.

Malaysia's other industrial policies implemented in the 1980s included the Industrial Master Plan (IMP) for the period 1985–95, with new long-term objectives such as increasing the indigenous technological capability through further utilization of the country's comparative advantage and development of its resource-based industries. The IMP has also encouraged the export of manufacturing exports by providing further export incentives such as tax and custom duties exemptions. As a result, there has been a significant performance in manufacturing exports in all of Malaysia's industrial sectors, which in most industries exceeded the IMP export targets (*Far Eastern Economic Review*, 1989).

In 1991, a National Development Policy (NDP) replaced the New Economic Policy (NEP) whose targets were unlikely to be achieved by 1990. The NDP's main objective proposed by the Prime Minister, Dr Mahatir Mohammad, as a new vision was for Malaysia to become a fully industrialized country by the year 2020. This objective is supposed to be achieved by implementing a number of strategies including more investment in R&D activities (increasing R&D expenditure per GNP to 2 per cent by the year 2000), further support policies for human resource development, attracting more FDI by allowing up to 100 per cent foreign equity in the export oriented sector, and continuing the promotion of indigenous technological capability through the diffusion and assimilation of foreign technologies.

In sum, having surveyed the success factors of Malaysian economic and industrial development during the past three decades, one can refer to some general reasons such as its rich endowment in natural resources, the existence of relatively adequate infrastructure and industrial facilities, the high level of FDI, and the role of the government in directing the industrialization process through a set of effective industrial and technological strategies. Therefore, one can generally say that like the first-tier NICs such as Korea and Taiwan, Malaysia's experience of industrialization may also have valuable lessons for other developing countries in particular for those with similar characteristics.

Thailand

Thailand is another fast growth economy in Southeast Asia with an averaged real growth rate of 7 per cent over the past three decades. Thailand is also a resource-rich country with various agricultural and mineral resources which put this country among the world's leading exporters of rice in the 1970s, and the second and third largest producer of tungsten and tin. Like Malaysia, Thailand has achieved most of the criteria which are required to join the ranks of the first-tier NICs to become the fifth tiger, since about 1988. Some of these indicators include a period of double-digit GDP growth rate (11 per cent and 13 per cent in 1988 and 1989), its share of industrial sector per GDP (32 per cent), and the share of manufactured output in GDP (76 per cent). However, some of the other elements, in particular its social indicators such as enrolment in education, per capita GNP and income distribution were not adequate enough and needed to be improved.

It can be said that Thailand has pursued relatively similar industrial policies in comparison with those of neighbouring Malaysia. For example, Thailand began its industrialization programme by choosing the usual pattern of import substitution aimed at creating an industrial sector producing for the domestic market. Following its capability to meet local needs to some extent, and the saturation of the domestic market with Thai-made products, the industrial policies in Thailand shifted to export promotion policies in the early 1970s. Various export incentives have been given to Thai producers such as tax exemptions, low interest loans and credits in order to encourage them to export their products. These effective measures and incentives resulted in a significant increase in Thailand exports and particularly manufactured exports. Manufactured exports increased from 10 per cent of total exports in 1971 to 66 per cent of total exports in 1988. The value of exports of processed goods increased from 23 billion baht in 1973 to 67 billion baht in 1978 (Cho, 1990). It is also believed that Thailand favourable policies, along with its adequate infrastructure and low cost of labour which led to a massive relocation of export industries from Japan and the East Asian NICs, and also attracted a huge inflow of foreign investment, have been among major factors affecting its success in expanding exports (Pathmanathan, 1985).

Unlike Malaysia which implemented a heavy industrialization drive in the 1980s, heavy industries have been relatively underdeveloped in Thailand. The Thai industrial sector in the 1980s had a higher proportion of light industries, particularly food processing, beverages, leather and rubber products and textile industries. Thailand also lagged behind other East Asian first and second-tier NICs in science and technology education. Several statistics and figures indicate a lack of qualified human resources at all educational levels in Thailand, which acts as a major constraint on the development of technological capability. For example, the number of high school graduates has been only 30 per cent of the population in Thailand, compared with 94 per cent in South Korea, 91 per cent in Taiwan, 53 per cent in Malaysia, 71 per cent in Singapore and 68 per cent in the Philippines (Ismael, 1990). According to another statistic, the number of scientists and technicians per 10 000 of the population was only 14 for Thailand, in comparison with 524 for Korea, 256 for Singapore and, 78 for Indonesia. It is estimated that by the year 2000, Thailand's shortfall of engineers will range between 10 000 and 30 000 (World Bank, 1980).

It is argued that industrial and technological development policies in Thailand have followed more the Taiwanese model of industrialization. Therefore, unlike Malaysia which adopted the Korean model and relatively neglected the development of an efficient local supply base of parts and components and suffered from a high dependency on foreign parts and components, Thailand has established a strong industrial base which is less dependent on the importation of foreign parts and components. In 1988, Taiwan allocated the highest share of foreign direct investment (FDI) and technology to Thailand with about 28.6 per cent of its total foreign investment (Figure 9.3). Taiwanese investment in Thailand has been more concentrated in labour intensive industries such as footwear, electrical appliances, ceramics, food processing, textile and toys, due to Thailand's cheap labour as well as the similar cultural background and the existence of a large Chinese community (UNIDO, 1992).

Despite the significant role of foreign investment in the industrial development and transference of technology and managerial skills in the later stages to Thailand, however, it is believed that most technology has been transferred through other channels such as technical assistance agreements, licensing, joint ventures, and purchase of machinery and equipment, in the earlier stage of its industrialization.

In sum, Thailand's successful experience of a rapid transition from an agricultural economy to a newly-industrialized country (NIC) can be attributed to some specific factors such as its strong export promotion policies, its rich natural resources, its effective state role in directing the industrial development process, its relatively stable

Figure 9.3   Foreign direct investment in Thailand, 1998

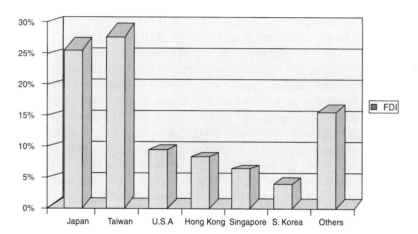

Source: UNIDO, United Nations Industrial Development Organization, 1992.

political and macroeconomic conditions, and the massive flow of FDI and technology.

Indonesia

Indonesia is another resource-rich country which is also classified in the second-tier NICs, with a total population of about 200 million living in more than 13 000 islands. The industrialization of Indonesia started much later than other Southeast Asian countries, because it took a longer time for the country to obtain a stable macroeconomic and political situation. Indonesia pursued an import substitution industrialization (ISI) policy during the period between (1965–85), financed largely by oil incomes and foreign aid and loans and directed through protection of domestic industries.

Indonesia entered the second stage of its ISI process in the 1970s, emphasizing more the expansion of intermediate and capital goods. The ISI strategy of the 1960s and 1970s was also accompanied by importing substantial qualities of foreign technology into Indonesia, much of which replaced older technologies. Increase in its oil revenues in the 1970s also enabled Indonesia to invest more in improving the infrastructure and general education needed for better acquisition of foreign technologies. The intensive transfer of technology also led to rapid modernization of both labour and capital intensive technologies in Indonesia during the 1970s. As a result of the relatively successful implementation of an import substitution policy, Indonesia achieved an annual average GDP growth rate of 7.9 per cent during the period 1973–81. According to another figure, the rate of growth in manufacture during the period 1967–81 increased 14-fold, which was mainly concentrated in the construction, transport and communication industries (Servaes, 1990).

However, because of a serious depression in the oil market and the general world recession of the early 1980s, the average annual growth rate of GDP decreased to 4.2 per cent during the period 1980–84. The rapid decline of oil prices in the mid-1980s eventually forced Indonesia to change to an export-oriented policy, emphasizing more the promotion of non-oil exports, particularly manufactured products. Following the adoption of the export promotion policy a series of policy measures including an effective currency devaluation, privatization and deregulation policies have also been introduced which resulted in an average annual increase of about 29 per cent in non-oil exports during the late 1980s (*Far Eastern Economic Review*, 1990).

The Indonesian government also encouraged the flow of foreign investment into the country in order to attract high technology and managerial expertise. Various measures have been introduced to encourage both domestic and foreign private investment. For example, one can refer to the recent privatization programme announced by the Indonesian government during late 1993 and early 1994, in which the shares of several state-owned companies were sold on the domestic and foreign capital markets. In addition to being an attractive place for foreign investors, mainly because of rich natural resources, cheap labour and large market size, the government in Indonesia also introduced some other incentives such as tax exemptions and establishing export-processing zones in order to attract more foreign investments. As result of these effective policy measures, the flow of FDI increased from $1.5 billion in 1987 to about $8 billion in 1993, mostly concentrated in export-oriented manufacturing industries (Lim and Fong, 1991).

Despite an important contribution of foreign investment in transferring technology and managerial expertise in the Indonesian manufacturing sector, other methods of acquisition of foreign technology such as importing capital and intermediate goods, joint ventures and licensing agreements have also been used. According to a survey of technology transfer through multinational companies (MNCs) in 12 manufacturing companies in Indonesia, the degree of local technological effort for achieving indigenous technological capability has been greater in the case of national companies which have purchased technology through licensing agreements than in the case of joint ventures between MNCs and Indonesian private or state-owned enterprises (Booth, 1992).

There are several common features in the industrial and technological development policies of Indonesia and other East Asian NICs. These policies include allowing unrestricted imports of machinery and equipment, massive investment in infrastructure and human resources, the acquisition of foreign technologies through appropriate selective channels and through limited well-considered government intervention, and introducing various export incentives measures in order to expand the export of manufactured products. However, as indicated earlier, Indonesia adopted an export-oriented industrialization policy later than other East Asian NICs.

SUMMARY AND CONCLUSIONS

The successful experiences of East Asian first and second-tier NICs in rapid industrial and technological development can be mainly attributed to the adoption of a set of appropriate policies. These have included a strong export-orientation industrialization strategy, massive investment in development of their human resources, education, technical training and infrastructure, and the development of their indigenous technological capability through the selection of appropriate methods of technology transfer. It should also be noted that the state in these countries has also played a vital role in directing these policies through providing an effective and supportive environment for their successful implementation.

Although it is realised that the successes of these countries are not the result of a single factor, it seems that the adoption of an export-promotion industrialization policy along with the acquisition of foreign technologies have contributed most to their industrial and technological development. As explained earlier, the very rapid growth rate of exports, and particularly manufactured exports, in these countries play a significant role in their success – and export promotion policies has greatly assisted this. Against this, these countries have had to be very efficient in the acquisition and absorption of foreign technology in order to remain competitive in the international market, which in turn has required massive investment in their technical human resources at all levels. In other words, the governments of countries like this need to play a visionary leadership role, with the efficient support of the private sectors, and governed and directed effective macro-industrial and technological policies incorporating massive investment in the accumulation and acquisition of foreign technologies, and upgrading of the skills of their labour forces.

One of the major lessons which other developing countries can learn from the success of these countries is that the importing of foreign

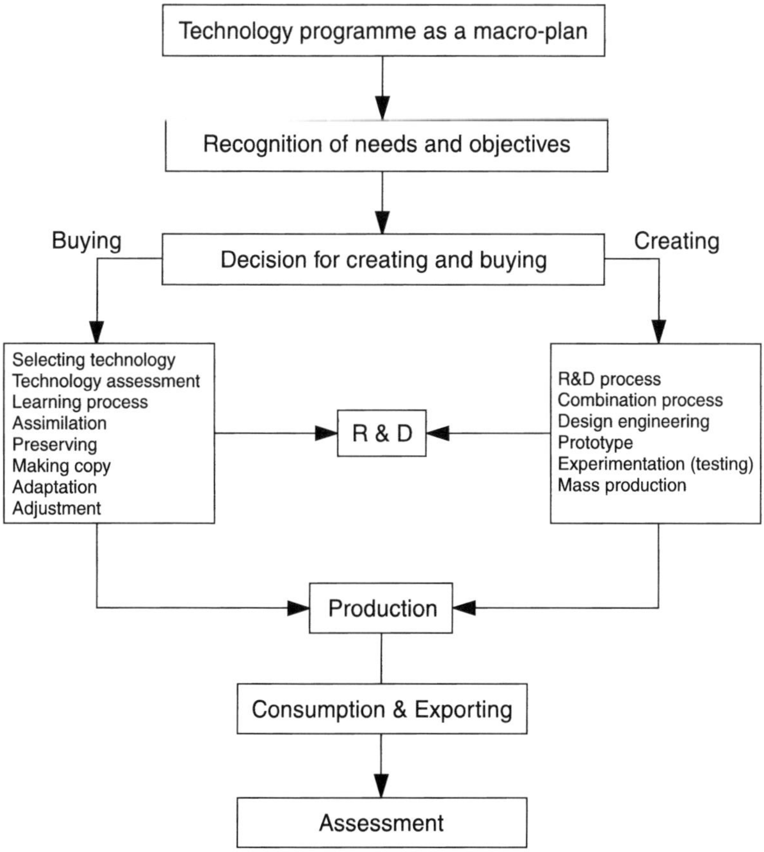

Figure 9.4   Self-sufficiency strategy for technology transfer

technology and the development of local technological capability has not been an alternative strategy but rather a complementary one. We can conclude that less-developed countries (LDCs) should adopt a strategy of technological transformation which pursues the following two closely related and mutually compatible objectives:

- Firstly, they must strengthen their indigenous technological capability through the creation of a research and development infrastructure with appropriate linkages to the production structure and thereby lessen their technological dependence;
- Secondly, they should adopt open policies toward the massive acquisition and diffusion of foreign technologies which promote their capability to compete in international markets.

If both of these processes are achieved simultaneously – importing technology from abroad, and strengthening their domestic technological capabilities – then each can help the other in the manner illustrated in Figure 9.4.

References

Adeoba, A. (1990) 'Technology Transfer and Joint Ventures: The Nigerian Experience', in UNCTAD (eds), *Joint Ventures as a Channel for the Transfer of Techonology*, United Nations, pp. 107–20.

Amsden, A.H. (1989) *Asia's Next Giant: South Korea and Late Industrialisation* (Oxford: Oxford University Press).

Booth, A. (1992) *The Oil Boom and After: Indonesian Economic Policy and Performance in the Suharto Era* (Oxford: Oxford University Press), p. 13.

Brick, A.B. (1992) 'The East Asian Development Miracle, Taiwan as a Model', *Issues and Studies*, vol. 28, no. 8, (August), pp. 1–12.

Buckley, P.J. (1985) 'New Forms of International Industrial Co-operations', in P.J. Buckley and M. Casson (eds), *The Economic Theory of the Multinational Enterprise* (London: Macmillan), pp. 39–59.

Chang, H.J. (1993) 'Political Economy of Industrial Policy in Korea', *Cambridge Journal of Economics*, vol. 17, pp. 131–57.

Chesnais, F. (1986) 'Science, Technology and Competitiveness', STI Review.

Cho, G. (1990) *The Malaysian Economy: Special Perspective* (London: Routledge), p. 200.

Choi, H.S. and Mok, Y. (1986) 'Technology Development in a Developing Country', Asian Productivity Organization, Tokyo, p. 145.

Choi, Y.B. (1994) 'Industrial Policy for Economic Development: Lessons from the South Korean Experience', *Human System Management*, vol. 13, pp. 111–21.

Chou, T.C. (1985) 'Industrial Organisation in the Process of Economic Development, The Case of Taiwan, 1950–1980', *Ciaco*, p. 37.

Cooper, C. and Sercovich, F. (1971) *The Channels and Mechanisms for the Transfer of Technology from Developed to Developing Countries*, UNCTAD: (TD/B/AC.11/5).

Dollar, D. and Sokoloff, K.L. (1994) 'Industrial Policy, Productivity Growth, and Structural Change in the Manufacturing Industries: A Comparison of Taiwan and South Korea', in J.D. Surrey, Aberbach, D. Dollar and K.L. Sokoloff (eds), *The Role of the State in Taiwan's Development*, (Eastgate Publishers) pp. 5–25.

Edwards, C. (1992) 'Industrialisation in South Korea', in T. Hewitt, H. Johnson and D. Wield (eds), *Industrialisation and Development* (Oxford: Oxford University Press), p. 125.

Erdilek, A. and Rapoport, A. (1985) 'Conceptual and Measurement Problems in International Technology Transfer: A Critical Analysis', in A.C. Samli (ed.), *Technology Transfer, Geographic, Economic, Cultural, and Technical Dimensions* (London: Quorum Books), pp. 252–3.

Far Eastern Economic Review (1989) 'The Industrial Master Plan of Malaysia', 7 September, p. 96.

Far Eastern Economic Review (1990) 'Thailand: Education Policy May Stall Economic Boom', 8 March.

Gee, S. (1981) *Technology Transfer, Innovation and International Competitiveness* (London: John Wiley), p. 10.

Haliday, J. (1987) 'The Economies of North and South Korea', in J. Sullivan and R. Foss (eds), *Two Koreas – One Future?* (Lanham, Md: University Press of America), p. 36.

Hong, W. (1993) 'Trade and Development: The Experience of Korea and Taiwan', in G. Hansson (ed.), *Trade, Growth and Development, The Role of Policies and Institution* (London: Routledge).

Ismail, M.Y. (1990) 'Export Competitiveness: Objectives and Performance of the Industrial Master Plan', *Journal of the Faculty of Economics* (Journal Ekonomi Malaysia), vols. 21 & 22, pp. 99–118.

Kanayak, E. (1985) 'Transfer of Technology from Developed to Developing Countries: Some Insights from Turkey', in A.C. Samli (ed.), *Technology Transfer, Geographical, Economic, Culture and Technical Dimensions* (London: Quorum Books), pp. 155–6.

Karake, Z.A. (1990) *Technology and Developing Economies: The Impact of Eastern European versus Western Technology Transfer* (London: Praeger), p. 52.

Kim, I. (1993) 'Managing Korea's System of Technological Innovation', Interfaces, vol. 23, no. 6, November–December, pp. 13–24.

Kim, L. (1990) 'Korea: The Acquisition of Technology', in H. Soesastro and M. Pangesto (eds), *Technological Challenge in the Asia-Pacific Economy* (London: Allen & Unwin), pp. 150.

Kim, L. (1991) 'Pros and Cons of International Technology Transfer: A Developing Country View', in T. Agmon and M.A.V. Glinow (eds), *Technology Transfer in International Business* (Oxford: Oxford University Press), pp. 223–39.

Kuo, S.K.Y. (1983) *The Taiwan Economy in Transition* (Boulder: Westview Press).

174   *International Technology Transfer to LDCs*

Kuznets, P.W. (1994) *Korean Economic Development: An Interpretative Model* (London: Praeger), p. 8.

Lall, S. (1993) 'Promoting Technology Development: The Role of Technology Transfer and Indigenous Effort', *Third World Quarterly*, vol. 14, no. 1, pp. 95–109.

Lim, L.Y.C. and Fong, P.E. (1991) *Foreign Investment and Industrialisation in Malaysia, Singapore, Taiwan and Thailand* (Development Centre, Paris: OECD), p. 50.

Lin, O.C.C. (1994) 'Development and Transfer of Industrial Technology in Taiwan', in O.C.C. Lin, C.T. Shih and J.C. Yang (eds), *Development and Transfer of Industrial Technology* (London: Elsevier Science), pp. 1–29.

Lucas, R. (1993) 'Making a Miracle', *Econometrica*, vol. 61, no. 2, pp. 251–72.

Madu, C.N. (1988) 'An Economic Decision Model for Technology Transfer', *Engineering Management International*, vol. 5, pp. 53–62.

Marton, K. (1986) 'Technology Transfer to Developing Countries via Multi-nationals', *World Economics*, vol. 9, no. 4, December, pp. 409–26.

Nelson, R. and Winter, S. (1977) 'In the Search of a Useful Theory of In-novation', *Research Policy*, vol. 6, pp. 36–76.

Olukoshi, A.O. (1990) 'The Dynamics of Corporate Technology Transfer to Nigeria', in M. Chatterji (ed.), *Technology Transfer to Developing Countries* (London: Macmillan), pp. 366–7.

Osada, H. (1994) 'Trade Liberalisation and FDI Incentives in Indonesia: The Impact on Industrial Productivity', *The Developing Economies*, vol. 32, no. 4, pp. 479–91.

Pang, C.K. (1992) The State and Economic Transformation: The Taiwan Case (London: Garland Publishing), p. 273.

Pathmanathan, M. (1985) 'Malaysia in 1984: A Political and Economic Sur-vey', *Southeast Asian Affairs*, pp. 211–321.

Perlmutter, H.V. and Saghafi-nejad, T. (1988) *International Technology Trans-fer: Guidelines, Codes and Muffled Quadrilogue* (London: Pergamon), p. 9.

Pilat, D. (1994) *The Economics of Rapid Growth: The Experience of Japan and Korea* (Cheltenham: Edward Elgar), pp. 218–19.

Prasad, A.J. (1981) 'Technology Transfer to Developing Countries through Multinational Corporations', in R.G. Hawkins and A.J. Prasad (eds), *Technology Transfer and Economic Development: Research in International Business and Finance*, vol. 2 (Greenwich Conn: JAI Press), pp. 151–73.

Prasad, A.J. (1981) 'Licensing as an Alternative to Foreign Investment for Technology Transfer', in R.G. Hawkins and A.J. Prasad (eds), *Technology Transfer and Economic Development: Research in International Business and Finance, ibid.*, pp. 193–218.

Servaes, J. (1990) 'Technology Transfer in Thailand: For Whom and for What?', *Journal of Contemporary Asia*, vol. 20, no. 2, pp. 277–86.

Simon, D.F. (1992) 'Taiwan's Strategy for Creating Competitive Advantage: The Role of the State in Managing Technology', in N.T. Wang (ed.), *Taiwan in the Modern World*, (Surrery: Eastgate Publishers) p. 98.

Song, B.N. (1990) *The Rise of the Korean Economy* (Oxford: Oxford Uni-versity Press).

Stewart, C. T. and Nihei, Y. (1987) *Technology Transfer and Human Factors* (New York: Lexington Books), p. 2.

Telesio, P. (1984) 'Foreign Licensing in Multinational Enterprises', in R. Stobaugh and L.T. Wells (eds), *Technology Crossing Borders of International Technology Flows* (Boston, Mass.: Harvard Business School Press), p. 178.

Tsai, G.W. (1993) 'Taiwan's Economic Modernisation and its Implication for Other Developing Countries', *Issues and Studies*, vol. 29, no. 6, June, pp. 61–79.

Tsai, G.W. (1995) 'Industrial Restructuring and the Development of Human Resources in the Republic of China', *Industry of Free China*, vol. 83, no. 3, March, pp. 55–66.

Tsang, E.W.K. (1994) 'Strategies for Transferring Technology to China', *Long Range Planning*, vol. 27, no. 3, pp. 98–107.

UNIDO (1992) *Thailand, Coping with the Strains of Success* (New York: The United Nations Industrial Development Organisation), p. 52.

United Nations Centre on Transitional Corporations (1995) *Transitional Corporations and Technology Transfer: Effects and Policy Issues* (New York: UNCTC), pp. 1–2.

Vakil, C.N. and Brahmanda, P.R. (1990) 'Technical Knowledge and Managerial Capacity as Limiting Factors on Industrial Expansion in Underdeveloped Countries', in A. Robinson (ed.), *Economic Progress*, 2nd edn (New York: St Martins Press), pp. 153–72.

Wade, R. (1992) 'East Asian Economic Success', *World Politics*, vol. 44, January, pp. 270–320.

Westphal, L.E. (1990) 'Industrial Policy in a Export-oriented Economy: Lessons from South Korea's Experience', *Journal of Economic Perspectives*, vol. 4, no. 3, pp. 41–58.

Wie, T.K. (1990) 'Indonesia: Technology Transfer in the Manufacturing Industry', in H. Soesarto and M. Pangestu (eds), *Technological Challenge in the Asia and Pacific Economy* (London: Unwin Hyman), p. 231.

The World Bank (1980) *Thailand: Industrial Development Strategy in Thailand*, (Washington, DC: World Bank Country Study), p. 8.

The World Bank (1992) *Indonesia: Developing Private Enterprises* (Washington, DC: World Bank), pp. 6–8.

The World Bank (1993) *Global Economic Prospects and the Developing Countries* (Washington, DC: IBRD).

The World Bank (1993) *The East Asian Miracle, Economic Growth and Public Policy*, A World Bank Policy Research Report, Washington, DC, p. 38.

Wu, R.I. (1987) 'The Economic Development of the Newly Industrialised Countries in East Asia', in P. West and A. Von Geusau (eds), *The Pacific Rim and Western World, Strategic, Economic and Cultural Perspectives* (London: Westview Press), pp. 179–97.

Yu, T.S. (1995) 'Industrial Policies of Republic of China on Taiwan: Review and Evaluation', *Industry of Free China*, vol. 83, no. 6, June, pp. 49–59.

Zahid, S.N. (1994) *Intra-Regional Investment and Technology Transfer: A South Asian Perspective* (Tokyo: Asian Productivity Organisation (APO), p. 57.

10 Techonological Change: The Impact of Different Cultures, Institutional Frameworks and Organizational Imperatives

R.L. Ritchie, L. Zhuang, R. Hudson-Davies and W. Williams

INTRODUCTION

Three elements may be identified as key determinants of success in the adoption and development of new technologies, which lie at the heart of economic development:

1. cultural contexts;
2. institutional frameworks; and
3. organizational imperatives.

This chapter develops a model to explore the impact of these factors. The model is set in the context of changes in the global economy, and developments in Singapore are examined to illustrate the model.

The first section provides a brief review of the background to the issues involved in discussing technological change within the global economy, including some of the myths that are commonly held. This is followed by an outline of the model that illustrates the three key elements under consideration and the potential impact of cultural differences and other contextual factors on the pace of economic growth and development. Finally, the chapter considers the effects of cultural differences, institutional frameworks and organizational imperatives on the adoption of new technologies.

BACKGROUND

The conventional ethnocentric view is that western countries do not suffer from a lack of creativity but they are considered to be very poor at innovation. Far-eastern countries, on the other hand, have displayed a considerable capacity to copy western ingenuity but are generally perceived to be less creative. Central and Eastern Europe is regarded as both a creative and innovative wasteland.

However, these 'bar-room' beliefs are being rapidly eroded by two forces. Firstly, western academics, who dominate the written and spoken word in the areas of creativity, innovation and entrepreneurship, are increasingly beginning to realise that 'Far-eastern' collectivist, incremental and adaptive innovative processes are as effective and perhaps more sustainable than western individual, competitive means of creating and taking product to the market (Drucker, 1985; Thorne, 1992; Tatsuno, 1990). Secondly, it is recognised that the Far East is becoming more creative in terms that western observers can readily identify and relate to. Thorne states that, *'there have been few totally new products initiated in Japan by Japanese. This is changing. They are changing'* (Thorne, 1992, p. 182). The concerns within Europe about these issues and their impact on the competitiveness of European industry are reflected in the recent publication of the European Commission's Green Paper on Innovation. In introducing the paper, the Commissioner responsible, Edith Cresson, stated that *'What the authorities must do is to provide an environment where the spark can, as it were, catch light, and to remove any obstacles that can dampen the flame'* (Cresson, 1996, p. 5).

Global competition has created, and will continue to create, pressure on business enterprises to increase their resource efficiency. This leads to pressures to develop technological and new forms of innovation. *'Innovation has become like motherhood in business. There is overwhelming evidence that it is a key factor in success'* (Trapp, 1995, p. 8).

An example of the responsiveness of Far East organizations to the competitive pressures can be seen in the communications field. One of the latest examples is the development of 'dual-mode phones'. A report in the *Financial Times* (Cole, 1996) commented on the innovations in this area in the Far East:

Thousands of telephone users in Japan are discovering that one handset is better than two. They are using cordless phones designed

to act both as a mobile phone and a conventional fixed-line tele-
phone in a home or office. Meanwhile, dual-mode handsets for
European markets are being developed by Siemens and Motorola,
with the latter planning also to launch a system for its home US
market.

The report went on to reveal that

Other Asian territories, including Hong Kong and Singapore, are
planning to launch PHS services. China, Indonesia, Malaysia and
Thailand are studying the system. In October, NTT and the UK's
Cable and Wireless formed a joint venture to promote PHS outside
Japan (*The Financial Times* (Internet version), 25 January 1996).

This is an example of Japan leading the way in innovation, with its
Asian neighbours following suit while western countries lag behind.
What is interesting about this is not the nature of the technological
change and innovation but, rather, the vivid manifestation of the shift
of economic power from the West to the Far East, especially Japan
and the newly-industrialised countries (NICs).

Clearly the rise of Japan's economic power and the subsequent
emergence of the four Asian NICs (Shibusawa *et al.*, 1992) is connected to their ability to utilise technology to boost economic growth.
However, the traditional and superficial association between economic
development and technological change needs to be re-evaluated if we
are to understand this relationship. Similarly, the division of the world
into two camps, the East and the West, according to the somewhat
over-exaggerated differences of social systems and political ideologies
must be re-examined.

OUTLINE OF THE MODEL

Innovation is the specific tool of entrepreneurs, the means by which
they exploit change as an opportunity for a different business or a
different service. It is capable of being learnt, capable of being prac-
tised (Drucker, 1985, p. 17).

Drucker's view that the practices and processes involved in successful
innovation are capable of transfer to other organizations and situations provides an important tenet for the approach adopted in this
chapter. The model developed places more emphasis on the contextual

Figure 10.1   A model of technological change

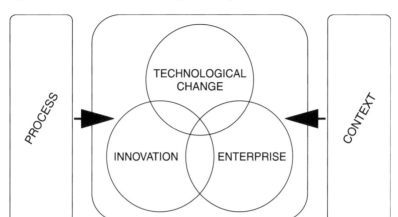

variables than the process variables, and recognises that the successful application of these are contingent on the particular organization, country and society. Figure 10.1 illustrates a general view of global competition whilst Figure 10.2 provides a more detailed view of the contextual variables and their impact on the dimensions of technological change.

Technical change, innovation and enterprise are closely interrelated and the effectiveness of managing this interrelationship is arguably the key to success in global competition. There are two broad perspectives from which this interrelationship may be considered, the process view and the contextual situation within which these processes take place. It would be foolish to argue that these may be considered in total isolation from each other as the context will clearly influence the nature and outcome of the process. It may also follow that the nature of the processes involved in innovation and adopting technological developments may lead to changes in the context, especially at the organizational level (for example modification to the organization structure, or changes in the attitudes and culture of those employed).

The model in Figure 10.2 represents an adaptation of a model by Hofstede (1984). The model introduces cultural variables, institutional frameworks and organizational imperatives as determinants of technological change. The questions that this type of model pose include:

- How effective are the diffusion processes in terms of technological developments across international boundaries?

Figure 10.2   Technical change – the cultural mechanisms

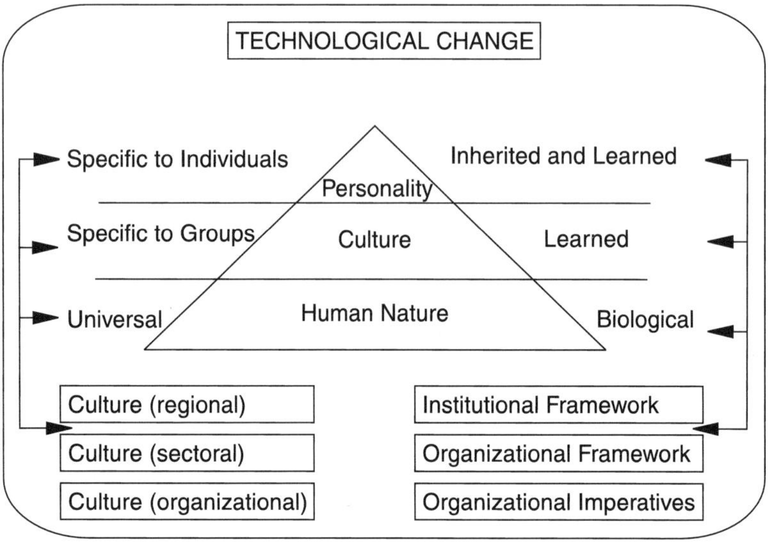

- Given the knowledge and availability of technological developments are there particular barriers or facilitators to adopting these?
- Are certain cultures more conducive to generating ideas?
- Do particular cultures enhance organizational capabilities in adopting and adapting technologies and effectively implementing them?
- What role does enterprise culture play in successful technological
  change?
- Can these various elements be disaggregated to allow their relative
  importance to be assessed?

Within the contextual view of this model of global competition there
are three different though integrated sets of factors:

- *Cultural differences* – especially the business culture.
- *Institutional frameworks* – the legal, political and economic factors
  at the national, regional and international levels.
- *Organizational imperatives* – the strategic importance of the innovation process to the particular organization at differing stages
  in its evolution.

ECONOMIC GROWTH AND CULTURAL DIFFERENCES

The initial approach to analysing the influence that cultural differences may have on technological change and hence global competition examines the link with economic growth. The earlier discussion on the background to the paper suggested a set of universally held beliefs that there may be an association between economic growth and culture.

There have been a number of documented attempts to study the relationship between national economic growth and cultural differences (Weber, 1904; Schumpeter, 1934; McClelland, 1976; Wiener, 1981). The latest study of this kind with a scale matching these previous studies was conducted by Lynn (1991) to test the theories previously devised, namely Weber's work ethic, Schumepter's concept of the culture of competitiveness, McClelland's achievement motivation, and Wiener's status of the land-owner. A questionnaire was assembled involving these four sets of variables and was administered to university student samples in 43 countries, two of which were later dropped (Lynn, 1991, p. 15). Questionnaire results achieved from the 41 countries were then correlated to their respective annual national rates of economic growth over the period between 1970 and 1985 (Lynn, 1991, p. 47).

Among the four sets of variables, only competitiveness showed a positive association with rates of economic growth. The relationship between competitiveness and growth is illustrated in Table 10.1.

Table 10.1 Comparison of economic growth and competitiveness

Country	Score on competitiveness	Economic growth (1970–1985)%
Korea	13.66	8.4
Taiwan	13.39	7.8
Hong Kong	12.64	8.4
China	12.37	7.3
Japan	12.21	4.5
Singapore	11.38	8.3
Belgium	10.75	2.5
France	10.19	2.9
Britain	10.04	2.1
Norway	9.60	4.3
Germany	9.10	2.3
Sweden	9.05	2.0
Switzerland	8.99	1.4

Source: Lynn 1991.[13]

These results seemed to suggest that a high level of competitiveness was responsible for rapid economic growth. However, it is not clear if a competitive culture leads to growth or whether the reverse is true. During the early days of industrialization, many Japanese companies had the reputation of copying everything from the West. At this time, few countries in the West regarded the Japanese as serious competitors, but through the adoption of western technologies and the implementation programmes of continuous improvement Japan achieved its highest national economic growth and soon became a world-class economic giant rivalling the USA (Chen, 1995, p. 25). It is possible that the development of a competitive culture is the effect of high economic growth. At least, cultural variables such as competitiveness alone cannot fully explain economic growth.

Other Factors Contributing to Economic Growth

Economists have generally agreed that the following are the most important factors affecting growth (Lynn, 1991, p. 24):

- the strength and stability of demand;
- the rate of technical progress;
- the growth and level of capital stock;
- international diffusion mechanisms;
- structural changes in employment patterns.

Almost all the above factors are affected one way or the other by innovation and technological change. Their combination usually reflects the priorities national governments place on the development of their national economy. This is where cultural differences, together with such factors as ideological differences and national resource capacities, can influence economic development. For example, Pheysey (1993) makes the following comparison between China and the UK:

> *In China, the leadership tends to give priority to ideological goals, but is forced to concentrate on order when disaffection shows itself and on economic goals when order has been restored, for only when the economy is growing is there a base from which to push further ideology. In the UK, governments tend to give priority to economic goals, but have to respond to political pressures of an ideological kind when social divisions grow* (p. 19).

Different Types of Capitalism

The rise of East and South Asian nations as major economic powers has caused many authors to question the basis for the Weberian thesis that associates economic prosperity with the Protestant work ethic. According to Chen (1995),

> *The same set of values blamed for the lack of capitalist development in East Asia began to be used to explain why a particular kind of entrepreneurial spirit prevalent in East Asia had been so successful in developing a competitive edge against the West* (p. 28).

Tu (1984) has argued that western capitalism is largely based on individualism, mastery over the world, the *laissez-faire* economy, the market mechanism, and the quest for specialized knowledge. Whereas eastern capitalism is based on the Confucian ethic that regards the self as the centre of relationships, thereby leading to a new kind of entrepreneurial spirit and management style. In other words, the central difference between capitalism in the West and in the East is that one is based on the individualistic approach whilst the other is founded on a more collective approach (Child and Bate, 1987, p. 20).

The influence of individualism or collectivism over the economic behaviour of individuals in their respective cultural environments is so deeply rooted that it is often taken for granted. For example, the proper way of addressing an envelope in the Orient is to follow the order of country, province, county/city, main street, side street, house number, surname and forename whilst in the West the order is reversed. However, few people stop to question the origin of these social and cultural conventions. Moreover, the same type of differences exist in the behaviour of organizations and they are largely conditioned by different cultural environments.

Hofstede (1980) has developed the most famous model of cultural differences in which he identified four dimensions:

1. *Power distance* – the extent to which the less powerful expect and accept that power is distributed unequally.
2. *Uncertainty avoidance* – the extent to which uncertain or unknown situations are perceived as threatening.
3. *Individualism/collectivism* – the extent to which individuals and families are expected to look after themselves.
4. *Masculinity/femininity* – the extent to which 'masculine' values such as assertiveness, ambition or achievement, dominate as

opposed to 'feminine' values, such as relationships, quality of life and service.

In more recent works Hofstede has added a fifth dimension, *long-term orientation* to his model which, according to Goffee (1996), '*appears to be a particular distinctive feature of East Asian cultures*' (p. 2).

TECHNOLOGICAL CHANGE AND STAGES OF ECONOMIC DEVELOPMENT

The remarkable economic growth achieved in many countries, such as the USA, Japan and the NICs, has been accompanied by a series of governmental and entrepreneurial initiatives that sought to encourage technological change. Depending on the stage of economic development, some of these initiatives are directed towards improving productivity whilst others are directed towards developing value-added features for products and services.

In the early stage of industrialization in Asian countries, a strategy of mass production of low-tech products to take advantage of their low labour cost was followed (Bernard and Ravenhill, 1995). These products were then exported to the developed countries in exchange for foreign currency and technical and managerial know-how. Whilst foreign direct investment (FDI) was encouraged – perhaps not so much in Japan – technological innovations at this stage usually fell into the category of technology transfer. Many developing countries, such as China and Indonesia, are currently at this stage of development (Shibusawa *et al.*, 1992).

As the domestic economy continued to grow, so did the standard of living and hence labour costs. The loss of comparative cost advantage then forced companies to shift to high-tech manufacturing. In order to justify the premium prices charged for their products, the focus of innovation at this stage tended to be the continuous improvement of product and process design (Chen, 1995, p. 199). The development and modification of the Walkman from the initial tape recorder provides a perfect example. Both Japan and the four Asian NICs went down this path at various stages of their development. As factor costs continued to rise, many successful companies sought to build on their competitive advantage by other means. This usually took the form of overseas investment and outward technology transfer. As far as FDI is concerned, Japan has now become indisputably the most dominant Asian power. The four Asian NICs were also not slow in redirecting their financial resources and technical expertise to the less-developed countries (MIDA, 1995, p. 1).

TECHNOLOGICAL CHANGE AND INSTITUTIONAL FRAMEWORKS

Different cultures utilize different forms and structures in creativity and innovation. Academics have attempted to identify the causes of such differences (Child, 1994; Parsons, 1951; Hofstede, 1984, 1991, 1995; Kluckhohn and Strodtbeck, 1961; Nonaka, 1991a, 1991b; Hampden-Turner, 1983; Trompenaars, 1993). Studies such as these have focused on individual and group psychological factors that result in national and regional characteristic behaviour, that combine to form culture.

An analysis of how culture, institutional and organizational frameworks are related in the process of technological change provides a wider appreciation of the process than studies that focus on individual and group psychological factors. Hofstede found that culture is specific to groups and is learnt. Organizational and institutional frameworks allow groups to be targeted and the culture, via 'learning', to be altered. This can then be channelled into increased technological creativity and innovation.

Drucker's premise is that innovation can be learnt and that the 'systemization' of innovation processes evident in a country like Japan should be adopted by the West, if the West wishes to remain competitive. He states: *'this, however, requires that innovation itself be organised as a systematic activity'*. Kirton (1989, p. xvii–iii) identifies innovation as involving both the 'new' and 'novel', but also change, albeit of the 'breakthrough' variety. He also concludes that innovation can be learnt, in that 'preferred cognitive styles' can be altered to induce innovative solutions to problems.

Silvano Arieti (1976, p. 229) suggests several possible causes for creativity, all of which are inextricably linked with the key cultural components necessary for innovation within a particular societal grouping:

- availability of the physical means by which cultural factors can affect creativity;
- cultural enlightenment and tolerance;

- vision in society;
- open access;
- variations in levels of access;
- contrasting cultural stimuli;
- interaction of significant people; and
- incentives and rewards.

Arieti proposed that only the first factor was an absolute requirement, the others were observations of factors that seemed to boost creativity. Although it is unclear that one can have the cultural means without one or more of the other factors.

   However, a dilemma present itself – that is, whether organizational and institutional frameworks are a product of culture or do they develop the culture? Drucker's stance seems to indicate that these frameworks are part of the process of developing an innovative environment. However has there got to be a 'cultural ignitor' to set up these institutions? In Singapore the cultural ignitor for technological change has come in the form of a single political party and its two leaders.

SINGAPORE – A CASE STUDY OF SYSTEMATIZED TECHNOLOGICAL CHANGE

Singapore is one of the best examples of systematized (via the development of a preferred cognitive style) technological change. Since independence from the UK in 1958, Singapore's economic growth has been extraordinary. In 1994 growth was 10.1 per cent (1993 – 9.9 per cent), with inflation at 3.6 per cent (1993 – 2.4 per cent), and this has coincided with full employment. Over the past decade growth in GDP has averaged around 9 per cent (DTI, 1995). In the absence of any substantive natural resources, except its location and a deep water harbour, Singapore has developed one of the most advanced manufacturing and commercial centres in the world. Manufacturing contributes 27 per cent to the GDP, and financial services a further 26 per cent. Both sectors, successes have been based on strong technological innovation, led by electronics in the manufacturing sector. In 1995 the Swiss-based International Institute for Management Development ranked Singapore as second in terms of world competitiveness.

   The links between economic success, technological innovation, culture and institutional and organizational frameworks are perhaps easier to identify in Singapore because of the overt intervention and social management by the state.

CULTURAL FRAMEWORKS

In studies by Hofstede (1995) and Trompenaars (1993), Singapore's culture has been characterized by :

- a high regard for authority and the hierarchy (unlike Japan, the UK and US);
- a very low tolerance of ambiguity (more like the UK and US, less like Japan);
- high collective ethos (unlike the UK and the USA and to a certain extent Japan); and
- a less masculine approach, not open to expressing emotions (unlike Japan, the UK and the USA).

These are generalizations and such conclusions from subjective measures are always open to question, especially when the researchers both happen to be from the same European country. However, the findings are interesting in that the frameworks that have developed in Singapore to enhance technological change and innovation seem to either be the products, or the determinants, of the cultural types identified by Hofstede and Trompenaars. A study by Kirton (1989) on the characteristics of people who can adapt and innovate can be linked to the Hofstede and Trompenaars findings. Kirton identified the main characteristics of a successful adapter and they bear close correlation to the Singaporean cultural 'elements' identified by Hofstede and Trompenaars. Moreover, according to Arieti (1976) a concept of key cultural components for innovation can also be applied in Singapore's case.

Political figures, especially Lee Kuan Yew, have provided a strong vision of what type of culture is helpful for encouraging economic development. Furthermore, Singapore's geographic position and openness to foreign investment has allowed a relatively freeflow of ideas, and the multicultural make-up of the population has undoubtedly encouraged creativity. This process has been assisted by a capitalist model that has rewarded innovative endeavour. Singapore is criticized for obsessive control of its population, but nevertheless the underlying conditions have allowed a culture of creativity and innovation to be developed.

INSTITUTIONAL FRAMEWORKS

Undoubtedly the 'indigenous' ingredients that create the culture in Singapore have been utilized but it is also apparent that the institutional framework has been manipulated so that certain cultural elements have been more fully exploited or even new factors have been introduced – *'much of the culture of Singapore was created in the years after independence'* (Prewitt and Reinhardt, 1993, p. 6).

Since 1958 Singapore has been governed by a single party, the People's Action Party, and until 1990 it was led by Lee Kuan Yew, who was succeeded by Goh Chok Tong, as Prime Minister. The country is a parliamentary democracy and even the government's critics agree that the vast majority of the population support the incumbent administration. Both Lee and Goh have spear-headed one of the most, if not the most, successful 'interventionist' economies in the world, against the backdrop of the failures in Central and Eastern Europe and the former USSR. This has been achieved by careful economic and social conditioning. Lee Kuan Yew can best be described as a pragmatist. Although he was the leader of the communist party pre-independence, he allowed and, more importantly, promoted and developed an economy based on free market principles. However, the government has controlled the direction of the key market drivers; for example it has acquired strategic stakes in major enterprises and thus has maintained control of the commanding heights of the economy.

The government has established a number of institutions through which it has sought to transform its vision for Singapore into reality. In the 1960s and 1970s the primary concern was job creation. Full employment was achieved in the early 1970s. However, as low labour cost advantages were eroded the emphasis shifted towards value-added through technological improvements both to products and to processes.

This shift has been helped by the development of key institutional mechanisms. The government has encouraged foreign inward investment, whilst assisting indigenous companies through the Development Bank of Singapore (owned by the Economic Development Board, EDB). The bank has made investments in companies that by the 1970s amounted to 25 per cent of equity investments in the economy. Thus the government had a mechanism to channel capital into areas of the economy at will (Prewitt and Reinhardt, 1993).

Wage rises in Singapore are controlled by the administration through the National Wages Council. In 1979 the government departed from its previously very tight control on wage rates by allowing a significant wage increase (14–20 per cent), thus forcing companies to develop export-based high-technology manufacturing and services. This helped to offset the increased cost of labour. This high-risk strategy has appeared to be successful:

> *Our strategy is to induce entrepreneurs and managers of capital to increase efficiency of production by restructuring, automation and rationalisation . . . we also encourage them to upgrade into higher-technology industries that can generate more value-added products* (Goh Chok Tong, 1979).

The control and manipulation of wage rates to induce technological innovation showed the visionary macroeconomic view of the government without which it is unlikely that Singapore would have achieved its current level of development.

In 1985 a severe recession led to negative growth and unemployment. The government concluded that in addition to unfavourable global conditions, Singapore had certain structural deficiencies. In particular, it was felt that the government had become too interventionist in the private sector and changes were instigated that allowed greater freedom for market forces to produce a more self-regulating system.

The institutional frameworks established since independence appear to have been driven by the government's desire for Singapore to be competitive. To achieve this the structure has been market-driven, but with state intervention where it appears that the market does not provide sufficient stimuli in a particular area, for example EDB's Manufacturing 2000 programme. 'Social Engineering' in the form of mechanisms such as the Central Provident Fund (CPF) and the Housing Development Board (HDB) ensure that the population as a whole realizes that the country has to remain competitive to maintain the relatively high standards they enjoyed.

Education is held at a premium and the government seeks to promote innovation through schools, colleges and higher education facilities, as well as specialist institutions such as the National Science and Technology Board. The policy is based on stressing high standards and the achievement of excellence in all aspects of education.

ORGANIZATIONAL FRAMEWORKS AND IMPERATIVES

In Singapore it is difficult to divorce state institutions from organizational frameworks and imperatives. Organizational imperatives have

been set by the institutional framework. Commercial organizations
are export and value-added driven. Singapore is no longer a source of
cheap labour and, moreover, the superior infrastructure and stable
political situation has encouraged foreign companies to invest in the
economy.

Limitations on the power of trade unions, although initially heavy
handed (several trade unionists have been imprisoned) has allowed
organizations to introduce more flexible working and employment
practices.

Morita (1987) has observed that the Japanese economic success is a
product of their perceived and actual need to survive at the very basic
level. There has been some debate that this basic instinct has been
diluted in recent years. However, in Singapore the overwhelming
impression from the media (albeit government controlled) is that the
competitive environment is operating and the population is working
hard to maintain the levels of prosperity enjoyed in the past 20 years.

The Uniqueness of Singapore

The influence of the government upon all aspects of Singapore's existence cannot be underestimated. However, the Singapore 'system'
has its critics:

> *Has the price of creating a country that works been a crushingly dull
> society? Are Singaporeans too regimented to make the shift from
> serving others – in shipping, tourism, banking and so on – to a society
> where more value is added by individuals with entrepreneurial flair?*
> (Prewitt and Reinhardt, 1993, p. 15).

It is unsurprising that Singapore's cultural pattern as identified by
Hofstede and Trompenaars does not necessarily fall into the normal
Far East or western 'categories'. Singapore is very much a unique
entity with a singular political, economic and social history. Thorne
concludes from his review of the key literature in the area of culture
that

> *The outcome of these studies shows a striking consistency between the
> qualities of national culture and the strengths and weaknesses of their
> innovators. The Anglo-Saxons are the competitive individualists. The
> people who create and who are applauded are the Edisons, the
> Franklins, the Flemings. Very few people from Anglo-Saxon countries*

will think creative talents in terms of more than two at a time. This competitive individualism is appropriate to basic research, to isolated inventors . . . Different countries adapt their creative output to fit their national psyche.

In contrast to this competitive individualism of the West he goes on to describe collectivist societies as, '*the adaptive, the incremental culture, as being where creativity will have most effect economically, at least for a few more years*'. The collectivist societies, such as China, Japan and Singapore, that do not seek after the 'Truth' and are more concerned with long-term vision than short-term gain '*will inevitably corner the world of creative science and technology*' (Thorne, 1992, p. 184).

In attempts to identify global systems at the cultural, institutional and organizational levels that will encourage technological change, it should be remembered that '*culture is learned, and can be considered only relative to other cultures. There is no absolute right or wrong in cultural preferences*' (Hoecklin, 1995, p. 48). Thus, although Singapore has undoubtedly been very successful in the structuring of its technological innovative processes, this can only be used as an indicator of a possible system that might be applied. Greater consideration of the individual circumstances of a country's cultural mechanisms have to take place before wholesale adoption of 'foreign' systems can be recommended.

CONCLUSION

This chapter started from the premise that global competition is significantly influenced by technological change, and by the ability of organizations to adopt and develop these technologies. Technological change is also the major driving force behind innovation, though not all innovation is technology related. Previous authors (for example Drucker, 1985) concluded that the processes and practices of successful innovators could be learned and applied to other organizations. The model in this paper sought to focus on the contextual variables in the organizational setting rather than the processes, though recognized that the two are closely interrelated. The three dimensions of the model related to organizational culture, institutional frameworks and organizational imperatives.

The study of Singapore illustrates the importance of the cultural element. It might be concluded that culture in Singapore is predominantly inherited and hence difficult to implant or transfer to other countries. The interesting finding is the extent to which the government and business organizations are actively involved in sustaining and promoting the innovative culture. This was evidenced not only in the expected areas of creating an economic infrastructure to promote, encourage and sustain inward investment, ease of trade and political stability, but equally in the other dimensions of the nation's life. Singapore raises interesting questions about how countries can create and maintain an innovative culture in the face of global competition. The uniqueness of political, social and economic conditions in Singapore indicates that to seek to directly transfer a Singaporean model would not be successful. However, Singapore provides an interesting case of the interactions between culture, institutional frameworks and organizational factors that influence technological adaptation to the pressures that arise from the increase in global competition.

References

Arieti, S. (1976) *Creativity: the Magic Synthesis* (New York: Basic Books), p. 229.

Bernard, M. and Ravenhill, J. (1995) *World Politics*, vol. 47, January, pp. 171–209.

Chen, Min. (1995) *Asian Management Systems – Chinese, Japanese and Korean Styles of Business* (London: Routledge), pp. 25, 28.

Child, J. (1994) *Management in China During the Age of Reform*, Cambridge Studies in Management (Cambridge: Cambridge University Press), pp. 287–310.

Child, J. and Bate, P. (eds) (1987) *Organization of Innovation – East–West Perspectives* (Berlin: Walter de Gruyter), p. 20.

Cole, G. (1996) 'Technology News: Two Ways to Ring In', *The Financial Times* (Internet version), 25 January.

Cresson, E. (1996) 'Towards a European Innovation Policy – The Debate Begins', *Innovation and Technology Transfer*, February, pp. 3–5.

Drucker, P. (1985) *Innovation and Entrepreneurship* (London: Butterworth-Heinemann), p. 17.

Department of Trade and Industry (DTI) (1995) *Singapore – General Information Pack*, July (London: DTI), p. 2.

Goffee, R. (1996) 'Organisational Behaviour – Cultural Diversity', Mastering Management, *The Financial Times*, Friday 26 January, p. 2.

Goodhart, C. and Xu, C. (1996) 'The Rise of China as an Economic Power', *National Institute Economic Review*, pp. 56–80.

Hampden-Turner, C. (1983) 'Is There a New Paradigm? A Tale of Two Concepts', *Personnel Management Review*, 56.

Herbig, P.A. and McCarty, C. (1995) 'Lessons to be Learned from the Soviet and Chinese Socialist Experiments: A Cross-Cultural Comparison of Innovative Capabilities', *Journal of East–West Business*, vol. 1, no. 1.

Hoecklin, L. (1995) *Managing Cultural Differences: Strategies for Competitive Advantage* (London: Economist Intelligence Unit and Addison-Wesley Publishing), p. 48.

Hofstede, G. (1984) *Culture's Consequences* (Beverly Hills, Calif.: Sage Publications).

Hofstede, G. (1991) *Cultures and Organizations: Software of the Mind* (London: McGraw-Hill).

Hofstede, G. (1995) 'Managerial Values: The Business of International Business is Culture', in T. Jackson (ed.), *Cross-Cultural Values* (Oxford: Butterworth Heinemann), pp. 150–65.

Kirton, M. (1989) *Adapter and Innovators*, (London: Routledge), pp. xvii–xviii.

Kluckholm, F. and Strodtbeck, F.L. (1961) *Variations in Value-Orientations* (Connecticut: Greenwood Press).

Lynn, R. (1991) *The Secret of the Miracle Economy – Different National Attitudes to Competitiveness and Money* (London: The Social Affairs Unit), esp. p. 15 and p. 47.

McClelland, D.C. (1976) *The Achieving Society* (Princeton: Van Nostrand).

Mida (1995) 'Taiwan Emerges as the Top Investor in Malaysia', *Malaysia Industrial Digest*, January–February, p. 1.

Morita, A. and the Sony Corporation (1987) *Made in Japan* (Glasgow: Collins).

Nonaka, I. (1991a) 'The Knowledge-Creating Company', *Harvard Business Review*, November–December, vol. 69, pp. 96–104.

Nonaka, I. (1991b) 'Towards a New Theory of Innovation Management: A Case Study Comparing Canon Inc. and Apple Computer Inc.', *Journal of Engineering and Technology Management*, vol. 8, pp. 67–83.

Parsons, T. and Shils, E.A. (1951) *Toward a General Theory of Action* (Cambridge, Mass.: Harvard University Press).

Pheysey, D.C. (1993) *Organisational Cultures – Types and Transformations* (London: Routledge).

Prewitt, E. and Reinhardt, F.L. (1993) *Singapore*, Harvard Business School Case Study.

Ramqvist, L. (1994) 'Innovation Generated by Professionalism, Respect and Perseverance', *The UK Innovation Lecture* (London: Dept. of Trade and Industry).

Schumpeter, J.A. (1934) *The Theory of Economic Development* (Oxford: Oxford University Press)

Shane, S. 1993, 'Cultural Influences on National Rates of Innovation', *Journal of Business Venturing*, vol. 8, pp. 50–73.

Shibusawa, M., Ahmad, Z.H. and Bridges, B. (1992) *Pacific Asia in the 1990s* (London: Routledge).

Takyi-Asiedu, S. (1993) 'Some Socio-Cultural Factors Retarding Entrepreneurial Activity in Sub-Saharan Africa', *Journal of Business Venturing*, vol. 8, pp. 91–98.

Tatsuno, S. (1990) *Created in Japan: From Imitators to World-Class Innovators* (US: Ballinger Publishing).

Trapp, R. (1995) 'Fresh Insight on New Ideas', *Independent*, 8 October 1995, p. 8.

Tu, Wei-ming (1984) *Confucian Ethics Today – The Singapore Challenge* (Singapore: Federal Publications).

Thorne, P. (1992) *Organising Genius – The Pursuit of Corporate Creativity and Innovation*, (Oxford: Blackwell), esp. pp.182–4.

Trompenaars, F. (1993) *Riding the Waves of Culture* (London: Economist Books).

Weber, M. (1904) *The Protestant Ethic and the Spirit of Capitalism,* trans. T. Parsons (New York: Scribner, 1929).

Wiener, M.J. (1981) *English Culture and the Decline of the Industrial Spirit 1850–1980* (Cambridge: Cambridge University Press).

World Bank (1993) *Development in Practice: Sustaining Rapid Development in East Asia and the Pacific* (New York: The World Bank).

Part 4
Implications for Organizational Change

11 Privatization, Shareholding and Efficiency Arguments

Andrei Kuznetsov and Olga Kuznetsova

INTRODUCTION

This paper addresses a major and yet under-researched issue of the disciplinary mechanism in corporate systems of transition economies with a particular emphasis on Russia. The importance of this issue follows from the fact that privatization and hence creation of corporations is the core process in the institutional restructuring in the economies of Central and Eastern Europe and the CIS. The successes of privatization in terms of the absolute decrease in the number of state-owned enterprises and the growing share of privatized firms in GNP are often interpreted as the most important indication of advance towards a market economy. This has important practical implications too. For instance, progress in privatization is an important element of conditionality on assistance provided by international financial institutions (Ners, 1995).

There are several theories defending the critical importance of privatization, most notably the 'political' theory (Boycko *et al.*, 1996), the 'competence' theory (Pelican, 1995) and the 'microeconomic' theory (Winiecki, 1991; Jackson, 1993). The latter is probably the most traditional and popular, and in this paper we will mostly refer to this concept. It is based on the belief that when assets are owned and controlled by those individuals in the society who value them the most highly, the assets will also generate the highest discounted present value of net returns from the society's point of view. This line of reasoning is also known under the name of the 'classic efficiency argument' for private ownership.

The 'classic efficiency argument' has a long history but the organizational theory which has been growing in importance very quickly in the last 30 years has detected a serious problem with it. In modern capitalist economies, the smallest companies apart, enterprises are rarely owner-operated. In other words, to use the famous phrase by, there is a separation of ownership and control. This creates the agency problem, that is a situation characterized by a conflict of interest between owners and managers regarding the ways the assets of the company should be best utilized. Clearly, in this situation the classical argument for private ownership may prove valid only if there is a mechanism in place that guarantees that ultimate control remains with the owners.

Such a mechanism, known as the mechanism of corporate governance, has been successfully developed in market economies. Its structure may vary from country to country depending on the prevailing concept of corporation, and indeed from this point of view the United States seem to be very different from Germany or Japan. The managerial literature makes a distinction between market-oriented or monistic corporate systems (Anglo-Saxon countries mainly), and network-oriented or pluralistic systems (Japan, Germany), and currently there is a discussion as to which of the two will prevail in the next century (Yoshimori, 1995; Moerland, 1995). But what system emerges in transition economies? This is a question of considerable practical and theoretical importance. From an academic point of view answering it is essential to determine what elements of the standard managerial, agency and financial theory are relevant to transitional corporate systems and what should be revised. From a practical point of view an answer may help to avoid frustration caused by 'inadequate responses' by firms to governmental reforms, which has happened so often in transition economies in the last years.

Reports on enterprise behaviour in Russia (Ash and Hare, 1994; Fan and Fang, 1995) indicate that newly-privatized enterprises in terms of their policies and responsiveness to market signals differ very little, if at all, from their state-owned counterparts. One possible explanation could be that changes in ownership need time to affect performance. On the other hand, firms established as private from new do behave differently (Fan and Fang, 1995). Usually these are small and medium companies where the owner's control is more direct than in huge and organizationally complex companies with dispersed ownership which emerge when formerly state-owned companies become privately owned. It is commonplace that an average Soviet enterprise used to be considerably bigger in terms of industrial capacity and employment than an average firm in the West. Even when 51 per cent of shares remain in the hands of the 'working collective', which is not uncommon, there are, due to the sheer size of the enterprise, thousands and sometimes dozens of thousands of shareholders. This suggests that variation in the degree of owners' control may be at least partially responsible for dissimilarities in the performance of private and newly-privatized enterprises. In turn, the corporate governance system may be crucial for big companies to meet the classical efficiency criterion. In the next section we will look at different types of corporate governance and evaluate their relevance to the situation in Russia.

THE COMPOSITION OF SHAREHOLDERS

The bulk of Russian medium-sized and large enterprises have become joint stock companies. Already in 1994, the private sector produced 62 per cent of officially recorded GNP. Give-away voucher privatizations have created 41 million shareholders within the period of only 18 months. The way ownership rights were distributed in Russia favoured members of 'working collectives' who had the right to decide on the method of privatization of their enterprise. Not surprisingly this resulted in a situation in which the bulk of shares was distributed within the 'working collective'. Figure 11.1 shows that insiders clearly dominate Russian stock companies, although in many cases the controlling power of the state is far greater than its quota of the equity capital may suggest. Through legal arrangements the state has reserved for itself the so-called 'golden share' in firms operating in strategic industries or industries important for national defence. This share gives the state the control of a majority shareholder irrespective of the actual weight of public ownership in the firm's capital. Therefore, a relative decline in public shareholding which may be observed over the past two years would not necessarily transfer into less control.

The role of small shareholders-outsiders in terms of company ownership has been at most modest and, according to predictions, will remain so in the foreseeable future. This is not surprising as far as the initial, voucher-based, phase of privatization is concerned, considering that this method of privatization put at a disadvantage everyone who had no direct links with privatized enterprises. At the same time, the fact that the importance of small shareholders-outsiders has been slow to grow after privatization entered, in 1995, its more advanced stage indicates some serious weaknesses in the process itself. The privatization plan in Russia foresaw that as soon as the initial free distribution of ownership rights was over, the shares would be traded in the secondary market leading to changes in the structure of ownership. These designs, however, have been late to materialize as far as the majority of

Figure 11.1   Russian privatization: major groups of shareholders

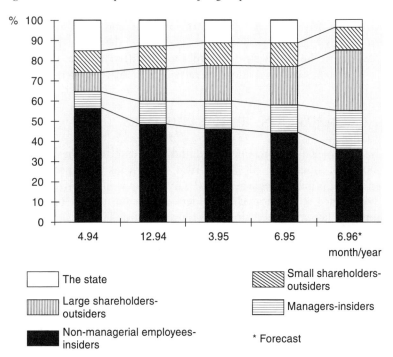

The state

Large shareholders-outsiders

Non-managerial employees-insiders

Small shareholders-outsiders

Managers-insiders

* Forecast

Source: *Voprosy ekonomiki*, no. 10, 1995, p. 53.

the Russian population is concerned. Their activity in the capital market remains very low as a consequence of, first, the fact that the economic situation in the country is not helpful for ordinary citizens to make savings; second, lack of confidence in existing institutional arrangements; and, finally, inadequate development of the financial market's infrastructure. Some of these factors may be held responsible for slow changes in the position of large shareholders-outsiders as well. These, of which a considerable part are foreign investors, appear to be particularly affected by implications of an unstable political climate in the country. In this respect the years 1995/96 have proven to be especially difficult as these may become the years of neo-communists re-ascending to power. After a period of buoyant trade, operations in shares on Russian stock exchanges plunged dramatically in the late summer of 1995 in anticipation of parliamentary elections and have never recovered since.

PATERNALISTIC MANAGEMENT AND INTER-ENTERPRISE RELATIONS

Although changes in the composition of Russian shareholders are under way, in most newly-privatized companies the shape of the agent problem is determined by relations between managerial and non-managerial employees. Despite many changes caused by transition processes these relations still bear the stamp of the social organization of production in the Soviet enterprise. Recent research based on previously inaccessible information describes them as essentially paternalistic (Kapelushnikov and Aukutsionek, 1995). In the Soviet Union managers tended to play the role of the representatives of workers in securing the best conditions under which they could carry out their productive tasks (Clarke, 1995). Such paternalism had evolved as a reaction to the rigidities of the official Soviet production system with its emphasis on technological determinism, leaving very little space for a human factor. To compensate this, certain structural, cultural and ideological forms came into existence to provide an informal hierarchy cementing together the 'working collective'. As a result the Soviet production system relied on its informal arrangements and networks as much as on the formal ones (Kuznetsov, 1994; Popova and Sørensen, 1996).

The legacy of the Soviet period remains very much visible in the behaviour of many newly-privatized firms. In the Soviet era it was characteristic of 'good' enterprises under 'good' directors that active and committed core-workers (*kadrovye* workers) strongly identified their value to the society as well as their own well-being with the enterprise they worked for. As a result the relationship between workers and managers developed into a long-term alliance strengthened by the fact that for both categories the enterprise itself was more than just a place of work but a medium of self-realisation. Indeed, still now, five years into reforms, the preservation of the labour collective in general and the core-workers in particular rate high in the list of priorities of both state-owned and newly-privatized enterprises in Russia (Kapelushnikov and Aukutsionek, 1995). In many cases the latter continue to be providers of important social services to their own workers and their families. With the mentality and spirit of paternalism still being very strong, on many occasions managers continue to enjoy the support and trust of their workers as far as strategic decision-making is concerned. The material proof of this is the fact that the boards of directors of newly-privatized enterprises are hugely dominated by managers and persons selected by managers (Radygin, Gutnik and Mal'ginov, 1995). In effect the board of directors in the majority of cases does not fulfil its role as an instrument of control of shareholders over the management.

The common interests of workers and managers based on the importance of preserving the 'working collectives' was particularly characteristic of the initial period of reforms and privatization. In terms of business conditions this period was marked by the highest degree of uncertainty, lack of communication and confidence which made firms follow a strategy of survival rather than expansion or restructuring. This strategy had risk-aversion and rent-seeking as its central principles. Experts within the country and abroad have found much evidence that the objectives of Russian enterprises' directors were focused, in that period of time, on the conservation of the existing status of institutions they represented till some 'next period' after the normalization of the economy.[1]

According to the evolutionary theory, innovative behaviour is strong when there is a mechanism in action rewarding those firms which are effective in adopting new organizational practices (Nelson and Winter, 1982). Uncertainty about the future and partial ignorance are the two factors retarding changes in behavioural routine. Managers are either in doubt which of the possible outcomes will materialize or simply unaware of some of them. Under these circumstances sticking to traditional routines and values may be chosen as a logical, though not necessarily optimal, strategy of self-protection. In Russia in the first years of transition the degree of uncertainty and ignorance were strong enough to justify managers sticking to old values, including the integrity of the working collective, even after privatization. But this was not the only factor. Labour overhang was helpful for firm managers in strengthening their resistance to the pressure of macroeconomic policies aimed at introducing hard budget constraints. In the absence of a conventional social safety-net, mass lay-offs could lead to a critical outburst of protest in the country. Consequently the government was compelled to acknowledge the significance of social functions fulfilled by enterprises and tolerate continuation of 'soft' or 'semi-soft' budget constraints, thus helping to preserve dated organizational practices as well as essentially conflictless relations between managers and the working collective at the enterprise level.

And yet conflicts did not take long to manifest themselves. The decline of a manufacturing sector in Russia following a 50 per cent drop in industrial output has made the burden of supporting the working collective, as inherited from the central planning days, unbearable for most newly-privatized firms. Still, only a relatively small part of the labour force was made officially redundant. Often managers would leave the employees for whom there was no work an option to retain a formal association with the enterprise by taking unpaid vacations, for example. As working conditions and remuneration deteriorated many employees showed readiness to give up their positions voluntarily thus sparing the managers some painful and unpopular decisions. The situation started to change, however, when those workers who still had work faced the situation when the real value of their wages fell below a certain minimal acceptable level, often because payments were delayed, sometimes for months, while price inflation soared. When employees held their directors responsible for this occurrence they discovered that their powers as shareholders allowed them to make prompt replacements. If, in 1994, according to some studies, only one out of ten directors of newly-privatized enterprises lost their position, the authors' own interviews in the former Ministry of Textile Industry in Moscow revealed that, in 1995, almost one-third of directors within the industry were replaced, mostly following disputes concerning late payments.

These instances may indicate the first cracks in the paternalistic system described above. They are also examples of successful proxy fights in which shareholders used their authority to discipline the management or, rather, a particular manager (director) since it is extremely rare that a new appointee comes from outside the core management team of the firm. From the point of view of the 'classical efficiency argument', however, these actions can hardly be seen as justifying large-scale privatization mainly because there is a widely shared concern that when control of the firms stays with employees it does not translate into a type of efficiency usually associated with private ownership. Theoretically it is not impossible that shareholders-employees may pursue same interests as shareholders-outsiders. For example, Mario Nuti proposed a model demonstrating that an insider's long-term interests as a shareholder are likely to prevail over his short-term interests as a wage-earner if this employee has a higher share of company equity than of labour input supply (see Uvalic, 1995). But it is quite clear that privatizers' hopes for improving the economic performance of the former state-owned enterprises were placed on bringing into play the self-interest and motivations of non-insiders. This makes it appropriate to look at the instruments of corporate control available to this category of equity owners.

MECHANISMS OF CORPORATE CONTROL

The firm organization theory suggests that managers should be disciplined by a mechanism that allows owners to dispose of their services if they feel that the capital underperforms in the hands of the managers. For companies with a large number of small owners the theory usually stresses as the most important the following mechanisms: a board of directors; proxy fights; hostile take-overs; large shareholders; and financial structure (debt finance) (see for example Williamson, 1985; Milgrom and Roberts, 1992; Hart, 1995). Since the composition and status of the board of directors in newly-privatized firms in Russia is dealt with in the preceding section, here we concentrate on other forms of corporate control.

Proxy Fights

In a proxy fight an unsatisfied shareholder puts up his or her own candidates to oppose current managers, and tries to persuade other shareholders to vote for these candidates. By their nature proxy fights put a lot of pressure on the dissident shareholder. This person must meet the cost of gathering and analysing information proving that the firm may do better under a new management and then invest money and effort in convincing other shareholders to give their support.

Even in societies with a long tradition of shareholding there are reasons to believe that a threat of a proxy fight has only very limited effect as a governance mechanism. A small shareholder is unlikely to venture a proxy fight if only because he would have to incur the cost of launching it individually while, if it were successful, its results would be a public good available to all shareholders. In Russia the chance of a proxy fight appears even less plausible. On the one hand, for obvious reasons the majority of small shareholders have no previous experience or relevant cultural background or awareness which may encourage them to contemplate and then put through a successful proxy fight. On the other hand, the direct and indirect cost of such an action is going to be a multiple of what it could be in a western economy mainly because of the absence of an adequate institutional framework. Gaining reliable information about the firm's performance already looks like an impossible task for anybody outside a very close circle of top managers, and even finding the names and mailing addresses of other shareholders may prove to be extremely difficult because the registry is again held by the firm (that is the managers) and there is a record of frequent abuse of shareholders rights (see, for example, *The Financial Times*, 16 November 1994).

Hostile Take-overs

In a hostile take-over the raider benefits from buying the controlling interest in the underperforming company at a low price and then selling this at a higher price after the company is successfully re-structured under a new management. In theory this is a more powerful controlling device than proxy fights in that the raider gets a con-siderable reward for his effort; but not necessarily so under Russian conditions though. Once again, the information problem for a raider-outsider appears to be enormous. Inasmuch as the issue of reliable economic information is important for the present analysis it is ap-propriate to look into this matter in more detail.

The central planning system was notorious for the scale on which economic information was distorted and falsified both deliberately and involuntarily. Concealing and distorting data was an important ele-ment of bargaining between central authorities and enterprise directors whereby each side tried to use its knowledge to its own advantage at the cost of the other side (Ellman, 1989). Modern Russia inherited this perverted tradition of under- and over-reporting, as well as a chaotic state of enterprise statistics. To make things worse the most important financial indicators, including prices, costs and depreciation, used to have very little economic content following the subdued role of money under socialism. Liberalization of prices, parallel circulation of na-tional and foreign currencies, and other changes, have made the task of getting to the real meaning of economic figures even more pre-carious. Conditions are generally unsuitable for meaningful market signals to emerge or to be received (Ickes and Ryterman, 1992; Kuz-netsov, 1994). To give just one example, a huge unpaid debt run by a Russian firm should not necessarily be taken as an indication of poor management. Because accumulated bad debt had grown out of pro-portion on the national scale and had become commonplace in all industrial sectors, dept performance has become separated from the business performance of the firm (Moss and Kuznetsova, 1995).

The other deterrent for hostile take-overs is the rudimentary state of the secondary market for securities. Accumulating a controlling share in the equity capital of a company may in many cases require a com-plex logistic operation. Since more than 50 per cent of the shares usually belong to those who are employed or used to be employed by the firm, the raider is likely to need to send his agents to the area where the firm is located and have them go from door to door convincing people to sell their shares. In the many remote factory cities in Russia these agents are often looked on as unwanted strangers while the top managers of the attacked firm, who are in charge of every aspect of life in such a city, are well positioned to make purchasing difficult. Without doubt, other considerations which are usually quoted in the literature to highlight the point that the threat of a hostile take-over may fail inits disciplinary role (the free-rider problem, invitation of 'white nights' and other responses from the management) fully hold their value for Russia as well.

Large Shareholders

Because small shareholders have little incentive or possibility to closely monitor the activities of managers, the literature on organizational theory suggests that the presence of one or several large (or core) shareholders may help put in place tighter control over the management (Phelps *et al.*, 1993; Shleifer and Vishny, 1986). The manner in which Russian privatization was organized produced three categories of large shareholders: top managers, investment funds and wealthy individuals. When top managers are core shareholders the agency problem ceases to be a matter of concern altogether. In the two other cases the situation is not so clear.

The impact of large shareholders on the corporate structure is determined eventually by what they perceive as the strategic objective of a particular investment. If this objective may be fulfilled without investing time and effort into exerting more control over the managers, it would be unlikely for such an effort to take place. There is no information, regular or representative enough, to warrant any accurate generalization on the behavioural pattern of large shareholders in Russia. Nonetheless, Russian sources typically picture them, investment funds and individuals alike, as opportunists setting and achieving short-term financial goals. Russian investment funds, to take one example, accumulated their investment portfolios by exchanging the privatization vouchers of the population for their own shares. In order to solicit voucher owners to place their vouchers with an investment fund, fund promoters usually promised quick and unrealistically high returns on investment (pledging 400 or 600 per cent dividends was not unusual). In reality, professionalism, competence and commitment to the interests of investors shown by these people often fell far too short of their promises. Not surprisingly, quite a few of the 600 funds have proved to be fraudulent. Others fail to display any particular interest in the performance of the managers of the firms they own, or in the firms themselves, seeking instead their fortune in financial speculations in order to boost the paper value of their own shares (*The Economist*, 8 April 1995).

Not all large shareholders are indifferent to the performance of firms they own, of course. Foreign producers investing in Russian industry are usually anxious to supervize decision-making, and actually see control over management as an important guarantee against certain investment risks. However, it is equally true that some large investors willing to play an active role in controlling management may face strong resistance from the managers. Individuals in particular may be at a disadvantage given the inadequate state of legal and institutional support one can rely on and poor enforcement of regulations. Cases are reported of managers applying simple but efficient means to prevent outsiders from voting at general meetings including summoning the meeting at very short notice or mailing out notifications *ex post*.

Financial Structure

Finally, yet another mechanism which the theory suggests may allow small shareholders to discipline managers hinges on the *financial structure* of the firm. According to this view, already at the point of incorporation, shareholders may arrange the debt finance of their company in such a way that a bank or a group of banks would have a substantial leverage on the company's management. Then, pursuing their own interests as lenders, the bankers would be expected to exert necessary guidance regarding the long-term financial performance of the firm, and hence push the managers of the firm towards decisions which would benefit the wealth of the shareholders as well. Not surprisingly, when one looks at developments in Russia, there is no evidence that this scheme can be operational there as far as former state-owned large enterprises are concerned. In the first place, and foremost, shareholders at the time of incorporation were not in a position to determine the financial structure. Newly-privatized firms simply inherited it from their predecessors, the state-owned enterprises. Besides, mass privatization took place in the period in which the national economy was besieged with the most severe arrears crises as a consequence of which the majority of firms were technically bankrupt anyway. The credit market itself was in a detrimental condition as a result of hyperinflation and general collapse of the economy. Short-term credit was prohibitively expensive while long-term finance was simply unavailable. This does not imply that a link between industrial firms and banks was severed altogether. As a matter of fact even before privatization quite a few large enterprises created their own banks or became shareholders in established ones (Pohl and Claessens, 1994). But obviously this has not led to the type of relationship which firm organization theorists have in mind when talking about the means of shareholders' control.

MANAGERS AS LARGE SHAREHOLDERS

The analysis above singles out only one occasion on which the agent problem appears to have a satisfactory solution in Russian conditions: when the top manager of a firm is at the same time a large shareholder in the firm. This once again focuses attention on the figure of the manager. As a matter of fact, the thesis that privatization puts former Soviet directors in a key position both in terms of control over property and strategic decision-making has strong support in Russian economic and managerial literature. Radygin provides a summary of such views when writing that initially mass privatization 'only legalises previously informal ownership rights which existed, for example, within the framework of principle–agent relations between the state and directors of state-owned enterprises' (Radygin, 1995, p. 64). This statement refers to the fact that under central planning directors enjoyed far greater freedom as managers, and extracted far more benefits from their status, than was ever accepted officially.

This chapter claims that in the course of privatization directors have indeed reinforced their control; first, by exploiting their position at the helm of the paternalistic enterprise system inherited from the Soviet economy in the situation when the majority stake is in the hands of the working collective, and, second, in many cases by accumulating significant personal packages of equity, sometimes as much as a fifth of the shares (Uvalic, 1995, p. 103). The transitional nature of the Russian economy and all its elements has been an extremely important factor influencing the agent problem. Reformers in the Russian government expected that by introducing hard budget constraints and exposing state-owned enterprises to competition and the impact of market forces they would bring about structural changes as well as organizational changes. In fact the importance of traditional networks only increased. Socialist planning could not be replaced by a capitalist market system overnight. The country entered the period of 'economic non-system' (Nuti, 1992) in which many informal networks constructed to overcome the deficiencies of the planning system filled the institutional gap created by the collapse of communism. Personal contacts and the reputation of the director became very important, and at times crucial, for the firm in terms of securing supplies, sales and financing (a banker interviewed by one of the authors in Moscow in the summer of 1995 revealed that, although her bank always evaluated performance-related data of their business partners, at the end of the day the personal reputation of a director was always a very strong and sometimes a decisive factor when the bank made a decision).

The newly-acquired prominence of networks increased the value of a 'good' director for the firm, adding up to other factors discussed earlier. Accordingly, directors benefited in terms of authority. Because of the inherited paternalistic system and the specific collectivist mentality of employees, the fact that insiders usually have majority ownership shields managers, as was shown, from efficient control by outsiders. On the other hand, insiders' majority ownership does not necessarily imply insiders' control as far as rank and file members of the 'working collectives' are concerned. Popova and Sørensen (1996) point out that in relation to privatization, the managers, workers and the local authorities and politicians form the core and interdependent group of control. This correctly identifies the principle beneficiaries of mass privatization. Now that it is almost over, struggle for control within this group will continue. Managers come as the strongest contenders. They had already entrenched themselves in the position of factual control even before privatization started and then legalized and consolidated it when the state gave up its ownership rights. Moreover, they are probably the only category who have some continual experience of economic power. As far as other categories are concerned, following a decline in living standards employees are increasingly forced to sell their shares to add to disposable income while the extreme volatility of the political process in society makes the position of individual politicians too precarious to guarantee a long-term status.

Having principle and agent as the same person may eliminate the agent problem but does this always sustain the efficiency argument? A positive answer is possible only if the manager-owner has competence to pursue efficiency maximization. A recent concept of firm efficiency stresses the point that economic competence is a rare asset. Developed by Pavel Pelican (1993), it argues that scarcity of this critical asset makes firms compete for competent managers. Those firms that fail to put competent Chief Executives in charge lose to their rivals and go under, and this is how the market provides the selection of managers in terms of an optimal allocation of competence.

This approach puts the issue of managerial control in Russia in a new perspective. The competence of Russian managers has its origins in the realities of an economic system which is no more. Many western experts assert that these people will never be able to transform enough to become adequate to the requirements of a market economy and must be replaced.[2] If this becomes a dominant attitude in society, managers will feel endangered. This may prompt a reaction aimed at preserving at least some of the elements of the system which gave them credibility, and respectively slowing down transformation. As a matter of fact in this situation well-entrenched owners-directors, who are also usually very active politically, would be more a deterrent to the imposition of market-based efficiency than support. Of course theoretically one may assume that in pursuit of income maximization the first generation of directors-owners will comprehend eventually the necessity to delegate executive functions to more competent managers than themselves. This scenario, though, does not account for political, social and economic realities in the country. New institutions, including the institution of private ownership, remain weak. In this situation managers cannot be expected to easily give up their current position of direct control over the firm. Uncertainties and the drama of a transitional period leave too little room for longer-term considerations. Russian directors appear to be locked in an uneasy situation in which their newly-acquired interests get into conflict with the origins of their authority. Together with other circumstances this adds to the climate which makes reforms in Russia look so insecure and half-hearted.

PRIVATIZATION IN RUSSIA AND THE THEORY OF PRIVATIZATION

Modern theories of privatization seek to provide a conceptual background to what their adherents see to be a strong message contained in the empirical findings of the last two decades, namely that privatization makes public enterprises more efficient.[3] Characteristically, references are mostly made to studies looking at developments in established market economies (see, for example, Boycko *et al.*, 1996, p. 309). However, one of the bitter lessons of post-communist reforms is that borrowed stereotypes can be misleading, sometimes with unfortunate consequences, when applied indiscriminately to transitional processes. Privatization is no exception. When after the initiation of reforms state-owned enterprises proved slow to restructure, the standard explanation offered by transitional literature hinged implicitly or explicitly on the assumption that they had never tried really hard, blaming their inadequate responses on poor managerial motivation, politicized employees' councils and general indiscipline. It took years before a more balanced approach became possible demonstrating that, in fact, many state-owned enterprises did have a potential for market success, were expertly managed and fully committed to restructuring, but were unable to succeed because the emphasis of reform policies was misplaced. As a result, even the most promising companies could not built upon their strengths and were overwhelmed by exposure to free market forces to which they had no time and resources to adjust (Amsden *et al.*, 1994).

Concern that axiomatic emphasis on privatization of large state-owned enterprises can actually delay restructuring becomes ever more common (see Ners, 1995, p. 113). It has been increasingly advocated now that more attention should be given to changes in the general economic environment (Pinto *et al.*, 1992; Amsden *et al.*, 1994). Analysis of some problems of corporate governance contained in this paper supplies more arguments in support of this point of view. It shows that mass privatization alone does not provide for higher efficiency. In fact, at least in early stages of transition, it helps to preserve the networks and centres of control which were already in place. Mass privatization of large enterprises changes little in their behaviour inasmuch as in real terms it does not expose them to new centres of control or provide them with means to restructure. Traditional mechanisms of corporate governance have so far been of little value because the institutional, legal and cultural environment they rely on to be effective is mostly missing. The practical implications of this are at least twofold. First, at least in the short term, responses of enterprises in Russia even after privatization cannot be expected to follow axiomatic conceptions based on a generalization of firm behaviour and practices in other countries. Second, benefits of privatization cannot fully reveal themselves in the absence of substantial progress in other elements of reforms.

Notes

1. See the article by B. Ickes and R. Ryterman (1992) in *Post-Soviet Affairs*, vol. 8, no. 4, pp. 331–61.
2. See for example A. Åslund's interview (1992) in *Transition: The Newsletter about Transitioning Economies* (Washington), vol. 3, no. 6, pp. 4.
3. Naturally, not all economists agree with this conclusion. For a recent overview of the debate see Aidan Vining and Anthony Boardman (1992) 'Ownership versus Competition: Efficiency in Public Enterprises', *Public Choice* (Virginia State University), vol. 73, no. 2, March, pp. 205–39.

References

Amsden, A., Kochanowicz, J. and Taylor L. (1994) *The Market Meets its Match* (Cambridge and London: Harvard University Press).

Ash, T.N. and Hare, P.G. (1994) 'Privatization in the Russian Federation: Changing Enterprise Behaviour in the Transition Period', *Cambridge Journal of Economics*, vol. 18, pp. 619–34.

Belianova, E. (1995) 'Motivation and Behaviour of Russian Enterprises' (in Russian), *Voprosy ekonomiki*, no., pp. 15–21.

Berle, A. and Means, G. (1993) *The Modern Corporation and Private Property* (New York: Macmillan).

Boycko, M., Shleifer, A.and Vishny, R. (1996) 'A Theory of Privatization', *Economic Journal*, vol. 106, no. 435, pp. 309–319.

Clake, S. (ed.) (1995) *Management and Industry in Russia* (Cambridge: Edward Elgar).

Ellman, M. (1989) *Central Planning* (Cambridge: Cambridge University Press).

The Economist (1995) 'Survey: Russia's Emerging Market' (London) p. 74.

Fan, Q. and Fang, B. (1995) 'Are Russian Enterprises Restructuring?', paper presented at the Joint Conference of the World Bank and The Ministry of the Russian Federation, 12–13 June, St. Petersburg, Russia.

Gurkov, I. and Abraamova, E. (1995) 'The Survival Strategies for Industrial Enterprises in New Conditions' (in Russian), *Voprosy ekonomiki*, no. 6, pp. 22–30.

Hart, O. (1995) 'Corporate Governance: Some Theory and Implications', *Economic Journal*, vol. 105, no. 430, pp. 678–689.

Ickes B. and Ryterman, R. (1992) 'The Interenterprise Arrears Crisis in Russia', *Post-Soviet Affairs*, vol. 8, no. 4, pp. 331–61.

Jackson, M. (1993) 'Property, Ownership, Company Organization and Managerial Behaviour in the Transition', paper presented at the Conference of the ACE Network on Company Management and Capital Markets, Prague, 25–26 April (mimeo).

Kapelushnikov, R. and Aukutsionek, S. (1995) 'Russian Industrial Enterprises in the Labour Market' (in Russian), *Voprosy ekonomiki*, no. 6, pp. 48–55.

Kuznetsov, A. (1994) 'Economic Reforms in Russia: Enterprise Behaviour as an Impediment to Change', *Europe–Asia Studies*, vol. 46, no. 6, pp. 955–70.

Milgrom, P. and Roberts, J. (1992) *Economics, Organization and Management* (Englewood Cliffs, NJ: Prentice-Hall).

Moerland, P. (1995) 'Alternative Disciplinary Mechanisms in Different Corporate Systems', *Journal of Economic Behavior and Organization*, vol. 26, no. 1, pp. 17–34.

Moss, S. and Kuznetsova, O. (1995) 'Modelling the Process of Market Emergence' (mimeo), paper presented at the workshop *The Economic Transition: Modelling and Reality*, Warsaw-Madralin, September 1995.

Nelson, R. and Winter, S. (1982) *An Evolutionary Theory of Economic Change* (London: Belknap Press).

Ners, K. (1995) 'Privatization (from Above, Below or Mass Privatization) versus Generic Private Enterprise Building', *Communist Economies and Economic Transformation*, vol. 7, no. 1, pp. 105–116.

Nuti, D.M. (1992) 'Economic Inertia in the Transitional Economies of Eastern Europe', paper presented at the conference, *Impediment to the Transition: The East European Countries and the Policies of the European Community*, Florence, European University Institute, 24–5 January (mimeo).

Pelican, P. (1993) 'Ownership of Firms and Efficiency: The Competence Argument', *Constitutional Political Economy*, vol. 4, no. 3, pp. 349–392.

Pelican, P. (1995) 'Les enterprises d'État après le socialisme: pourquoi et comment les privatizer repidement', *Revue d'études comparatives Est–Ouest*, no. 2, pp. 5–37.

Phelps, E.S., Frydman, R., Rapaczynsky, A. and Shleifer, A. (1993) 'Needed Mechanisms of Corporate Governance and Finance in Eastern Europe', Working Paper no. 1, European Bank for Reconstruction and Development.

Pinto, B., Belka, M. and Krajewski, S. (1992) 'Microeconomics of Transformation in Poland: A Survey of State Enterprise Responses', a report on 75 large Polish state-owned enterprises, World Bank Working Paper, June.

Popova, J. and Sørensen, O. (1996) *Economic Reforms in Russia: A Network Perspective on the Enterprises' Relations to the Reforms*, International Business Economics Research Paper No. 2, Aalburg University, Denmark.

Pohl, G. and Claessens, S. (1994) 'Banks, Capital Markets, and Corporate Governance: Lessons From Russia for Eastern Europe', Policy Research Working Paper 1326, the World Bank.

Radygin, A. (1995) 'On the Theory of Privatization in a Transition Economy' (in Russian), *Voprosy ekonomiki*, no. 12, pp. 54–67.

Radygin, A., Gutnik, V. and Mal'ginov, G. (1995) 'The Post-Privatization Structure of the Equity Share Capital and Corporate Control: "Managerial Counterrevolution?" (in Russian), *Voprosy ekonomiki*, no. 10, pp. 47–69.

Shleifer, A. and Vyshny, R. (1986) 'Large Shareholders and Corporate Control' *Journal of Political Economy*, vol. 94, pp. 461–88.

Uválic, M. (1995) 'Insiders' Privatisation in Central-Eastern Europe', paper presented at 1st International Conference on *Enterprise in Transition* Split, October 4–6. Published in Proceedings, pp. 101–108.

Walsh, J. and Kosnik, R. (1993) 'Corporate Raiders and their Disciplinary Role in the Market for Corporate Control', *Academy of Management Journal*, vol. 36, no. 4, pp. 671–700.

Williamson, O. (1985) *The Economic Institutions of Capitalism* (New York: Free Press).

Winiecki, J. (1991) *Resistance to Change in the Soviet Economic System: A Property Rights Approach* (London: Routledge).

Yavlinsky, G. (1994) 'Lessons of Economic Reforms' (in Russian), *Octiabr'*, no. 9, pp. 136–149.
Yoshimori, M. (1995) 'Whose Company is it? The Concept of the Corporation in Japan and the West', *Long Range Planning*, vol. 286, no. 4, pp. 33–44.

12 Enhancing Global Learning and Change in Multicultural Organizations through Valuing Diversity in Project Teams

Paul Iles and Paromjit Hayers

INTRODUCTION

In recent years there has been an increasing level of speculation and research on the need for managers and other key staff to work prod-uctively with others: whether working with people from other func-tions in interdepartmental, cross-functional or integrative project teams and task forces, managing across borders in culturally and na-tionally diverse strategic alliances and partnerships and transnational organizations (see for example Bartlett and Ghoshal, 1989), or work-ing in organizations characterized by increasing gender, racial, ethnic, physical ability and other forms of diversity (for example Kandola and Fullerton, 1994). Often team members hold very different theoretical perspectives and assumptions, use different languages (for example res-ident vs client vs patient vs. customer), employ different standards as to what counts as evidence (for example objective/quantitative vs in-tuitive/qualitative), and hold different expectations of one another's roles.

Different priorities, different statuses, different assumptions about each other's constituencies and pressures, and numerous other differ-ences also help to make working collaboratively with each other pro-blematic. Misunderstanding, miscommunication, mutual stereotyping of each other's competences and contributions, and a tendency to mutual blaming all create the potential for conflict, tension and dis-agreement.

215

Such issues of difference are likely to be multiplied when working with people who are culturally different and of different nationalities and when working with gender, racial and ethnic diversity. Diversity, if managed skilfully, may be a source of creativity and innovation; but the often-heard assertion by diversity trainers and others that diversity *per se* is an asset and a positive resource needs to be examined more carefully. It is the contention of this paper that diversity, whether of identity, nationality or functional background, can be such a resource, but only if skilfully managed. Learning to work successfully with difference is therefore becoming imperative, but the skills and strategies involved need to be clarified. In particular, closer attention needs to be paid to the nature of the difference, the nature of the task, the phase of the task or project, and the skills and competencies of the individuals involved. In this chapter we mainly explore cultural differences in international contexts. However, whilst recognizing the specificity of working with each dimension of difference, similar skills and strategies may also be relevant to working with differences of gender, functional background or professional identity.

MANAGING DOMESTIC DIVERSITY: A SOURCE OF COMPETITIVE ADVANTAGE?

A new perspective on differences in the workplace, 'managing diversity', emerged in the USA in the 1980s and is likely to also become very influential elsewhere in the 1990s. This perspective is often perceived as complementing or supplementing previous approaches to differences based on equal employment opportunity and affirmative action (EO/AA). These two approaches, rooted as they are in the particular social and political agendas of the 1960s and 1970s are increasingly argued as outdated and unable to meet the new challenges of the next millennium.

As Copeland (1988) points out:

> What has given great impetus to the managing diversity model has been increasing assertion that *valuing differences makes business sense*...Those who view diversity among employees as a source of richness and strength...can help bring a wide range of benefits to their organizations (p. 52).

It is likely that in Europe as well as in the USA 'managing diversity' will grow in importance, as it will be argued it makes good business sense. In common with the USA the focus is likely to move from discrimination *per se* to the full utilization of all potential resources in the organization and towards issues of enhanced mobility rather than access. It is likely to be an attractive concept, embracing a broader range of issues and groups than those traditionally encompassed by equal opportunity and positive action. It is also more likely to focus on organizational culture and management style than has the traditional EO/AA paradigm. This then is the basis of its appeal, but also the source of some of its problems and limitations.

There are several ways in which managing diversity may assist in the search for competitive advantage. Organizations which foster and encourage differences in perspective may well encourage learning, creativity and innovation in comparison to those which attempt to suppress such differences, avoiding such phenomena as 'groupthink' (Janis, 1977).

Organizations which seek to meet different cultural and religious demands in such areas as religious observance, diet and religious holidays as well as in terms of work flexibility in relation to family and lifestyle may also be more likely to enjoy a competitive advantage in the recruitment and retention of employees. Whilst some of these arguments posit positive benefits at the interpersonal and personal levels, most are couched in terms of the competitive advantage that managing and valuing diversity may bring to organizations (see for example Griggs and Louw, 1995). For example, Cox (1991) argues that there are six areas in which managing diversity effectively may generate organizational benefits – costs, resource acquisition, marketing, creativity, problem-solving and flexibility. Minority workers in particular will be more likely to be attracted, retained and motivated if cultural differences are valued, generating savings on turnover, absenteeism and legal costs. Such organizations will be more able to sample from a diverse talent pool, so that no potential is lost. Minority clients and customers in particular – a growing category – may be more likely to be attracted, and their needs more adequately met. Of particular relevance to global organizations is the contention that heterogeneous teams with diverse perspectives and resources are more likely to be creative and innovative, and therefore diversity is likely to give rise to greater organizational flexibility and adaptability. This is likely to be of significant benefit to enhancing learning and change in global organizations.

However, it should be noted that though there is some evidence for the propositions concerned with minority employee recruitment and retention, the evidence for the later more 'downstream' or 'indirect' benefits is much more sparse (Kandola and Fullerton, 1994). There has been little research to explore these benefits of adopting a managing diversity perspective, despite many of the claims made in the literature. There is some evidence that US firms employing more women managers perform better financially (Blackburn *et al.*, 1994). Shrader, Blackburn and Iles (1995) adopting a resource-based perspective on competitive advantage (for example Barney, 1991; Grant, 1991) have argued that the ability to capitalize on and apply corporate internal resources in dynamic and uncertain contexts – especially human resources and employee and management capabilities – is a key sustainable, hard to imitate, source of competitive advantage. Since firms that have employed more women managers may have done a better job of appraising and utilizing human resources effectively, the strategic use of women managers in particular may be of corporate benefit. Using archival data they showed that US company performance as measured by such profitability measures as net income and return on investment over the period 1982–93 was correlated with the firm's ranking on the *Wall Street Journal's* index of the percentage of women in management. However, such correlations only partially support the proposition that more utilization of the diverse talent pool available to organizations will generate improved financial performance.

Other research also supports, but does not confirm, this line of reasoning. Diversity may bring about a considerable number of strategic benefits. For example, Wiersema and Bantel (1992) again using US archival data from the banking industry showed that top team demography was related to corporate strategic change. In particular, heterogeneous top teams as defined by education, age and functional background showed a greater receptivity to change, a greater willingness to take risks, a greater diversity of information sources, a greater openness to diverse perspectives, and more creative and innovative decision-making. However, such findings have utilised dimensions of diversity – age, functional background and education – not usually considered in a diversity context (in part because top banking teams have historically been all-white and all-male). We will take up this issue further after considering research on managing international diversity.

MANAGING INTERNATIONAL DIVERSITY

The ability to manage diverse resources is likely to be of particular benefit to global organizations with global stakeholders, especially as systems theory predicts that internal complexity and diversity becomes increasingly important in diverse and complex external environments due to the demands of 'requisite variety'.

One approach to the successful management of international diversity has been through the concept of 'intercultural competence'. If companies can identify a profile of required international competencies they can assess and select candidates for specific roles against the profile, and seek to enhance these competencies through training and development. Such competencies are likely to be useful at many points of the international career cycle, as Figure 12.1 shows. Some researchers have tried to examine the international and pan-European competencies required for different roles and positions. For example, one influential framework derived by the Ashridge Management Research Group (Barham and Oates, 1991) distinguishes 'doing' competencies from 'being' competencies.

Assessing Inter-cultural Competence

Although many companies cite such qualities as relational skills, motivation, cultural empathy and adaptability as important qualities contributing to international effectiveness, they rarely seem to assess such qualities systematically, often using job or technical proficiency as a sole criterion for international assignments.

Managing International Diversity, Global Strategy and Organizational Life-cycles

As organizations become increasingly international in their operations, cultural diversity – and hence the need to manage it effectively – takes on increasing importance. Perlmutters' (1979) model of managerial orientations suggests that as organizations internationalize, their managerial mind-sets need to also change, especially in the areas of recruitment, selection, assessment, appraisal, training and development, and reward and compensation. An ethnocentric orientation – viewing home-country management styles as the only or the most effective forms – may be effective in a domestic organization but not as international operations become increasingly important. Here 'polycentric' orientations – prioritizing local responsiveness and therefore the need to take cultural diversity into account – become more appropriate. However, though such orientations may assist organizations in meeting the demands of responsiveness, they may impede their

Figure 12.1 Required competencies at different stages of internationalization

	Domestic/Export Stage	Multi-Domestic/ International Stage	Multinational Stage	Global/Transnational Stage
Structural Features	Functional divisions	Functional, with international divisions	Multinational lines of business	Global alliances, heterarchy
	Centralized	Decentralized	Centralized	Co-ordinated, decentralized
Culture				
• Sensitivity	Marginally important	Very important – especially with clients, customers and suppliers	Somewhat important, particularly for employees and managers	Critically important for executives
• Perspective	Ethnocentric	Polycentric, regiocentric	Multinational, geocentric	Global, multicentric
• Assumption	'One way'/'one best way'	'Many good ways'	'One least-cost way'	'Many good' ways simultaneously
Human Resources Priorities				
– Degree of rigour required	Low to moderate	Moderate to high	Moderate to high	Moderate to high

– Content emphasis	Interpersonal skills, local culture, consumer values and behaviour	International skills, local culture, technology transfer, stress management, local business practices and laws	Interpersonal skills, two-way technology transfer, corporate value transfer, international strategy, stress management, local culture, and business practices.	Global corporate operations/systems, corporate culture transfer, multiple cultural values and business systems, international strategy, and socialization tactics.
– Training and development emphasis	Low to moderate training of host nationals; focus on understanding home-country products and policies.	Low to moderate training of host nationals; primary focus is on production/service procedures.	Moderate to high training of host nationals in technical areas, product/service systems, and corporate culture.	High training of host nationals in global corporate production/efficiency systems, corporate culture, multiple cultural and business systems, and headquarters.
– Staffing	International assignments rare; ethnocentric assumptions	Senior managers on international assignments; ethnocentric or regiocentric orientation	Local managers, polycentric staffing.	Senior and fast-tract managers on multi-cultural assignments, global resourcing on geocentric basis.

ability to meet other demands, such as those identified by Bartlett and Ghoshal (1989) as 'organization learning' and 'integration'. Polycentric orientations may be appropriate for multinational organizations (Adler, 1991; Bartlett and Ghoshal 1989) others may require regiocentric (taking the region as the reference point for human resources policy decisions, as in developing a pan-European strategy, or even geocentric orientations. As an organization becomes more geocentric, global or transnational, the importance of cultural diversity, and therefore the need to manage it effectively, becomes more important.

It is not only expatriates and those on short-term assignments that need diversity training, as in the multinational/polycentric organization, but managers and staff at all levels as customers, markets, stakeholders, project teams and management composition (including the composition of senior and top management teams in all parts of the organization) become increasingly diverse and multicultural. Hence the need for the effective management of diversity, and the need to develop management skills in this area, becomes more pressing.

Inter-cultural Competence and International Diversity

Many organizations, especially parochial and ethnocentric ones, have attempted to either ignore or suppress the cultural differences presented by multicultural organizations. It is true that initially, at least, such organizations may present difficulties of communication and comprehension, perhaps leading to tension, conflict and confusion. However, if actively managed cultural differences may be an asset and a resource, especially where an organization needs to devise new ideas, entertain new perspectives, and expand on existing plans. If cultural differences are recognized, valued and used to the organization's advantage, then greater synergy may result. If this is to be realized, then organizational members will need to display both cultural self-awareness and crosscultural awareness – a crucial 'diversity competence' necessary for working with difference.

Cultural diversity at all levels of an international organization may lead to a greater understanding of diverse markets and customer preferences. More culturally appropriate marketing and human resource practices are likely to result, especially in the areas of such things as leadership style, communications, training, appraisal and recruitment. Employees are more likely to be attracted to an organization, and more likely to be retained, if they see their cultural background valued rather than ignored or disparaged. Many international organizations have, therefore, recognized that valuing cultural diversity and incorporating it into the business is likely to be a source of competitive advantage. Diversity competencies may as a result come to play a key role not only in such areas as recruitment, selection, training, development and performance-management practices, but also in building multicultural teams and in crosscultural negotiations. For example, British Airways has sought to develop in its European operations a valuing of cultural difference by its staff (for example Lauermann, 1992), whilst in its Egyptian operations it has sought to ensure that its cabin products and services reflect local culture, helping to attract both high-potential local recruits and local customers (Iles and Mabey, 1994).

VALUING DIVERSITY: SOME CAVEATS

Adler (1991) suggests that culturally diverse groups can perform either extremely well or extremely poorly, compared to homogeneous groups. Work done at INSEAD supported this notion by showing that culturally diverse teams either performing very poorly (if they try to downplay or minimize their differences) or very well (if they try to acknowledge, affirm and use their differences). Adler also suggests that diversity may well be an asset in the creative, divergent thinking phase of a task, but a source of friction and misunderstanding in convergent thinking, decision-making phases. Diversity may, because of its potential for tension, misunderstanding and friction, be less of an asset in routine tasks (for example, implementing strategy and evaluating options) as opposed to creative tasks (such as developing new products or services).

However, many enthusiasts for diversity have not only glossed over the complexity of its relationship to task 'phase', but also over the kind of diversity being considered, generalizing illegitimately from differences in personality or cognitive style to differences of gender, race and culture. One helpful distinction in terms of diversity dimensions is made by Alderfer and Thomas (1988) who distinguish between task/role (that is function) and identity (that is race/gender, nationality) differences, to which we could add individual differences (for example personality, cognitive style). Research which appears to support the positive benefits of differences along one dimension (for example cognitive style or team role) does not necessarily support claims made for other dimensions (for example race, gender, or nationality).

LEARNING TO WORK WITH DIFFERENCE IN MULTINATIONAL PROJECT TEAMS

If the potential synergies available from cultural diversity are to be realized, organizational and team members need to be inter-culturally competent, able to understand their differences, but also to continue to communicate effectively and integrate across these differences. These competencies are likely to involve empathy, negotiation, the ability to create a shared reality through collective participation, the open re-solution of conflicts, and the ability to use cultural differences as a resource. Diversity *per se* is unlikely to generate the benefits often claimed for it unless it can be worked with effectively to realize those benefits. Some of the skills involved and the steps necessary to use differences as a positive asset can be illustrated by an analysis of a multiculturally diverse project team in action.

Case 1   Developing Competencies to Work with Diversity in Multicultural Teams: the Case of Whirlpool

Managing international diversity has become an imperative for the Whirlpool Corporation based in Benton Harbor, Michigan in the USA with 38 000 employees scattered across the world. In 1988 Whirlpool bought the white goods section of the Dutch giant, Philips, establishing its European headquarters in Italy at Comerio.

One of the ways the company has attempted to facilitate global-ization has been through training and development to foster a common framework of international project teams. Cross-national, crossfunctional team-working in such areas as delivery teams and product business teams is an established practice in Comerio, whilst Whirlpool managers from many different countries interact in lea-dership courses such as those run at Ury just south of Paris. Out-door development activities and team-building initiatives have been commonly used alongside more traditional, classroom-based team-building and educational sessions to develop individuals and organ-izations and to help them better manage cultural diversity. Here a variety of activities including outdoor activities are used to create awareness of team dynamics and individual styles of behaviour.

Once self-awareness has been enhanced, greater self-confidence is built-up through mental strategies, psychometric instruments and trust-building exercises. For example, the project team at Ury uses a measure known as DISC to identify preference for different types of behaviour style. DISC identifies four broad areas of behaviour, dominant (D), influential (I), steady (S) and compliant (C). However, it is possible that such routes to self-awareness could lead to a masking rather than a valuing of cultural differences. For instance, in the language of DISC two managers – one from Denmark and one from Spain – might assume affinity with each other because they both score highly on the 'dominant' scale; yet we would anticipate that their ways of expressing this style would be very different due to the power distance and uncertainty avoidance indices associated with their respective national cultures (Hofstede, 1980). In addition, there is the further crosscultural complication of importing North American training assumptions, models and facilitators into a European training event (Iles and Mabey, 1994).

These kind of team-building and outdoor development initiatives may work best if participants come from cultures showing low power-distance because of the non-directive leadership styles often adopted by facilitators. Participants from low uncertainty cultures (given the frequent ambiguity of the task) and high individualism (given the nature of the individual feedback provided) may also benefit from such interventions. That is, such initiatives may work best in Anglo-American or Nordic cultures. Participants from other cultures, especially more collectivist ones with higher uncertainty avoidance and power distance, may find the process more threatening and less helpful. They may well be more comfortable in events where the trainer is more directive, where status is respected more, where tasks are more structured, and where feedback is less intense, more anonymous and less personal.

Case 2 Learning to Work with Difference in Multicultural Teams: the Case of Raleigh International

A group of eight international managers from difference parts of Europe and North America engaged in the 1994 international management challenge for the youth development charity Raleigh International were filmed, observed and interviewed as part of the 'People' Unit of the Open University MBA course B890 'International Enterprise' (Iles, Thompson and Altman, 1995). The aims of the two-week project were both to help Raleigh organize a community and conservation project for young people in Botswana by drawing on the global management experience of the participants, and to help the participants and their sponsoring organization learn more about multicultural teams and cross cultural negotiations by working on a 'real life' project. The team consisted of four male and four female managers drawn equally from the public/charity sectors (the UN, the Red Cross, the British Council and the Gradua Institute), and the private/commercial sectors (Hewlett-Packard, Statoil, BP and Lever Brothers). One manager was African-American, another Czech, another Scandinavian and another North American. The others were British, as was the Raleigh project director.

The two-week programme consisted of several phases:

- A prior two-day-team building/outdoor development programme held at Ashridge Management College in the UK.
- A three-day-stop-over in Zimbabwe to orient the group to Raleigh's work, including a project to build a house for a Save the Children Fund community health worker.
- Sub-group meetings in the capital, including a radio station appeal and a meeting with the Vice-President.
- An assessment of three potential community/conservation projects in Botswana (a rhino sanctuary, a wilderness school and a community hall/bus stop in a remote village).

The team appeared to leave for Africa unclear about their goals, ground rules and ways of working. Shock at the basic accommodation offered to them in Zimbabwe created doubts over Raleigh's performance. At the initial orientation with Raleigh, the director raised more doubts when he stressed how much he had accomplished in a short time in numerical terms (109 meetings in 21 days, 40 meetings in 5 days). Presented with a large folder of objectives and details, a split began to emerge in the team, not on *national* but on *sectoral* lines. A private sector group (75 per cent male) wished to press on with the task, whereas the public sector group (75 per cent female) wished to hang back to discuss the plans in more detail. This split remained an issue for the whole two-week period. Some of the public sector managers disputed the implications that they were afraid of the task and had backed away from it.

Despite these internal tensions, the group as a whole felt satisfied with their work for Raleigh, an illusion cruelly shattered by the Director. The team eventually recommended that all three projects they had assessed should be supported, and Raleigh eventually seemed happy with the outcome, accepting their recommendations.

The members of the team also seemed to feel that they had learned some valuable lessons about teamwork and negotiations in a multicultural setting and about themselves as international managers, such as the necessity of valuing and managing diversity and resolving tensions and conflict over preferences.

LEARNING TO WORK WITH DIFFERENCE IN MULTICULTURAL TEAMS AND ORGANIZATIONS: A MODEL

Taken together, the case studies illustrate the key role of a variety of diversity competencies, including managing stress, managing risk, managing ambiguity and humility. What is of particular interest here are five key competencies, namely:

- *cultural awareness*: understanding the differences present in a team;
- *communicative competence*: communicating across these differences;
- *cognitive competence*: acknowledging stereotypes over such differences;
- *valuing differences* as an asset and resource; and
- *gaining synergy* from the differences.

These appear to be crucial competencies involved in learning to work with difference, whatever the nature of the differences (whether oriented for example around gender, race, ethnicity, function or culture).

Cultural Awareness: Understanding the Differences

The Raleigh case study shows the importance of being aware of cultural differences. For example, the director used extremely quantitative criteria to measure his effectiveness (how many meetings in how few days) – other cultures may use more qualitative criteria. Some cultures are very task-orientated, others more relationship-oriented. It was noticeable that the American manager from the most task-oriented of all cultures, the USA, tended to take the lead, chair meetings, and try to push the group along. When the team engaged with local people in assessing the need for a village bus-stop, they also asked the very task-oriented question 'why do you want a bus-stop', which may be a very offensive way of first approaching people from relationship-oriented cultures.

Communicative Competence: Communicating Across the Differences

Language and communication, including non-verbal communication, play a key role in learning to work with difference, Hill (1965) noted the importance of silence in cultures in the early 1960s. This point is borne out in the Raleigh case, where the Czech manager couldn't add anything to the decision as she didn't understand the process and wasn't able to follow the conversation.

However, other team members seemed not to ask her what she thought, whether she agreed, or how she saw things, and did not particularly try to pull her into discussions. They seemed to feel that her silence signified agreement, which it did not necessarily imply.

Cognitive Competence: Acknowledging Stereotypes over the Differences

Mutual stereotyping and 'groupthink' in multicultural teams is always likely. However, what is important for crosscultural interactions is that stereotypes are acknowledged and make explicit, open and shared – not a process apparent in the Raleigh case study.

Valuing Diversity as an Asset

In the Raleigh case study the introduction by the director or by the UK facilitators failed to give early legitimization to the acknowledgement and positive valuing of diversity and difference. As a result, team members quickly looked for similarities and things in common, not differences – such as we're all in Africa together, we're all foreigners, we all have a job to do (Adler, 1995). This attention to the forces drawing them together may have blinded them to their differences and to ways of using them to their advantage. In many cases team members appeared to assume agreement where non existed, taking silence and disengagement as signifying assent.

Obtaining Synergy from the Differences

As a result, given the lack of significant 'drivers' for the group (their jobs or careers did not depend on their effectiveness), cultural synergy did not appear to be obtained in the Raleigh project. Figure 12.2 shows that this may only be achievable if members of a multicultural team are sufficiently 'inter-culturally competent' at the affective, cognitive and communicative levels and can master the earlier steps so as to enable communication and integration across acknowledged differences and explicit stereotypes to occur in a climate which values diversity rather than seek to ignore, suppress or disparage it. Such skills are more likely to be developed using experiential methods like multicultural team-building, presentation and negotiation activities and the use of multicultural outdoor development and cross-functional project teams as in the Whirlpool case, and the team building and action learning projects in the Operation Raleigh case. These can address not just individual learning but also team and organizational learning, and are methods which focus not just on cognitive awareness and problem-solving but also on more open-ended, experiential, personal and self-

Figure 12.2   The impact of task nature diversity and member intercultural competence on team synergy

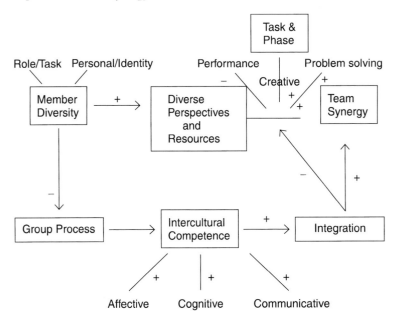

Figure 12.3   Matching cross-cultural programmes and processes to the qualities being developed in diversity training

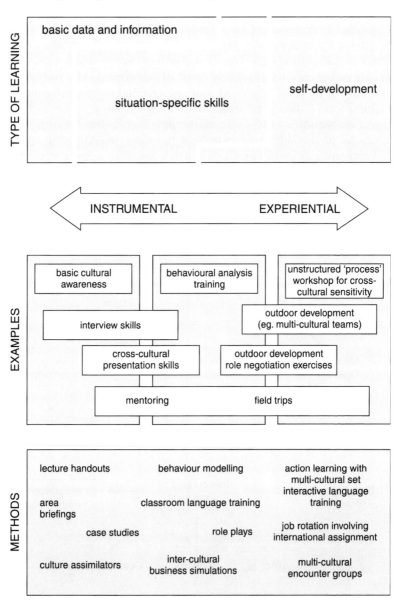

development processes in a multicultural setting, whilst also dealing with 'real life' issues (see Figure 12.3).

CONCLUSION

This chapter has developed an argument that learning to work with difference will be an important managerial skill. The chapter has critically reviewed the management of cultural diversity in domestic and international contexts to develop a model of working with difference which is applicable to individuals teams and organizations. The model recognizes the significance of types of diversity – individual, task/role and identity of task phase, and of task nature – for understanding the relationship between diversity and team and organizational outcomes, and hypothesises that synergy and integration across diversity is more likely to occur if team and organizational members display intercultural competence at the affective, communicative and cognitive levels. In particular, members will need to understand their differences, communicate across them, acknowledge stereotypes, and actively value diversity and use it as a resource. Strategies for developing such skills involving 'experiential' methods that address the affective, cognitive and behavioural dimensions of working with differences have also been reviewed.

References

Adler, N.J. (1991) *International Dimensions of Organisational Behaviour* (Boston, Mass.: Kent Publishers).
Adler, N.J. (1995) Commentary on *The Survival Guide*, BBC/Open University video.
Alderfer, C. and Thomas, D. (1988) 'The Significance of Race and Ethnicity for Understanding Organisational behaviour' in C. Cooper and I.T. Robertson (eds), *International Review of Industrial and Organizational Psychology* (Chichester: Wiley).
Barney, J.C. (1991) 'Firm Resources and Sustained Competitive Advantage', *Journal of Management*, vol. 17, pp. 99–120.
Bartlett, C. and Ghoshal, S. (1989) *Managing across Frontiers* (London: Hutchinson Business Books).
Black, L.S., Gregersen, H.R. and Mendenhall, M. (1992) *Global Assignment* (San Francisco: Jossey-Bass).
Blackburn, V.L. Puran, B.M. and S. Hrader, C.B. (1994) 'Investigating the Dimension of Social Responsibility and the Consequences for Corporate Financial performance', *Journal of Managerial Issues*, vol. 16, pp. 195–212.

Barham, K. and Oates, D. (1991) *Developing the International Manager* (London: Business Books).

Copeland, L. (1988) 'Managing Diversity, parts 1 and 2', *Personnel*, July, pp. 44–60.

Cox, H. and Blake, S. (1991) 'Managing Cultural Diversity: Implications for Organisational Competitiveness', Academy of Management Executive, vol. 3, pp. 45–56.

Evans, P., Doz, Y. and Laurent, A. (1989) (eds), *Human Resource Management in International firms* (London: Macmillan).

Grant, R.C. (1991) 'The Resource-Based View of Competitive Advantage: Implications for Strategy Formulation' *California Management Review*, vol. 133, pp. 114–135.

Gertsen, M.C. (1990) 'Intercultural Competence and Expatriates', *International Journal of Human Resource Management*, vol. 1, no. 3, pp. 241–62.

Griggs, L.N. and Louw, L.L. (1995) (eds) *Valuing Diversity: New Tools for a New Reality* (New York: McGraw-Hill).

Hill, E.T. (1965) *The Silent Language* (Greenwich, Conn.: Fawcett).

Hofstede, G. (1980) *Culture's Consequence* (London: Sage).

Iles, P.A. and Auluck, R. (1989) 'From Racism Awareness Training to Strategic Human Resource Management in Implementing Equal Opportunity', *Personnel Review*, vol. 18, pp. 24–32.

Iles, P.A. and Auluck, R. (1991) 'The Experience of Black Workers', in M. Davidson and J. Earnshaw (eds), *Vulnerable Workers* (Chichester: John Wiley).

Iles, P.A., and Mabey, C. (1994) 'Developing Global Capabilities through Management and Organisation Development Strategies', paper presented to British Academy of Management Conferences Lancaster University, September 1994.

Iles, P.A., Thompson, A. and Altman, Y. (1995) *International Enterprise* (Milton Keynes: Open University).

Janis, I. (1977) *Groupthink* (Boston: Houghton Mifflin).

Kandola, R. and Fullerton, J. (1994) *Managing the Mosaic* (London: Institute of Personnel and Development).

Lauerman, E. (1992) 'British Airways in Europe: A Human Resources Viewpoint of Development', *European Management Journal*, vol. 10, pp. 85–86.

Perlmutter, H. (1979) *Multinational Organisation Development* (London: Addison Wesley).

Rhinesmith, S. (1992) *A Manager's Guide to Globalisation* (Arlington: American Society for Training and Development).

Ronen, S. (1990) 'Training the International Assignee', in Goldstein, I. (ed.), *Training and Development* (San Francisco: Jossey Bass).

Shrader, C.B. Blackburn, V.L. and Iles, P.A. (forthcoming) 'Women in Management and Firm Financial Performance', *Journal of management issues*.

Thomas, R.R. (1990) 'From Affirmative Action to Affirming Diversity', *Harvard Business Review*, vol. 68, pp. 107–12.

Thomas, R.R. (1992) *Beyond Race and Gender: Understanding the Power of your Total Workforce by Managing Diversity* (New York: Amacom).

van Houten, G. (1989) 'The Implications of Globalism: New Management Realities at Philips', in Evans, P. *et al.* (eds), *Human Resource Management in International Firms: Change, Globalisation, Innovation* (London: Macmillan) pp. 101–12.

Wiersema, M. and Bantel, K. (1992) 'Top Management, Team Demography and Corporate Gtrategic Change', *Academy of Management Journal*, vol. 35, pp. 91–112.

13 Patterns of Legitimation in Times of Change: How People in an East German Organization are Coping with the Transformation Process

Thomas Steger

THEORETICAL BACKGROUND

Introduction

The transformation process taking place in Central and Eastern Europe is doubtless one of the most exciting topics for social scientists today, not only for the people in the countries concerned, but also for all those interested and involved in processes of social change (Edwards and Lawerance, 1996).

In this current discussion (Lang, 1996) we can identify three processes which characterize the transformation process of change in former socialist societies:

- Change from a socialist economy to a market economy at the economic level.
- Democratization at the political level.
- Modernization at the level of the individual enterprise.

Some authors (Gutmann, 1991) consider that transformation has taken place when the first two processes are complete. But change at the level of the individual enterprise and at the level of the individuals can be considered to take at least the next generation to work through, and are changes that are often underestimated and need to be integrated in a much wider perspective that focuses not only simply on the systems that get developed, but also on the social dynamics that take place (Offe, 1991; Reißig, 1994).

There is no doubt that during the last decade in East Germany (and prior to that in the former GDR) a process of value change was taking place. The transformation process, therefore, produced a special input and – on the other side – has been influenced itself by the long-range changes in values. These changes in values can be seen as one of the major reasons of, and the background to, the change of attitudes and perceptions of the people and, furthermore, for changes in action strategies and behaviours. On the other hand, the various experiences of success or failure with these behaviours had a major impact on the changes in values and are, moreover, reproducing these values at both the meso- and the micro-level.

The different kinds of legitimation processes can be considered, therefore, to be a focal point at the crossing between values/attitudes and behaviour. This is true especially with regard to the ongoing transformation process which has brought into question a lot of opinions and beliefs taken for granted over decades. Moreover, the legitimation strategies in use give us important information about how people try to cope with their personal situation.

The changes in values in East Germany constitute the background for understanding and interpretation, and therefore function as a starting point of this chapter. After a few theoretical considerations about legitimacy, a case of a small East German enterprise will be presented focusing on the legitimation strategies in use and the relationship towards the new legal system. With the help of a model by Suchman (1995) and a self-developed typology, these strategies will be classified and rearranged. In the final part the major findings are summarized and reflected against the background of the changes in values. Some consequences for practise and for further research will also be discussed.

Changes in Values in East Germany

During the last few years there has been a vivid discussion about changes in values in East Germany and former GDR (Böhm, 1994). Because of limited space, we would like to focus here on Klages and Gensicke (1993) who have undertaken the largest research activities on this topic and can, therefore, be considered as one of the major references.

Klages and Gensicke consider four dimensions as important for the interpretation of value development in East Germany before and after the *Wende* of 1989:

- Have there been any changes in values in the GDR between 1949 and 1989?
- Was there a modernization input connected with the changes in values?
- Have the changes in values in the GDR been persistently influenced by the political regime?
- Are there fundamental differences in values to be expected in the long run between East and West Germans?

Starting from these dimensions, they first identify three different interpretations for the development of values:

- The first (we call a 'totalitarism' approach) states that in the GDR any changes in values were mainly characterized by the socialist system and the rules of the communist party – the SED (Maaz, 1990).
- The second ('niche' approach) position denies a decisive influence of the regime on the value structure of people in the GDR, and suggests that the substance of values dominating the German middle class in the middle of this century has been by and large conserved through the socialist decades (Senghaas-Knobloch, 1992).
- The third ('modernization' approach) is strictly opposite to the first position, but also the second, assuming that there were strong changes in values in the GDR – in fact not parallel to the development in the western part of Germany – which created, as an effect of the political–ideological strategy of the SED a secularized and levelled workers' society (Gensicke, 1991).

Based on this background the two authors develop a fourth scenario that can be considered as the most differentiated and which is validated by numerous wide-ranged research projects. It is characterized by four phases as shown in Table 13.1. From this background Gensicke (1995) identified, along with three groups of values, five types of people as shown in Table 13.2. It might be interesting to ask which types we will find later on in our case study.

Table 13.1   Changes in values model

Phase 1	Two decades (minimum)	Ideologically-based processes to break down traditions, and running in parallel an exaggeration of certain traditional values
Phase 2	Late 1960s and the 1970s	Growing emancipation towards the system from the inside, and the development of a private niche
Phase 3	The 1980s	Growing estrangement of the majority of the people from an increasingly less trustworthy system
Phase 4	Time of the *Wende*	Attempts to anticipate new demands and chances by revitalization of conventional values

Source: Klages and Gensicke, 1993.

Table 13.2   Preferences for values of five types

	Convention-alist	Resigned	Realist	Hedo-materialist	Idealist
Conventionalism	high	low	high	low	low
Idealism and engagement	low	low	high	low	high
Hedonism and materialism	low	low	high	high	low
West 1990	20%	15%	33%	15%	17%
East 1990	23%	10%	32%	20%	15%
East 1993	21%	16%	35%	14%	16%

Source: Based on Gensicke, 1995, pp. 137ff.

Legitimacy

When discussing the legitimacy of a certain attitude or behaviour, Weber (1980) distinguished between three types of legitimacy:

- legitimacy of rational character;
- legitimacy of traditional character; and
- legitimacy of charismatic character.

Suchman's (1995) distinction goes even further, as can be seen in Table 13.3. Although he focused on the legitimacy of organizations his

Table 13.3   A typology of legitimacy

	Actions	Essences
Pragmatic	Exchange	Interest
Legitimacy	Influence	Character
Moral	Consequential	Personal
Legitimacy	Procedural	Structural
Cognitive	Predictability	Plausibility
Legitimacy	Inevitability	Permanence

wider differentiation makes it an interesting basis for our study. Therefore, it will be used here for the self-legitimations of the people in our case study. The first step, therefore, is the adoption of Suchman's definition. According to it we say:

> Legitimacy is a generalized perception or assumption that the own actions are desirable, proper or appropriate within some socially constructed system of norms, values, beliefs and definitions (cf. Suchman, 1995, p. 574).

This usage changes Suchman's 'the action of an entity', replacing it here with 'the own actions'.

It is not possible here to discuss Suchman's model in detail. Therefore, I should like to provide the reader with some short explications of the most important distinctions it draws (Suchman, 1995, pp. 577ff).

Pragmatic legitimacy rests on the self-interested calculations of a person's most immediate audiences; moral legitimacy reflects a positive normative evaluation of the person and his/her activities; and cognitive legitimacy is distinct from evaluation and involve acceptance as necessary or inevitable based on some taken-for-granted cultural account.

In addition to this trichotomy Suchman arrays legitimation dynamics along two cross-cutting dimensions: the first reflects the focus of legitimation, dividing dynamics that focus on the person's actions from dynamics that focus on the person's essence. The second separates dynamics that operate in episodes – the horizontal dimension in Table 13.3. from those that are continual – the vertical dimension in Table 13.3.

CASE STUDY

Method

Considering the high level of complexity of the research area, it would not be a good idea to deal with East Germany on the basis of rigidly designed research programmes. According to Feyerabend (1975), a certain freedom of choice and a wide range of methods might be a good medicine even (or especially) for social science research.

Our project is based on the interpretative paradigm focusing on describing and understanding people's positions and meanings. As Wollnik (1995) declared, there is a chance for a better approach to an organizations' reality by using such a perspective because of:

- the emphatic interdisciplinary focus;
- the native-view perspective;
- the highly reflective research methodology; and
- the good plausibility of most results.

Therefore, our project is not intending to gain representivity but contains a case study of a small East German firm where six qualitative interviews (duration 50–90 minutes) were conducted with different people from a wide social spectrum. The interviews followed the form of a so-called 'issue-focused interview' (Sackmann, 1991) that provides a stimulus to respondents to make interpretations based on their cultural framework.

To discover typical patterns of thinking and acting the interviews were analysed following the 'grounded theory approach' (Glaser and Strauss, 1967). Moreover, an analysis of many internal and external documents supported and complemented the data work. Here we will focus on one important topic identified during the research project.

History of the Firm

The firm in our case study was the so called 'Engineering bureau for rationalization' of the cosmetics combine situated in Chemnitz (former Karl Marx Stadt). Its duty was to maintain and support the technological part of the combine. It employed about 130 persons in the three branches of construction planning, electronics and special equipment.

After the *Wende* the electronics branch was closed, and the two others faced a completely unsure future. Therefore, three important employees of the special equipment branch left the firm in summer 1991, founded their own firm, and managed to develop albeit at a low level to about 6–7 employees.

Meanwhile, the construction-planning branch benefited from good conditions in comparison to the special equipment branch in the old firm where the staff numbers decreased to about 6 persons. They struggled to survive and finally got in contact with a firm from West Germany which was interested in leasing a part of the firm's real estate and promised to take over the employees of the special equipment branch. The Treuhandanstalt, still owner of the whole firm (at that time), was against this idea and preferred an independent special equipment firm to a leasing company, which the directors of the old firm wanted to establish. Therefore, they made an agreement in autumn 1992 that the new firm of the former employees would buy the whole firm.

This situation provoked a mixed reaction amongst the staff. The employees of the construction-planning branch, who still had a good market situation, all left the firm, while the special equipment staff had to accept the new owners. Moreover, after six months one of the three co-owners of the firm left in disagreement with his two colleagues.

The following two years were characterized on the one hand by a continuing legal struggle between the new owners and the Treuhandanstalt over the 'fair' sales price (the decision of the judge was not yet known at the moment when this article was written). On the other hand the firm developed step by step to about 15 employees and managed to obtain a certain number of orders (even from the United States), but continually faced severe financial problems that often provoked wage payment delays.

Interviewed Persons

All names in the following have been changed.

Mr Adler, about 40 years old, lathe operator, was an employee of another firm in town and was put on part-time work as early as spring 1990. After almost 9 months at home he managed to find a new job near Augsburg (West Germany) where he worked till Mr Graf offered him a job in the new firm in November 1992.

Mr Graf, about 45 years old, engineer, persuaded his two colleagues to leave with him in 1990 (the new firm, therefore, also carries his name). He is dealing with the commercial side of the business and is without doubt the strong man of the firm.

Mrs Huber, about 45 years old, technical designer, was put on part-time work in 1991 and was dismissed in September of that year. She began a re-education programme in January 1992, which she broke off in April to take over a job in the new firm where she is now dealing with material requirements and various administrative affairs.

Mr Klaus, about 45 years old, engineer, left the old firm in autumn 1990 and became co-owner of the new firm. He concentrates on the technical side of the business.

Mr Stark, about 55 years old, constructor, has been in the old firm all the time, and became chief of the workshop during that time.

Mr Wild, about 35 years old, bricklayer (and all-rounder), worked in the old firm till 1985, then was in different jobs in different firms in the cultural sector and came back in February 1993. He is the field worker of the firm and – if necessary – is also helping his colleagues in the workshop.

Legitimation Strategies

During the interviews it became obvious that the six interviewees are different from each other in many respects. We would like to develop and highlight the profiles of these persons in respect to the ways they try to gain legitimacy for their attitudes, behaviour and actions. We can by no means give here a complete overview of the data stemming from the interviews, but the short portraits presented here may provide the reader with some central insights.

Adler seems to be a normal worker who is not highly affected by the processes going on inside or outside of the firm: he just does his job. What is central for him is the experience of the change of behaviour. These problems are the main source for his legitimacy. In spite of attributing most problems to outside causes he is not arguing on a moral level: '...formerly, everybody did rely on the state...and had to rely ...There are a lot of people who lost their jobs, it happened to me, in fact it wasn't their fault, so that you are suddenly standing there, without any salary or, let's say, without a job...'.

But Adler was able to get a new job quite fast, he went over to West Germany and seemed to have no problems there, additionally his wife held her job all the time. So he is not bitter and he has an optimistic attitude, even towards the future. 'You have to continue with these things optimistically. If I take on a certain thing saying "it will end up in nothing anyway" then I can forget it. And you can always see, that there is progress. There are little steps, that's clear...'.

Graf is what we imagine when speaking about small firm entrepreneurs. In spite of the cooperation with Klaus he is a typical individual fighter, with typical individual fighter's ethics: 'It's not
possible to serve everybody, was my saying . . . you can do what you
want, I say, in the end, money has to come out of it . . .'. He is watching
the surrounding world in a very critical, grim manner. What were
formerly the firm's director and the political system, are now the
Treuhandanstalt, the competing firms (especially from West Germany)
and the legal system: '. . . today they fight with, let's say, a jargon in
order to deceive others, not to pay the bills, in any way . . . that's very
grave. Thus, one finds oneself doing the same things, out of necessity'.

Nevertheless, he is looking forward quite optimistically and self-
consciously based on his high-level professional skills as an engineer
and his belief that he cannot be blamed for what he has done in the
past: 'I could handle this problem in a quite easy way, I can say, because we had never to be ashamed about our professional competencies and about our relations, and we are still convinced, that we
have not done anything wrong, otherwise we would perhaps already
have been blown up somewhere'.

Huber is highly influenced by her bosses, Graf and Klaus, and what
they are doing. By leaning upon their behaviour she tries to legitimate
herself: 'The boss is the best example for it, Mr Klaus is extremely
active, so I must do the same . . .'. Another important source of legitimacy is the development of the company's business; as long as it goes
on and the company's size is increasing, she considers herself as having
made a good contribution: 'The most important thing for him is that it
is going forward around here. And I think or I hope that I can myself
make a little contribution to it'. Nevertheless, her doing and thinking is
in fact not aggressive. She is concentrating on the firm and all things
happening outside or stemming from outside obtain a certain fatalistic
character in her words: 'First of all it was luck, that I could stay . . . . in
fact, we have been extremely lucky, to have survived for more than two
years now . . .'.

A lot of aspects and facts are ignored; for example what has happened to old colleagues, what was going on during the first round of
dismissals in the old firm and so on.

Klaus, as one of the founders and the actual boss of the firm, can be
characterized as highly action-oriented. He is not as dominant as his
colleague Graf, and his attitudes and opinions seem to be more calm
and careful, but his orientation is quite similar. The main source for
his legitimacy is his opposition to some negatively perceived groups

and persons, such as the former secretary of the firm who was a member of the former board of directors, the Treuhandanstalt or the GDR system's framework in general: '... in the current situation with the board of directors, the chief executive, people introduced by the Treuhand, we said: If we want to survive, it is better, with this background, to privatize'.

On the other hand Klaus, as an engineer, has a high level of professional pride. Together with Graf he has saved the special equipment industry in this place and has become a real pioneer: '... in the mechanic's garage we constructed the first machine, we relied on the cooperation and support of the artisans in the surrounding area for we had no possibility to do lathe and milling work ...'.

On this background he takes dismissals as '*a fact*', and he was never worried because of his high-level skills.

Stark is a typical representative of the old artisan tradition – highly experienced, loyal to the firm, with a high level of duty values. He was one of the leaders during the hardest time of the fight for survival, but his concepts and ideas have been broken by the come-back of Graf and Klaus: '... with support of the firm "Reich", we thought, now we can do it, now it's our turn. And then came the cut by Mr Graf, he bought us. And then it started again from new'.

Therefore, he is disappointed and holds a quite defensive position. He stands especially in opposition to Graf, the entrepreneur type, and they had a special relationship that has developed over many years: 'Well, you know, Mr Graf was my former boss, and we know each other for such a long time now, so that our personal relationship, it is a bit different than it is to the other colleagues'. His strategy, therefore, is quite defensive, also connected to little belief in the support of external institutions. 'There are institutions to address, like the trade union or the labour court, but you know well that most people don't do it because they say, until I get through there ... in the end, it's not worth it. Thus, you duck and try to work so that you don't give offence to your employer, so that he cannot say: "Well, I must dismiss that man ..."'.

Wild is a different kind of an individual fighter. He has a lot of experience in completely different jobs and is, therefore, able to do what is wanted of him. Nevertheless, he shows a clear ethical attitude concerning what is happening in his surroundings: '... well, it wasn't as unfair in some respects compared with what one experiences today, and I think we could keep that, we don't have to do everything like they do it in West Germany'. This does not include a negative assessment of the actual surrounding world, he rather holds a kind of a positive–fatalistic view: '...in some respect, nevertheless, as a minimum at the beginning, all wanted it like this, whether they had any different conceptions or not, I don't know anybody who is able to make a better proposal...'. The main source of his actions – this can also be seen in his professional past – is the personal (intrinsic) work satisfaction: 'Nevertheless I'm glad about how it is, it is somehow more active, the time, more things are going on...therefore it is a complete difference. It is more performance dependent'.

Table 13.4 shows what kind of legitimacies could be found in the data. A few aspects seem to be quite interesting: only one person (Huber) is using only one type of legitimacy; on the other hand Wild is using four of them. Graf and Klaus are only using action-oriented types of legitimacy, which could be connected to their position as entrepreneurs. Stark is only using pragmatic legitimacy types, maybe a consequence of his disappointment. One type of legitimacy could not be identified in the data and one can assume – according to Suchman – that cognitive legitimacy can hardly be found with individuals. The fact that one type of cognitive legitimacy could be found with Graf and Klaus can be interpreted as an indication of their higher self-consciousness, that in fact should be the basis of this self-legitimacy type.

Table 13.4   Legitimacy types in the data

	Actions	*Essences*
Pragmatic Legitimacy	Adler, Graf, Klaus, Stark, Wild	Adler, Stark, Wild
Moral Legitimacy	Adler, Graf, Klaus, Wild	Huber, Wild
Cognitive Legitimacy	Graf, Klaus	

THE LEGAL SYSTEM

There is no doubt that the legal system constitutes a special framework influencing peoples' legitimation strategies. Moreover, when we have a situation with a complete change of the system as happened in East Germany, it might be interesting to focus on this special relationship to validate and/or accentuate the findings from above study.

Starting with the currency union (1 July 1990) and especially with the German re-unification (3 October 1990), people in the former GDR have been confronted with a legal system completely different in many aspects to that which they had learned and had lived with for almost 40 years. Therefore, one should ask how people are feeling and reacting toward this new system that has come overnight and that has influenced from one moment to another a lot of the various aspects of their daily life.

Our data show that completely different people still have some problems with the new system five years after the *Wende*. They all know that they have to accept it but they have not yet got used to it. The strategies they use to cope are therefore completely different: on the one hand there are people (like Huber or Stark) who are extremely defensive and take the system as something that can beat them over-night: 'Well, you always have to be on the alert, that you are always awake, otherwise, someone who is once absent will never be saved anymore, he goes down . . .' (Stark). On the other hand there are people like Graf who are quite grim and think they are forced to fight against an evil enemy for their rights: 'There were a few sleepless nights and very intensive travels between Halle and Chemnitz, and it ended up that I myself had to investigate the dusty documents in the govern-mental archives . . .' (Graf). In between the two we can find people (like Klaus or Wild) with the attitude that it is firstly a learning pro-cess. 'The current situation is that you have to stand your ground . . . a thing that you do have to learn, and in this direction . . . we, all of us, have to fight in order to cope with the facts' (Klaus).

The level of activity of the people in our case study seems to be highly dependent on the possibility of finding a source for a certain

Figure 13.1   Typology of coping strategies

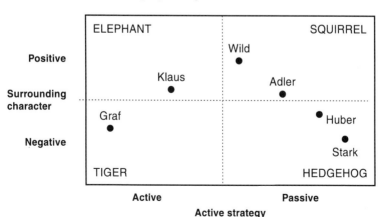

self-consciousness or even safety. This can be based on their professional skills (Graf, Klaus), on the cooperation with important people
in the surrounding (Huber), on a secure family situation (Adler), or on
the flexibility to always come up again (Wild). One person (Stark)
must be considered as an example that lacks all these traits: the consequence is high feelings of insecurity and very defensive behaviour.
Figure 13.1 concludes an attempt at a typology for the coping strategies based on what we have found and discussed so far. The central
questions are therefore:

- How do people interpret the character of their surrounding (pos-
  itive/negative)?
- What is the character of their action strategy (offensive/defensive)?

CONCLUSIONS

We close the circle by questioning how our findings can be interpreted
against the background of the changes in values in East Germany. As
we stated earlier, Klages and Gensicke (1993) reported attempts to
revitalize traditional values for anticipating the changed surroundings.
It is very interesting to see how the people in our case study are doing
this: Wild and Adler are both more or less realists; they are profiting
by their past experiences to endure difficult situations without any
complaints, and they had to find work 400 km away (Adler) or they
often took on completely different jobs with bad salaries (Wild). Klaus
and Graf can also be identified as realists; they at first refer to their
flexibility (especially technical) and their experiences of how to find
some gaps in the ruling system. Graf also shows some attributes of the
hedo-materialists: he tries to be successful using all his power, subord-
inating a lot to reach his goals. Huber seems to be a conventionalist,
revitalizing duty values and leaning upon authority. Stark could belong to the group of the resigned; he feels quite isolated and frustrated
and hides so as not to stand out.

One can assume therefore that the situation of the interviewees – in
accordance with their coping strategies – could differentiate even more
during the next few years. It is already obvious in our data that there
are some kinds of winners and losers in the transformation process (in
spite of the fact that we have not included unemployed persons). Actually this does not cause any problems, because of – as one could
assume – the adverse economic situation which is taming any critical

and obstinate people. Nevertheless, in the future there could arise a problematic source for employer–employee conflicts (Fiedler and Steger, 1996).

Another interesting aspect is the kind of surrounding interpretation, that is still quite negative. As Aderhold *et al.* (1994) pointed out, this can be the basis for a community conception of 'friend–enemy', referring to the former 'top-down' differentiation in the GDR working culture. However, it needs to be questioned whether this concept may be a fruitful fundamental for developing long–standing relationships with the firm's stakeholders.

Consequences for Management Practice

What are the consequences of our findings for practical management in times of massive change? Changing processes in organizations are always risky for they provide a lot of situations which can cause losses and losers. As we pointed out, management is well-advised to watch these affected employees carefully, otherwise a decrease of work motivation or obstructive actions can be the consequences. This highlights the high importance of social competencies especially for executives. There are much more and better possibilities than purely monetary ones to cushion such situations. Organizational and personnel development should, therefore, go hand in hand.

A second recommendation could be to direct change-strategies more towards value-oriented policies. Especially in huge transformation processes as in East Germany, the organizational culture can take an important role by creating a common identity and providing some guidelines for action to the organizational members. For management this means a need to question which existing values could support the changing process even more than to propagate a complete breakdown of the 'socialist shed'.

Consequences for Further Research

Although the findings seem to be quite interesting and perhaps sometimes surprising, it has to be taken into account that they are of an explorative character and, therefore, should not be overestimated. They should be validated on the one hand by integrating more interviews and different firms in the analysis, and on the other hand by using more extended qualitative methods for the whole material.

Nevertheless, the case study presented gives a concrete impression of some interesting aspects of the transformation process which could probably not be observed when only using traditional quantitative methods. Therefore, it is to be hoped that the full range of qualitative methods, of which those used above are only a fraction, will be used more often not only by sociologists or psychologists but by management researchers as well. The final criteria whether to use a certain method or not should not be any 'scientific tradition', but the adequacy of the method in relation to the subject.

Note

1. The author wishes to thank Ramona Alt, Rainhart Lang, Neil Thomson and Elke Weik for their helpful comments on earlier drafts of this chapter.

References

Aderhold, J., Brüss, J., Finke, M., Hanke, J., Heidenreich, M., Kirchhof, F., Schölzel, T., Schrott, M., Schwingeler, S. and Sievers, M. (1994) *Von der Betriebs zur Zweckgemeinschaft* (Berlin: Sigma).
Böhm, I. (1994), 'Auswertung empirischer Untersuchungen 1989–1992 – "Katalog" – Übersicht und Wichtung', in Heyse, V. and Erpenbeck, J. (eds), *Management und Wertewandel im Übergang* (Münster/New York: Waxmann), pp. 15–66.
Edwards, V. and Lawrence, P. (1996) 'Transition in Eastern Germany: A British View', *Journal for East European Management Studies*, vol. 1, no. 1, pp. 28–42.
Feyerabend, P. (1975) *Against Method* (London: New Left Books).
Fiedler, A. and Steger, T. (1996) 'Das Verhältnis der Werktätigen zur Arbeit in Ostdeutschen Industriebetrieben – Beharrung oder Neuorientierung?', in Becker, M., Lang, R. and Wagner, D. *Personalarbeit in den Neuen Bundesländern* (München/Mering: Rainer Hampp), p. 91.
Gensicke, T. (1991) 'Werte und Wertewandel im Osten Deutschlands', unpublished paper (Speyer: Hochschule fur Verwaltung).
Gensicke, T. (1995) 'Pragmatisch und Optimistisch: Über die Bewältigung des Umbruchs in den neuen Bundesländern', in Bertram, H. (ed.), *Ostdeutschland im Wandel: Lebensverhältnisse – Politische Einstellungen* (Opladen: Leske & Budrich) pp. 127–54.
Glaser, B. and Strauss, A.L. (1967) *The Discovery of Grounded Theory* (Chicago: Aldine).
Gutmann, G. (1991) 'Zur theoretischen Grundlegung von Transformation', *Gesamtdeutsche Eröffnungsbilanz*, vol. 2, pp. 29–59.
Klages, H. and Gensicke, T. (1993) 'Wertewandel in den neuen Bundesländern', in Klages, H. (ed.), *Traditionsbruch als Herausforderung* (Frankfurt am Main/New York: Campus), pp. 215–38.

Lang, R. (ed.) (1996) *Wandel von Unternehmenskulturen in Ostdeutschland und Osteuropa* (München: Mering).

Maaz, H.-J. (1990) *Der Gefühlsstau. Ein Psychogramm der DDR* (Berlin: Argon).

Offe, C. (1991) 'Das Dilemma der Gleichzeitigkeit: Demokratisierung und Marktwirtschaft in Osteuropa', *Merkur*, vol. 4, pp. 279–92.

Reißig, R. (1994) 'Transformation: Theoretisch-konzeptionelle, Ansätze, Erklärungen und Interpretationen', *BISS public*, vol. 15, pp. 5–44.

Sackmann, S.A. (1991) 'Uncovering Culture in Organizations', *Journal of Applied Behavioral Science*, vol. 27, no. 3, pp. 295–317.

Senghaas-Knobloch, E. (1992) 'Notgemeinschaft und Improvisationsgeschick: Zwei Tugenden im Transformationsprozeß', in Heidenreich, M. (ed.), *Krisen, Kader, Kombinate* (Berlin: Sigma), pp. 295–309.

Suchman, M.C. (1995) 'Managing Legitimacy: Strategic and Institutional Approaches', *Academy of Management Review*, vol. 20, no. 3, pp. 571–610.

Weber, M. (1980) *Wirtschaft und Gesellschaft*, 5th edn (Tübingen: Mohr).

Wollnik, M. (1995),'Interpretative Ansätze in der Organisationstheorie', in Kieser, A. (ed.), *Organisationstheorien* (Stuttgart: Kohlhammer), pp. 303–20.

14 Aspects of the Transition to the Market Economy in the Czech Republic and Hungary

Tom Lupton, Gyorgy Kauscek,
Eva Hrabitova and Richard Thorpe

In this account we summarize our findings of research into aspects of the transition process in the Czech Republic and Hungary. In both these countries primary research data was collected by native professionals working in their own language. The research design and the methods employed were worked out through discussion and debate with two western partners who together coordinated the work and managed the logistics of the study – support for the research was through the European Community.

Our enquiries focused on the consequences of foreign investment for the labour market in the Czech Republic and Hungary and for the management of enterprises both foreign and indigenous, the organization of work, wage levels and systems of wage and salary payment. Although the research reported here is specific to the Czech Republic and Hungary, the issues raised and lessons learned can be generalized to other Central and Eastern European countries.

RESEARCH DESIGN AND METHODOLOGIES

In each country the following procedure was followed. First a thorough survey was made of the academic literature, journals and newspapers seeking references to matters of interest to the project. Official documents and statistics were also referred to where appropriate and available. Interviews were then conducted in a small number of enterprises following an agreed format. Questions were posed to managers, management specialists, supervisors and blue-collar employees in order to gain a representative view from the whole of the workforce in each location studied. All the enterprises, save three, were foreign-owned or jointly-owned and controlled. The exceptions in each country were indigenous enterprises where for comparative purposes the same interview schedules were used. Because of the nature of the issues which concerned us, special attention was directed to developments in human resource management.

Towards the end of the project workshops were organized in Prague and Budapest to which we invited all representatives of all the companies where interviews had been conducted. The two 'western' coordinators attended (together with interpreters). Papers were presented and discussed in the native language in order that the findings of the interview programmes could be checked against the experience and perceptions of the participants – in order to provide a kind of validity check – from those workshops. Adjustments were made to our ideas and conclusions.

Finally, the Czech and Hungarian partners were asked in the context of their studies to make some predictions as to what changes would take place along some of the following dimensions in the next 20 years:

- Employment/unemployment;
- Labour market flexibility/inflexibility;
- Levels of nominal and real wages and salaries;
- The relationship between employment and productivity;
- The relationship between pay and productivity;
- Work organization and methods, for example job design, management control, team work, empowerment and so on;
- Management styles and structures;
- Human-resource management practices and styles;
- Problems experienced and the attitudes of managers and management;
- Professionals and what will be happening in further stages of the transition;
- Effects on governmental labour market policies and administration and the emergence of other labour market agencies;
- Effects on technology and know-how transfer;
- Effects on career patterns;
- Effects on labour unions and collective bargaining.

The responses received to these rather difficult questions will be presented and discussed towards the end of this chapter. The main body of the chapter aims to describe a picture of contemporary Czech and

Hungarian life uncovered by the researchers. This will focus on the period of transition described, and their judgements about the first stages of the process of transformation. Hungary will be examined first.

HUNGARY

The 'intelligence agents' of foreign capital appeared in Hungary before the political change. In fact foreign direct investment's (FDI) massive influx began in the early 1990s. It is a current success story of the Hungarian economy (the volume of FDI in Hungary alone is equal to that in the rest of the Middle and Eastern European countries together). Out of the 35 biggest multinational corporations, some 20 are present as investors including such giants as GE, GM and Ford. The volume invested by the 'giants' is considerable and their structural distribution is favourable. Green-field investments are typical, and the industries that do invest offer longer-term returns in manufacturing and services. Japanese investors – known for their extreme cautiousness – have a considerable share of FDI in the region, but mainly in Hungary. Of importance are the knock-on benefits of foreign direct investments, one is the message it sends to smaller companies that it 'is worth investing in Hungary'.

Perhaps the best way to attract further investment is the good image generated by those credible investors who are already there. There is also the multiplier effect. Incoming foreign capital brings with it more advanced technologies, organizational and management methods, and advanced marketing practices. This access to worldwide information and the marketing networks of multinational companies is indispensable for the modernization of the Hungarian national economy. The presence of multinational companies in Hungary has so far shown a positive balance. But it would be wrong to think that there are no negative aspect; one has been the possible under-utilization of domestic subcontractors. Some multinationals tend to act as islands separated from their surrounding economy, and there are signs of an uneven territorial distribution developing.

The FDI is concentrated in Budapest and in the western part of Hungary to take advantage of the north-western development that incorporates Vienna, Bratislava, Prague and Warsaw. However, the picture of their impact is far from being complete due to the rather short time they have been in Hungary.

Turning to the process by which development took place, the first period was dominated by illusions and fears. There were those who expected to be surprised by new, never-seen-before developments in technology, organization, and management. It was thought that privatized companies would be taken over by exceptionally talented managers and professionals. These expectations were also the source of fears. People worried that the arrival of western capital and western managers would result in the closing of companies, as all those newcomers wanted from their investment was the market. They expected that workers would be laid off, and those remaining would be subject to unbearable efficiency targets.

Following this period, the first couple of years brought a more sober outlook. It began to be noticed that most technological equipment (except of course green-field investments) was hardly any different from what had been used before. The methods used in organization and management by the new owners that had been feared were seen to be not really that new, being built instead on well-known methods which had been applied by good managers in Hungary in any case. The competence and knowledge of the incoming foreign managers and professionals were also not perceived to be superior to those of Hungarians who were not all that impressed. Occasionally it happened that it was the Hungarians that proved to be better qualified than their western 'teachers'.

In their first couple of years, the strategies of multinational companies did not show much uniformity in regard to their managerial and organizational approaches. There were places where the managers' independence had increased and there were examples where local people had been downgraded to merely operationalize or execute plans designed and developed by others. In some locations sensible organizational changes were implemented, whilst in others where there were already problems the new solutions simply made things worse. Where one inward investor company positively encouraged the Hungarian cultural characteristics and worked hard to capitalize on them, another did its best to remove them.

The conclusions of our research in Hungary could be summed up in the observation that the practices of the companies show diverse patterns of management and organization, and there are few significant common trends that can be perceived in the developments. Analysis at a deeper level, however, uncovers a clearly recognizable system of interrelations. To identify and interpret these, a different approach had to be used, and in order to introduce this approach we have had to re-examine the concept of *globalization*.

What is happening in Hungary has to be seen within the context of the irreversible wider processes of globalization promoted and accelerated by dynamic growth in electronic communication and transport, as well as in the development of financial markets. Multinational companies are only one aspect of globalization, perhaps as yet not the most developed. Product markets, capital markets and information networks are already global. If Hungary is not to be left out it must be aware of what is happening and respond appropriately.

The negative consequences for small countries undergoing a transition process are many, including placing national states and their governments in a vulnerable position. There are also the threats to local work cultures, traditional market networks and the possible devaluation of local skills.

We referred earlier to the diversity of the managerial and organizational techniques imported by the multinationals. However, in the context of globalization and their impact on the matters investigated in this research project, their broad similarities appear more significant than the differences, at least in the small sample of companies reviewed. These are summarized as follows:

1. *Pure profit orientation*   Although in the interviews with senior managers in the multinational companies other strategic aims were mentioned such as market-share and customer satisfaction, these were seen as means to the end of profit. Given that profit (defined broadly as the difference between income generated and costs incurred) is the aim, then the emphasis on individual and group performance is not surprising. This is in sharp contrast to management aims and behaviour in the previous command/semi-market economy.
2. *School of the market economy*   For many Hungarian workers and managers the adjustment to the ways of multinational companies has been a (sometimes painful) learning process. To see everything – community, family, leisure, working practices and relationships – as subordinate to the single aim of profit is something not easy to learn.
3. *Slowness in self-learning*   However, because the multinationals themselves are complex organizations scattered around the globe, they too are slow to learn. To 'learn about Hungary' is continually to discover and understand local characteristics, a long process

which has only just started. The contact between the researchers and persons in the companies and in the workshops has done a little to help this process along.

There are related similarities and some minor differences also in the managerial ways and organizational tendencies of multinationals in Hungary. These can be considered under the following headings :

1. *Managerial decision and action space* Because of the flat management structures introduced by the multinationals, Hungarian middle managers find themselves with more autonomy and independence. Consequently they must learn to be decisive; even creative. Those above them, however, are bound by the top management or find it difficult to influence decisions taken abroad. Those below them experience the tighter control implicit in the new management methods.
2. *Working culture* Managerial work cultures of incoming companies are in many respects similar to those in Hungary which makes contact between expatriates and local professionals easier. The workers seem resigned and obedient, mainly because of fear of job loss and lack of collective power to influence their working lives.
3. *Standardization* Inevitably, multinationals replace existing procedures with their own standardized documents and administrative procedures, since without them control from the centre would be difficult. The new standards are often no better than the existing local ones but have to be accepted as the price of integration with global enterprise.
4. *Type of ownership* However, a distinction can be made between foreign *professional* investors and *financial* investors. The latter leave a lot more to local management. They are interested less in the way things are done than in the financial outcomes, and emphasize the long term rather than the short term. The feelings of autonomy and pride in achievement outweigh (for the managers at least) the risks of working for a financial investor.
5. *Wages, salaries and incentives* In the multinationals the main guiding principle for pay levels is the labour market. In the case of managers and management professionals who are in short supply and whom companies wish to retain, salaries are high as are other benefits such as company cars, housing loans and pension schemes. The pay of white collar workers is determined by comparisons at national level, and the wage levels of blue collar workers are

determined by local labour market comparisons. As for incentives to work harder or smarter, the managers have prestige and the perks, the white collars and blue collars the fear of job loss.

6. *Productivity and work efficiency* Productivity in the multinational companies studied had undoubtedly improved. However, it appears that this is not so much the result of improvements in the organization of work. Rather, performance has improved by increasing pressure, in particular the better use of working time. Perhaps because labour is cheap, expensive solutions are eschewed. There is, it would seem, ample scope for further increases in labour productivity but measures to do this will only be taken if labour becomes more costly.

7. *Managerical strategy* Apart from reforming management structures and developing managerial skills, the burden of flexibility falls upon the labour force. The old paternalism has gone and while for management personal and professional development is part of company policy, for the labour force the policy is to adjust numbers according to the demands of the product market, with and intensive work for those who remain.

   Massive lay-offs have not been characteristic of Hungarian multinationals. They tended to react slowly to competitive pressures and to the characteristics of labour markets. The effect of the multinationals on general levels of employment has not been very significant.

8. *Work conditions* Working conditions remain basically unchanged, and where some improvements have been made they have been overshadowed by the pressure for performance. Complaints and conflicts are rarely overt because of job insecurity.

9. *Cultural adjustments* The everyday life of a multinational company in Hungary is a continuous test of adjustment to other cultures. The process of coming together is slow but sure, except in the case of companies from Asia where the process is more protracted.

10. *Learning to be global* The arrival of the multinationals has speeded up the process of globalization generally. Employees of the foreign multinationals and the emergence of Hungarian multinationals has meant that many Hungarians are learning foreign languages, travelling around the world, and making contact with other cultures.

11. *Relations with Trade Unions* By and large, the multinationals have not shown enthusiasm for bargaining with trade unions.

They prefer to make individual rather than collective contracts. In some cases, Hungarian senior managers will act as intermediaries between the owners and the Hungarian workforce.

12. *Company life and private life* During the interviews a recurring theme was the effect of working for multinationals on family and community life. From top managers to the shop-floor, people complained that the increase in work intensity and long and inconvenient working hours had robbed them of time and energy they used to have to devote to their homes, families and local community.

THE CZECH REPUBLIC

The economic situation prior to the reform was based on central planning and state ownership of productive assets. The reforms consequent on the change of regime have aimed at macroeconomic stabilization, price and trade liberalization and privatization. During the early period of the transition there was an economic downturn. However, so far the Czech Republic has emerged with the lowest rate of inflation and the lowest level of unemployment at 4.4 per cent amongst the former command economies of Central and Eastern Europe. It also has a good record on measures of institutional reform and foreign investment.

Foreign investors are attracted amongst other things by political stability, a skilled and adaptable labour force and well-developed infrastructures, but they are cautious because of incomplete legislative changes, bureaucracy and the 'Czech phobia' about the inflow of foreign capital. To date the leading foreign investors are US and German.

There is a continuing tendency for employment in mining, agriculture and forestry to decrease, and for employment in manufacturing, some parts of the service sector and public administration to increase. The rate of unemployment differs greatly from region to region. For the whole country there were in 1996 1.7 applicants for every vacancy, in Prague the figure was 6.8. In Prague recorded unemployment was 1.26 per cent and in Pibram 9.1 per cent. Between 1989 and 1995 the service sector absorbed redundant workers from other sectors. Tertiary sector employment grew and there were large workforce movements to the private sector.

Considerable regional differences occured in the growth of average wages between 1989 and 1995; for example in Prague it was 186.7 per cent, whereas in Bohemia over the same period it was 143.6 per cent.

The general relaxation of government controls, although in general having had positive effects, has also created problems. Although all organizations now have the freedom to develop new systems of wage and salary payment, and other structures and procedures such as performance appraisal, they lack the skill to take maximum advantage of them. The structures of salaries and wages have been influenced more by external labour market forces than by internal differentiation based on skill, responsibility and so on. 'Incentive' payments which account for as much as 50 per cent of the pay packet are not systematically related to performance, and compensation systems neglect to emphasize the responsibility of managers and supervisors for the work performance of their subordinates. If these issues go unaddressed many of the problems that occurred in Britain and the USA in the 1960s and 1970s may well be repeated.

These points refer of course mainly to Czech companies in the state and private sector, and as such are part of the legacy of the former regime. The multinational companies have brought with them more developed administrative and human-resources management practices and systems.

The findings from the Czech literature survey, the interviews in foreign multinationals and in Czech companies and the workshop are summarized under the same headings as in the Hungarian study.

1. *Pure profit orientation*   The point of profit orientation by foreign multinationals as described by the Hungarian partner is seen by the Czech partner as an 'emphasis on efficiency and competitiveness'. It is also pointed out that Czech companies are now intent to follow the same path.
2. *School of the market economy*   The difficulties of Czech adjustment to the ways of foreign companies are seen partly in terms of the foreigners causing some resentment by unfairly underestimating Czech managers. Personal factors, as in the Hungarian case, also play a part in the adjustment process.
3. *Slowness in self-learning*   There are many advantages for managers who work for foreign companies. They are trained in new ways of working and for new responsibilities. Often they go abroad for training where they have new experiences and see different locations and activities. This important developmental process is not

available to the same extent to managers who work for Czech organizations.

The Czech research suggests the following responses to the 13 points raised on the previous pages.

1. *Managerical decision and action space*   In the Czech multinational studies there was less emphasis on hierarchy than under the old regime. However (as in Hungary) because of the 'flattening' of organization structures and the emphasis on performance-evaluation, work pressure was more intense.
2. *Working culture*   Because of the low level of unemployment in the Czech Republic the response to this point is in some ways different from that of the Hungarians. There are fewer lay-offs and consequently more attention is paid to the training and development of the work force. This and the relative lack of fear of job loss makes better relationships but can also encourage a relaxed attitude.
3. *Standardization*   As in Hungary the multinationals import their own standards, procedures, controls and remove previous ones. The Czech interviews reveal no particular problems arising from such changes.
4. *Type of ownership*   Either because there are no financial investors in the Czech Republic, or because the sample of companies studied did not include one, the Czech report is silent on this matter.
5. *Wages, salaries and incentives*   As in Hungary the labour market is reported as the major influence both on wage and salary levels and structures.
6. *Productivity and work efficiency*   The multinationals in the Czech Republic introduce structures and processes that increase work intensity. There is much more emphasis on quality and greater and continuous attention to the job is required by everyone. Because of competitive pressure, this is beginning to happen in Czech companies also.
7. *Managerical strategy*   In some of the companies studied, cleaner work environments have been created and new machinery introduced. The pressure for organizational flexibility falls mainly on the lower levels of the organization in the shape of variable, sometimes long, working hours, new shift patterns, flexitime and the insistence on quality.
    Because labour markets are tighter in the Czech Republic than in Hungary, the people who have been laid off by multinationals

and Czech companies have been largely absorbed in the growing service sector. In the Czech workshop some company representatives saw the re-training of employees as a problem. In areas of high demand for labour foreign workers are imported.

8. *Work conditions*   Working conditions have in some cases improved but mainly in the 'hygiene' factors – cleanliness, lighting, subsidized meals and so on – less in work organization and in the enrichment of jobs. In some reported instances jobs have been enlarged but this is felt to increase responsibility and pressure.

9. *Cultural adjustment*   Exactly as in Hungary. There are no Asian investors in the Czech Republic.

10. *Learning to be global*   See 3 above.

11. *Relations with Trade Unions*   In the Czech Republic, as in Hungary, foreign managers brought the idea of individual contracts. However, the political climate and legislation are in general more favourable to collective bargaining and the trend is in that direction.

12. *Company life and private life*   Findings the Czech Republic research echo from Hungary's experience in many respects. It seems that whatever the political and economic shortcomings of the previous regime, job security, short hours, relaxed work pace and so on. meant that for everyone there was time and energy for family and community activities, particular the former. The new working arrangements driven by efficiency and competitive pressure, and sometimes requiring long journeys to work, reduce the time and energy available for other activities.

Turning now to the predictions around the factors raised at the beginning of the chapter, Table 14.1 brings out the main issues of importance.

CONCLUSIONS

As the Hungarian partners point out, multinationals need to be seen clearly as only one part of the process of globalization. The parallel process of privatization will eventually bring into the world competitive arena those locally-owned enterprises not subjected to the modernizing influence of multinationals. The state-owned corporations will also follow (more slowly perhaps) the managerial prescriptions inherent in the ideology of market economics. Suppliers in the local

Table 14.1 Predictions fourth Czech Republic and Hungary

Item	Czech Republic	Hungary
Employment	Unemployment will increase. There is over-employment in Czech companies. The level will depend on whether the shake-out will be absorbed in the service sector	The decline in employment due to the move to a full market economy will stop and un-employment will stabilize at around present levels
Labour market flexibility	Employees now realize that they do not have jobs for life any more, but most are well trained in transferable skills. However, mobility will be hampered by lack of housing, increasing rents and poor public housing	The labour markets will remain inflexible because of lack of retraining facilities, the constraints of housing shortage and trans-port. This may change if Hungary joins the EEC as many people will seek jobs in other countries
Nominal and real wages and salaries	Real average wages/salaries have only recently reached 1989 levels so there will be pressure from employees and unions for increases. How-ever, employers and government will be uncer pressure to keep costs down. How much growth there will be could depend on how collective bargaining will develop	For managers and specialists real salaries will grow quickly towards West European averages. For workers, growth will be much slower and for a long time their real wages will remain well below West Europe. Join-ing the EU could speed up growth
Relation between employ-ment and productivity	Competitive advantage of low labour cost is decreased by low productivity, so wage growth will be accompanied by productivity growth. This will mean more unemployment unless service sector or new activities like tourism can absorb surplus	Productivity will increase because there is room for growth, and employment will de-crease almost as quickly. The rate of in-crease/decrease will vary according to the economic sector

Pay and productivity	Growing competition means Czech companies must follow similar policies to the joint ventures. To keep the advantage of low labour costs they must improve productivity	There is no strong relationship between pay and productivity and this will continue to be the case. Wage levels will continue to be determined by the labour market
Work organization and methods	They will continue to move towards modern 'western' ways in management technologies and systems. This movement which emphasizes individual responsibility will come up against the collective thinking and dependence on central-ized control inherited from the past. To find a productive balance will take a long time	The next 15–20 years will see fast growth in the introduction of modern practices in job design, work organization (e.g. team work-ing) empowerment of employees, etc. The critical starting phase is over and attention can be focused on these matters
Management styles and structures	These should change to 'western' ways. In con-trast to previous styles, managers now concent-rate decision-making in their own hands. For transition this might be appropriate, but some managers will want to continue like this and must be trained to be more sensitive to the needs and wishes of employees. If unemployment continues to be low they may have to be	Managerial styles will improve in the sense that there will be a focus on problems and people rather than on the extremes of au-thority and *laissez-faire*. Management structures will become more flexible and adaptive to changing circumstances
Human resources practices	Will depend on the level of employment and on the policies of foreign investors. Low unemploy-ment will bring sophisticated methods of attracting new employees. With high unemploy-ment this will not be so necessary. It may be that if the intention is to benefit from cheap labour, to invest in training and development might not be considered worthwhile	These are likely to remain as they are, i.e. to develop human resources insofar as there ae economic payoffs

Table 14.1 (*contd.*)

Item	Czech Republic	Hungary
Problems experienced by employees at all levels in transition to market economy	Managers will have to become more flexible, more knowledgeable, and more capable of acting independently and more understanding of the interdependence of decisions	The multinationals can be a source of national tension although the new business 'aristocracies' will get on well together. In spite of the facade of good communication to others the manipulation will stay. Workers will lack information about the company. The gap between manager and workers will widen. Assimilation to imported ways has its dangers for indigenous culture
Labour market policy and administration	Will depend on the level of employment. In conditions of rising unemployment the policy and administration will become more active – job creation, consultancy, retraining, etc.	The governments' policies will remain hesitant and drifting. This will create opportunities for emerging private agencies

economy are drawn by the foreign investors into the globalization process. They are competing for the orders of the multinationals and against other suppliers worldwide.

Competitive pressures stimulate the search for structures and processes of managerial control to reduce costs and promote flexible responses to the changing demands of the environment. They also impel the enlistment of governmental assistance to legislate in favour not only of the multinationals but also private companies in the local economy, in particular with measures to create flexible labour markets. For example, the facilities for re-training, transport and housing. Pressures are also there to improve other infrastructures to create a favourable environment for business. The doctrines of the market economy and its managerial accompaniments see profit *via* efficient and flexible use of resources as a compelling single imperative.

The role of government according to these doctrines is to create and maintain the infrastructures of law and order, roads, railways, telephone and other communication networks, to the expense of which, through taxation, privately-owned companies as well as the public will contribute. However, if the costs of taxation and of other resources became a hindrance to the search for profit *via* cost efficiency, the multinationals may seek other less-costly and more helpful places to locate.

It is of course the case, as both the Czech and Hungarian partners say, that multinationals bring to the countries in which they locate new management methods and in copying these and implementing them the newly-privatized indigenous companies too enhance their competitive strength in local and foreign markets. This is plain from the responses of managers and others to questions put by the interviewers in local companies. It is one item on the positive side of the arrival of multinationals in the Czech Republic. Others are the importation of modern technology – particularly information technology. In the context of the transition to a market economy the multinationals have also met the transition costs of training in the disciplines of marketing, selling, financial management, accounting and human-resource management. In some of the reported cases they have also improved the physical environment – new buildings, cleanliness and so forth.

On the negative side, as seen from the point of view of the host countries, one can cite the reduction of some of the social benefits previously enjoyed by employees, the 'flattening' of organization structures leading to lay offs and limitations on career progression.

Rationalization of work processes are also leading to further lay-offs, thus importing the process of 'down-sizing' as a competitive weapon. From society's point of view this can be seen as contributing to unemployment. In the Czech case the processes of 'shake-out' and 'downsizing' have not gone far enough as yet to have much effect on the level of employment. However, as recent events show, for example the conflicts over rationalization on Czech railways, and as the Czech partner predicts, further 'down-sizing' could increase the level of unemployment unless, as has so far been the case, a growing service sector can continue to absorb the surplus labour.

Certainly improved management styles and systems have increased work pressures and reduced the time and energy that was previously devoted to family and to activities outside the company. The relation between managers and workers in the command economy has also changed. Everyone in that regime was a member of a collective, everyone had a job, the work pace was relaxed and there was time for 'leisure at work'. Now, as the Czech partner points out, the direction of movement is towards individual rather than collective responsibility, and the problem will be to try to strike a balance.

It is difficult to see how blue-collar and office workers can feel comfortable with the fact that they can no longer rely on having a job for life, that many have become unemployed and there is no noticeable difference in the purchasing power of their wages, and more families are becoming two job families. The same applies to many managers and professionals; their jobs too are intrinsically no more protected from competitive pressures but for the moment they are in short supply and they have good salaries and perquisites.

So the balance of advantages so far seems to be on the negative side. However, the Czech and Hungarian partners are on the whole optimistic and see in the long term that the globalization process (which includes the transition of the Central and Eastern European *via* foreign investment, privatization into the market economy, and so on.) will in the next century be beneficial materially to the countries and their people.

They are probably right so far as material prosperity goes. A concern is that the importation of foreign structures and procedures brings with it not only changes in working styles and ideas relating to production, marketing, financial management. It also carries with it cultural implications about individual and collective good and places a high value on individual competition for material things which may begin to erode traditional ways of life and the values of caring, welfare, family and community regional diversity and a breakdown of social cohesion. Should that happen it would be a pity, but it seems that some of the signs are already appearing.

Some of the economic and social processes already referred to are posing, and will continue to pose, problems and dilemmas in the political sphere – for central and local governments in the former command economies. The concept of flexible labour markets seems to have become an integral part of the dogmas of market economics. In its practical expression it can mean an increase in what Karl Marx described as the 'reserve army of labour'. The existence of such a pool of short-term or permanent unemployed people enables the employer to keep down labour costs and thus enhance competitive advantage. It is clear that this is consistent with the practical policies of the multinational corporations wherever they happen to be located. Indigenous companies which also are becoming driven by the competitive imperatives of the emerging global economy will follow those policies.

The resulting fragmentation of the workforce – the unemployed and the employed who fear for their jobs – makes collective action to improve matters more and more difficult. All this works to the competitive advantage of the employers but passes on the resulting costs and psychological consequences largely to the civil authority.In the advanced industrial societies these consequences include, for example, the escalating costs of policing the increase in crime and social disruption that follow from the alienation of long-term unemployed youth, the costs of social security for the unemployed, and the costs of labour market measures to promote flexibility of labour – job centres, job-creation programmes, re-training programmes and housing. State budgets for social security and such matters are cause for public concern because of their implications for taxation and political popularity. To the extent that such costs are levied on the companies whose decisions contributed largely to them, there arises another reason to contemplate moves to other climes of cheap labour, low taxes and access to other markets, where they would be welcome for their wealth-creating potentialities. The possible long-term negative consequences seldom seem to be considered and are hidden in the positive short-term glow. (Commentators such as Charles Handy see this split between the permanent core of corporate employees and the army of flexible 'floaters' as an inevitable and irreversible consequence of the global market economy but pay little attention to the social dimension.)

All this seems inevitable. The power of the multinationals seems greater in its economic and social impact than the political power of some nation-states to control their impact. There exists no international civil power to control the growth of the global economy in the interests of the citizens of the world. Perhaps this is a challenge for the twenty-first century.

Index